Integrating Qualitative and Quantitative Methods

3, 5 - Morgan

For Susan

Integrating Qualitative and Quantitative Methods

A Pragmatic Approach

David L. Morgan
Portland State University

Los Angeles | London | New Delhi
Singapore | Washington DC

Los Angeles | London | New Delhi
Singapore | Washington DC

FOR INFORMATION:

SAGE Publications, Inc.
2455 Teller Road
Thousand Oaks, California 91320
E-mail: order@sagepub.com

SAGE Publications Ltd.
1 Oliver's Yard
55 City Road
London EC1Y 1SP
United Kingdom

SAGE Publications India Pvt. Ltd.
B 1/I 1 Mohan Cooperative Industrial Area
Mathura Road, New Delhi 110 044
India

SAGE Publications Asia-Pacific Pte. Ltd.
3 Church Street
#10-04 Samsung Hub
Singapore 049483

Publisher: Vicki Knight
Managing Editor: Catherine Forrest Getzie
Editorial Assistant: Kalie Koscielak
Production Editor: David C. Felts
Copy Editor: Paula L. Fleming
Typesetter: C&M Digitals (P) Ltd.
Proofreader: Sally Jaskold
Indexer: Virgil Diodato
Cover Designer: Candice Harman
Marketing Manager: Nicole Elliott

Copyright © 2014 by SAGE Publications, Inc.

Printed in the United States of America.

Library of Congress Cataloging-in-Publication Data

Morgan, David L. (Sociologist)

Integrating qualitative and quantitative methods: a pragmatic approach / David L. Morgan, Portland State University.

pages cm
Includes bibliographical references and index.

ISBN 978-0-7619-1523-2 (pbk.: alk. paper)

1. Social sciences—Research—Methodology.
2. Social sciences—Statistical methods.
3. Qualitative research. I. Title.

H62.M6448 2013
001.4'2—dc23   2013000962

SUSTAINABLE FORESTRY INITIATIVE
Certified Chain of Custody
Promoting Sustainable Forestry
www.sfiprogram.org
SFI-01268
SFI label applies to text stock

13 14 15 16 17 10 9 8 7 6 5 4 3 2 1

Brief Contents

Detailed Contents

Preface

This is a book about research design. In particular, it is about research designs for projects that collect both qualitative and quantitative data so that using the combined strengths of qualitative and quantitative methods will accomplish more than would have been possible with one method alone. The approach presented here is broadly interdisciplinary because mixed methods research has interested social scientists from a great many fields, including anthropology, communication, criminal justice, education, evaluation, nursing, organizational behavior, political science, psychology, public administration, public health, social work, sociology, and urban studies.

Despite this widespread interest, what has been lacking is a truly practical discussion of strategies for bringing qualitative and quantitative methods together. In contrast to a belief that "anything goes" or a naive hope that "two methods are better than one," this book argues that projects using mixed methods research need to pay even more attention to research design than projects that rely a single method. Hence, the core of this book is a set of research designs that provide practical approaches to combining qualitative and quantitative methods. These designs are practical in two ways. First, they are accessible. Most researchers with a basic background in qualitative and quantitative methods will find the methods used here to be quite familiar. Second, they are dependable. As the empirical examples throughout the book demonstrate, these are well-proven research designs.

Because this book emphasizes practical research designs, it will be most useful to practicing researchers—including both students who intend to pursue such a career and those who already devote their energy to collecting and analyzing data. Whether you are a student or a more experienced researcher, you will learn how mixed methods research gets done in the real world.

This is not just a how-to book, however; instead, it concentrates on when and why to combine qualitative and quantitative methods. In particular, it emphasizes the importance of understanding and stating the motivations behind your decision to use both qualitative and quantitative methods. Once you have clarified your reasons for bringing these different methods together, the material here will show you how to match those goals to appropriate research designs.

Acknowledgments

The work behind this book has been going on for a number of years, and one of my oldest debts is to Duane Alwin, who first encouraged me to teach about combining qualitative and quantitative methods during a series of summer courses offered through the Institute for Social Research at the University of Michigan. At Portland State University (PSU), the students in my graduate courses on combining qualitative and quantitative definitely assisted in developing the content on this book. In addition, this book was completed after I left the College of Urban and Public Affairs and moved to the Department of Sociology, so I want to thank my colleagues in Sociology for the opportunities and encouragement they have provided. At PSU, I especially appreciate the conversations I have had with and the support I have received from Jutta Attaie, Paula Carder, Pete Collier, Nona Glazer, Bill Greenfield, Molly Griffith, Kim Hoffman, Leslie McBride, Jason Newsom, Bob Liebman, Margaret Neal, and Sue Poulsen. Further afield, I have also benefited from my contacts with John Creswell, Sharlene Hesse-Biber, Berit Ingersoll-Dayton, John Knodel, Bojana Lobe, Ray Maietta, Jan Morse, and my colleagues at the University of Alberta. Finally, I would to thank the Sage panel of reviewers for this book, including A. Victor Ferreros, Walden University; Greg S. Goodman, Clarion University of Pennsylvania; Bryan W. Griffin, Georgia Southern University Nancy N. Heilbronner, Western Connecticut State University; Charles A. Kramer, University of La Verne; Elizabeth L. Langevin, University of Phoenix; D. Patrick Lenihan, University of Illinois at Chicago; Laura Meyer, University of Denver; and Pamela M. Wesely, University of Iowa.

Part 1

The Logic of Mixed Methods Research

CHAPTER 1

An Introduction and Overview

Overview

This chapter is introductory in two senses. First, you should be able to read it quite easily, even if you have only a minimal background on the topic of combining qualitative and quantitative methods. In particular, the discussion of the literature is postponed until the later chapters, which means this chapter has few references. Second, this chapter is introductory in the sense that it summarizes the basic arguments for the book as a whole. Consequently, the chapter begins with summaries of the chapters in Part 1 followed by an overview of the four basic research designs that make up Part 2 of the book.

PART 1: THE LOGIC OF MIXED METHODS RESEARCH (CHAPTERS 1 TO 5)

An Introduction and Overview (Chapter 1)

Different methods have different strengths. Almost every argument for combining qualitative and quantitative methods relies on this basic insight, but the attraction of combining methods with separate sets of strengths has to be balanced against the complexity of research projects that use multiple methods. The additional value that you get by combining methods has a cost, which comes from the serious challenges in designing and executing this kind of research. In fact, combining two methods often involves more than twice as much work as using a single method, since you must not only use each separate method effectively but also integrate them effectively. Simply having more results or different kinds of results does not inherently improve your work; in addition, you must bring those results together in a way that demonstrates the value of your additional effort. Hence, research projects that use multiple methods are not automatically preferable to studies that use just one method.

Both the appeal and the difficulty of integrating multiple methods are especially obvious when you want to bring together qualitative and quantitative methods. On the one hand, using very different methods is appealing because these methods possess very distinctive strengths. On the other hand, combining qualitative and quantitative methods can raise difficult problems precisely because they are so different. You may thus be attracted by the separate strengths of qualitative and quantitative methods but end up frustrated by practical problems in integrating both their different procedures and their different results. Hence, it is important to avoid an "anything goes" approach to combining methods—sometimes called methodological eclecticism. Example 1.1 illustrates the kinds of problems encountered by those who hold the simplistic belief that merely using more methods will lead to better results.

Example 1.1   A Personal Experience With Methodological Eclecticism

My first experience in combining qualitative and quantitative methods was more than 25 years ago, when in my dissertation I studied how social networks influenced the sense of community in a retirement home. During the course of the research, I took extensive field notes, conducted in-depth interviews, collected two waves of surveys, kept systematic records of interaction patterns, and tracked a naturally occurring experiment as the home reorganized its basic structure.

Gathering this wealth of data was an exhilarating experience. Making sense of it was another matter. Ultimately, I used the different methods for a variety of purposes throughout my dissertation. For example, an early descriptive chapter began with global information from the survey data followed by several brief biographies from the in-depth interviews. The bulk of the data that I reported came from my participant observation, but one chapter presented complex statistical analyses of the interaction patterns as social networks.

> At the conclusion of my dissertation defense, I wanted to know what my committee members thought of my efforts. One of my advisers, who was known for his extended metaphors, compared it to a Jell-O salad in which a number of things were held together by something that wasn't nearly as interesting as the bits and pieces themselves. Sadly, he was right. I had relied on a naive faith that merely using more methods would lead to a better understanding of what I was studying. Even though both the qualitative "bits" and the quantitative "pieces" had much to offer, I hadn't found a successful approach to integrating them.

The best way to resolve this dilemma is to create a careful connection between your reasons for using both qualitative and quantitative methods and a research design that suits those purposes. Thus, the real challenge is to integrate the different strengths that qualitative and quantitative methods offer; hence, the title of this book is *Integrating Qualitative and Quantitative Methods*. It is also worth noting that there are any number of other labels for the general goal of using both qualitative and quantitative methods within a single research project. Up until this point, the label *mixed methods research* has been replaced by phrases such as "combining qualitative and quantitative methods" or "integrating multiple methods." The reason for avoiding the term is that it can feel too casual—as if combining multiple methods involves little more than putting them together in the same project. In contrast, the current argument is that *integrating* qualitative and quantitative methods can be a very demanding task, and a number of researchers made similar arguments when the name *mixed methods* first appeared. Since that time, the name *mixed methods research* has become so well entrenched that it would be almost impossible not to recognize its dominance; hence, that terminology will appear throughout the remainder of the book.

The book's subtitle also indicates a *pragmatic approach* to these issues. At the most fundamental level, this amounts to linking your *purposes* (in terms of research questions) and your *procedures* (in terms of research methods) at every step. Choosing an appropriate research design means finding a match between the purposes that motivate your research and the procedures you use to meet those goals. In some cases, your best choice will be to rely on a single research method; in other cases, an integrated combination of methods will best serve your purposes. In the end, any decision to combine qualitative and quantitative methods must start with a careful consideration of why you want to do mixed methods research before you can decide how to do so. Again, using two methods can be more than twice as difficult as using one method because of the additional effort required to integrate the separate sets of results. Example 1.2 shows what can happen if you don't plan for this additional work right from the start.

| Example 1.2 | A Personal Experience With Ignoring the Need to Integrate Results |

One of my first large-scale research projects combined data from focus groups and surveys to study the experiences of families who were caring for someone with Alzheimer's disease. The goal of the project was to compare the social support networks of family caregivers who were still providing care in the community with those who had placed their family member in a nursing home. At that time, there was little research on family caregivers in nursing homes, so the focus groups used open-ended discussions to explore differences in the experiences of community-based and nursing home–based caregivers. In contrast, the surveys relied on well-established procedures from the social support literature to measure the positive and negative relationships that the caregivers reported.

Everything went smoothly until I began to compare the data analyses. According to the surveys, there were many supportive relationships and few negative relationships. Yet, when those same caregivers discussed their experiences in the focus groups, they were more likely to mention negative relationships. A lengthy series of further analyses eventually led to the conclusion that negative relationships were indeed rare (thus matching the survey data) but they were quite important when they did occur (thus matching the focus group data). This additional analysis was a time-consuming process: Because my original research design did not include any plan for dealing with this kind of discrepancy, the only option was to "dig through" the data for an answer.

Looking back, it is easy to see that my original design provided a good justification for using a qualitative method (i.e., exploring something that was poorly understood) and an equally good justification for the quantitative method (i.e., relying on well-developed measurement procedures). The problem was that I hadn't paid enough attention to *why* I was combining these different methods and *how* I would do so. Either of these studies would have worked well on its own, but I did not have a plan for *integrating* the two of them into a coherent whole.

Once you have reached the conclusion that using both qualitative and quantitative methods does make sense, you then face the further choice about how to do it. Because integrating different methods requires extra effort and resources, it would be foolish to attempt such a complex task without a solid strategy for accomplishing your goals. At present, however, there is little consensus about how to bring together qualitative and quantitative methods. Hence, when you do mixed methods research, you need to pay even more attention to research design than when you use a single method. This book cannot promise to resolve all of those issues, but it will provide you with both a set of practical research designs and a broader conceptual framework for making decisions about when to use those designs.

Research design is all about making decisions. To make good choices about research design, you need to know both what your options are and how to evaluate those options. Consequently, the core of this book devotes a chapter apiece to four research designs that give you practical options for integrating qualitative and quantitative methods, along with guidance on the specific purposes that each of these designs can serve. Thus, you can choose a specific design only after considering the broader issues that are the subject of the chapters in Part 1 of this book.

Pragmatism as a Paradigm for Mixed Methods (Chapter 2)

Chapter 2 lays out the connections between pragmatism as a philosophy and mixed methods research as a way of doing social science research. The essence of pragmatism can be found in its root word, *pragma,* from the Greek word for "action," which indicates that knowledge comes from taking action and learning from the outcomes. From a pragmatic point of view, this principle applies to all of human experience, and research is simply a more self-conscious and careful effort to link actions with their likely consequences.

Within pragmatism, *inquiry* is the specific term that is applied to processes such as research. Inquiry is an explicit attempt to produce new knowledge by taking actions and experiencing their results. Inquiry occurs when you confront situations that fall outside your existing knowledge and then take action to extend your knowledge so you know how to proceed when you encounter similar situations. The products of inquiry are "warranted beliefs" about actions and their likely consequences. It is important to note, however, that human experience occurs within historical and cultural contexts, so your current warranted beliefs can evolve as you encounter new situations.

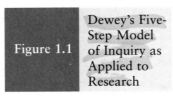

Figure 1.1   Dewey's Five-Step Model of Inquiry as Applied to Research

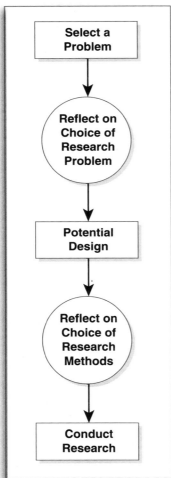

Examining inquiry as a formal process, Figure 1.1 shows that inquiry begins with a problem or question that needs to be answered. At the next step, you reflect on the nature of the problem as you seek possible solutions. In addressing research questions, these potential solutions typically take the form of a research design. Once you have generated this potential research design, you reflect further on what it implies about the actual methods involved in your research (i.e., the data collection and analysis that are the ultimate actions in any research project).

This summary of pragmatic inquiry highlights the importance of research design as a link between your broader purposes, as represented by the initial research question, and your specific procedures, as represented by research methods. Figure 1.1 points to this central role of research design as a pivot point between your purposes and your procedures. On the one hand, it is the key link to your research questions; on the other hand, it is the main determinant of your research methods.

As a paradigm, pragmatism gives mixed methods researchers a shared view of how to conduct research. The kind of consensus implied by a paradigm does not, however, apply at the technical level of research methods. Instead, it implies a more conceptual agreement about research in terms of both the purposes it pursues and the procedures it uses to pursue those purposes. In particular, mixed methods researchers follow a pragmatic path by consistently asking, What difference would it make to do your research one way rather than another? Pragmatism can thus be considered a "paradigm of choices," a description that is particularly appropriate for mixed methods research because of the complexity of the choices involved in integrating qualitative and quantitative methods.

Research Design and Research Methods (Chapter 3)

Chapter 3 compares *qualitative research* and *quantitative research* as opposed to qualitative methods and quantitative methods. These two approaches to researching the social world emphasize both different purposes and different procedures for meeting those purposes. As Table 1.1 shows, qualitative research concentrates on a set of purposes (or research goals) that are typically *inductive, subjective,* and *contextual,* while the purposes associated with quantitative research are typically *deductive, objective,* and *general.* In addition, both approaches use a set of procedures (i.e., research methods) that are particularly appropriate for their own purposes.

Table 1.1	Comparing Qualitative and Quantitative Research
Qualitative Research	Quantitative Research
Induction	Deduction
Subjectivity	Objectivity
Context	Generality

Saying that qualitative research uses induction means that this approach emphasizes using your observations to generate theory. Saying it relies on subjectivity emphasizes using your research experience to interpret the social world. Saying it relies on context emphasizes collecting detailed data that tell you about specific settings and circumstances. For example, when you do participant observation, you typically work within a particular location (context) to understand the lives of community members (subjectivity) in ways that help you describe their perspective on the social world (induction).

In contrast, saying that quantitative research uses deduction emphasizes using your observations to test theories. Saying it relies on objectivity emphasizes minimizing your impact as a researcher on the results. Saying it relies on generality emphasizes collecting data you can apply to a wide variety of settings and circumstances. For example, when you conduct a survey, you want the results to apply to a broad range of people (generality) in ways that treat every research participant alike (objectivity) so you can determine whether your observations match your hypotheses (deduction).

How are actual research methods related to these larger packages of purposes and procedures? The research methods covered in this book are primarily tools for collecting data. Qualitative methods, such as participant observation and open-ended interviewing, have strengths that are especially useful for inductive-subjective-contextual research, while quantitative methods, such as survey interviews and experimental interventions, are especially well suited to deductive-objective general research. Thus, both qualitative and quantitative research provide well-developed matches between a set of research purposes and a corresponding set of research procedures. Mixed methods research, however, is still developing a clear conception of both its typical research goals and the methods that match those goals. Hence, Chapter 4 considers three different motivations for integrating qualitative and quantitative methods.

Motivations for Using Mixed Methods Research (Chapter 4)

Social scientists have developed a range of reasons for integrating the different strengths of qualitative and quantitative methods. This chapter provides an overview of three broad purposes for combining qualitative and quantitative methods, but this book does not attempt to cover each of these motivations. Instead, it provides a detailed examination of research designs that fall within a single broad motivation for combining methods: *sequential contributions*. In research motivated by sequential contributions, your goal is to use the strengths of one method to enhance the performance of another method. This approach relies on a division of labor in which each method serves a different purpose and one method builds on what you learned from the other. For example, you might link qualitative methods as an input to designing a program intervention, or you might start with a preliminary survey to locate appropriate participants for a core qualitative study. Thus, in Figure 1.2, which compares sequential contributions to two other motivations, the symbol for sequential contributions is an arrow that links the two methods.

The goal of producing sequential contributions is not the only reason for combining qualitative and quantitative methods, however, and Chapter 4 also covers the two other basic motivations that are shown in Figure 1.2: *convergent findings* and *additional coverage*. It is important to understand how sequential contributions differs from these other options, because each results in conducting mixed methods research for fundamentally different purposes—which often leads to very different research designs.

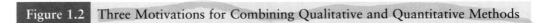

Figure 1.2   Three Motivations for Combining Qualitative and Quantitative Methods

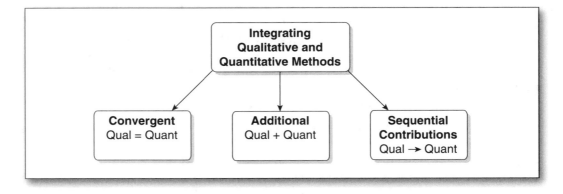

Among the various motivations for integrating multiple methods, one of the best-known goals is to produce convergent findings across different methods that each address the same research question, as symbolized by an equal sign. For example, you might want to examine the same research question using both a survey and qualitative interviews to determine whether the results are similar. This motivation, also known as triangulation or cross-validation, signals that your goal is to produce similar results from methods with different strengths. The main difference between convergent findings and sequential contributions is that the former compares the results from different methods that investigate the same research question, while the latter uses the results from one method to contribute to the needs of another.

In contrast, studies that pursue mixed methods through additional coverage, as symbolized by a plus sign, match the strengths of each method to a specific purpose or set of purposes and then use each method to study a separate part of the overall question. For example, you might collect most of your data for a case study of a community through participant observation and also conduct a small survey to cover a topic of special interest. Like research that uses sequential contributions, studies based on additional coverage also rely on a division of labor between methods. Therefore, you choose your methods according to their strengths for accomplishing specific tasks within the project as a whole. The difference is that additional coverage assigns each method to its own separate purpose within the larger project, while sequential contributions explicitly uses the results of one method to enhance the effectiveness of another.

Although sequential contributions, convergent findings, and additional coverage motivations all recognize that different methods have different strengths, each uses that basic insight in different ways to pursue different purposes. Yet the same message comes through in every case: The research design that you choose must link your purposes to your procedures. A research design that provides a useful combination of strengths for some purposes may be completely inappropriate for other purposes. Hence, it is crucial to begin with a clear understanding of the purposes that motivate your decision to integrate qualitative and quantitative methods.

The Sequential Priorities Model (Chapter 5)

In studies that are motivated by the goal of producing sequential contributions, qualitative and quantitative methods serve separate but closely linked purposes so that the results of one can enhance the effectiveness of the other.

This book concentrates on a set of research designs that use this basic logic to assign different roles to the qualitative and quantitative methods. These research designs arise from two fundamental principles:

1. *Prioritizing.* A division of labor assigns different roles to a *core method,* which supplies the key strengths your project requires, and a *supplementary method,* which contributes additional strengths to enhance the effectiveness of your core method. Either a qualitative or a quantitative method can serve as your core method, depending on which one best serves the overall goals of your project. The designs in this book match both a core method that is qualitative with a supplementary method that is quantitative and a core quantitative method with a supplementary qualitative method. For example, if your main purpose was to generate theory, then a core qualitative method would be most likely to meet that goal; alternatively, if your highest priority was generalizing to other populations, you would want to use a core quantitative method.

2. *Sequencing.* The methods are used in a specific order such that the supplementary method is either an input to or a follow-up on the core method. The place of the supplementary method within the sequence depends on whether your core method is more likely to benefit from a *preliminary input* or a *follow-up extension.* For the designs in this book, a sequence that begins with a qualitative method will proceed to a quantitative method, while a sequence that begins with a quantitative method will proceed to a qualitative method. For example, you might use a supplementary quantitative method that came either before or after a core qualitative method, depending on the strengths that the supplementary method was contributing to that core method.

Combining these two principles leads to four basic research designs for pursuing sequential contributions, as shown in Table 1.2. The columns in the diagram reflect the fact that the core method may be either qualitative or quantitative, depending on the goals of your project. The rows reflect the fact that the supplementary method can be either an input or an extension to the core method. Each of the four cells also contains a pictorial summary of the corresponding research design, using a notation developed by Janice Morse (1991). In this notation, the core method is shown in capital letters and the supplementary method in small letters, while an arrow shows the sequence.

Starting in the top row of Table 1.2, designs based on *preliminary qualitative inputs* begin with a qualitative study that contributes inputs to a largely quantitative project; for example, if you need insights into designing a program evaluation, you could use a set of focus groups as a first step. Equivalently, designs based

Table 1.2	Sequential Contributions Model for Integrating Qualitative and Quantitative Methods		
		Priority of Methods	
		Quantitative Priority	Qualitative Priority
Sequence of Methods	Preliminary Contribution	**Preliminary Qualitative** qual→QUANT	**Preliminary Quantitative** quant→QUAL
	Follow-Up Contribution	**Follow-up Qualitative** QUANT→qual	**Follow-up Quantitative** QUAL→quant

on *preliminary quantitative inputs* use a quantitative study as an input to a largely qualitative project; for example, if you need to locate specific categories of people for qualitative interviews, you could search for them in an existing database.

In the bottom row, designs based on *follow-up qualitative extensions* extend the results from a largely quantitative project with an additional supplementary qualitative study; for example, if you produced unexpected results from a survey, you could explore the sources of those results through in-depth interviews. Equivalently, designs based on *follow-up quantitative extensions* extend the results from a largely qualitative project with an additional supplementary quantitative study; for example, if you wanted to show the transferability of things that you observed in one location, you could use those conclusions to create a demonstration program in a similar setting.

One obvious question is whether these four designs are in fact the "best" way to combine qualitative and quantitative methods. The answer is that this book's emphasis on sequential contributions is *not a claim about how research should be done.* Nothing in this book claims that research using a sequential contributions approach is inherently superior to other motivations for combining methods. Instead, the goal is to provide a detailed description of a highly effective set of designs for how mixed methods research has been done and can be done. The main reason for emphasizing these sequential contributions designs is their practicality. The goal of this book is to systematize and develop a set of basic designs that are ready to be used in the field rather than to propose new but untested ideas.

* * *

Overall, Chapters 1 through 5 emphasize the importance of matching the broader purposes that guide your research with the specific procedures you use to pursue those goals to avoid the problems that can arise in combining multiple methods. Once you have a solid conceptual framework for integrating qualitative and quantitative methods, the next step is to evaluate the concrete research designs that might serve your specific purposes. The second part of the book consists of four chapters that not only describe each of the basic sequential contributions designs in more detail but also provide a wide range of examples from real world research.

PART 2: FOUR BASIC DESIGNS (CHAPTERS 6 TO 9)

Preliminary Qualitative Inputs to Core Quantitative Research Projects (Chapter 6)

This design represents a version of the sequential priorities model in which a preliminary qualitative study contributes inputs to a largely quantitative project (in Morse's notation, this is summarized as *qual* → *QUANT*). For example, if the core of your project is a survey, then a preliminary qualitative study would help you learn how the respondents think about the topics you want to cover in your questionnaire. Similarly, you might be able to increase the effectiveness of the intervention in an experimental design by beginning with a qualitative study that helps you understand the people whose behavior you want to change. Example 1.3 demonstrates how this design can be used to develop a new set of survey items.

Example 1.3   A Qualitative Input Design

One of the classic uses for preliminary qualitative data is to address a new area where few survey instruments or intervention projects exist. Krause (2002) used a series of qualitative studies as input to a larger survey researching the topic of religiosity among the elderly. This input was important for the project as a whole because the goal of the survey was to cover a wide range of feelings, experiences, and behaviors that were related to both formal religion and more informal aspects of spirituality. Because older Americans had rarely been asked about this aspect of their lives, the funders of this project specifically wanted Krause and colleagues to develop high-quality survey measures that other researchers could use as the basis for further research.

As a first step in generating qualitative inputs for survey, Krause (2002) and colleagues used focus groups to uncover the participants' perspectives on the topics they wanted to include in the survey and to discover new topics that should be added. As a second preliminary study, they conducted individual, open-ended interviews to develop the content for a set of questions that would "operationalize" the things he had heard in the focus groups. Finally, they conducted relatively detailed "cognitive interviews" to hear how potential respondents reacted to the wording of the questions and then refined those questions accordingly. Most survey instruments do not require nearly this much preliminary development. In this case, however, little guidance was available with regard to the basic issues related to religion, health, and aging, let alone the specific questions that would address each of those topics. Krause et al. thus used a series of qualitative methods first to discover likely content areas, then to develop questions for those areas, and finally to define the actual wording of the survey items.

In general, qualitative studies make a valuable contribution in preliminary qualitative input designs because quantitative methods typically require predetermined research protocols before they enter the field. This means that you have few options for modifying a quantitative study after you begin collecting data, so it is important to start with the best possible content for your survey instrument or experimental intervention. If you ask the wrong questions in a survey or implement an inappropriate intervention in an experiment, then the whole project may be jeopardized. Thus, in cases where you have doubts about the appropriate content for either a survey or an experimental intervention, even a small preliminary qualitative study can make a major contribution.

Preliminary Quantitative Inputs to Core Qualitative Research Projects (Chapter 7)

These designs use a quantitative study as an input to a largely qualitative project (*quant* → *QUAL*). For example, if you are planning to conduct a case study that relies on participant observation as your core method, you might examine statistical data to choose a research site that matches the needs of your study. Similarly, if you are planning to do qualitative interviews, you might use an existing survey sample or other quantitative database to locate specific categories of informants who match your research interests. Thus, the most common form of preliminary quantitative input design uses a preliminary quantitative study to help select the sources for in-depth qualitative data collection, as shown in Example 1.4.

Example 1.4   A Quantitative Input Design

Quantitative databases are often a useful way to locate cases that are both unusual and interesting. A good example of this process is a cover story in *U.S. News & World Report* that used a series of six case studies to illustrate the key traits of outstanding high schools (Toch, 1999). To locate these schools, the magazine commissioned a preliminary quantitative study that was done by the University of Chicago's National Opinion Research Center. The quantitative portion of the project analyzed data on a variety of indicators from public sources for over 1,000 high schools in 6 large American cities to identify schools where students' performance consistently exceeded what would have been expected from their socioeconomic backgrounds.

The goal of this preliminary quantitative work was to locate schools that could serve as "exemplars," that is, schools for which something about their unique character, rather than their location or the income level of their students, was responsible for their success. The article concentrates on six detailed case studies that demonstrate a valuable policy or practice. For example, a public school in Detroit illustrates the importance of insisting on high standards through a demanding and focused curriculum; the school overcame its lack of resources and sent 95% of its graduates to college. Alternatively, a Catholic school in the South Bronx neighborhood of New York City showed the value of a sense of community as evidenced by an emphasis on volunteerism and social justice that created connections between the school and the local area as well as within the school itself. Overall, the fact that this project began with a systematic search for schools that produced excellence was a strong justification for paying attention to the in-depth lessons that the article produced from its six central case studies.

The quantitative study in a preliminary quantitative input design helps to focus the data-gathering efforts for the core, qualitative study. Because qualitative studies typically rely on small Ns, such as one or two sites for participant observation or a relatively small number of informants for in-depth interviews, you can waste a great deal of time if you select an unproductive field site or run into trouble locating appropriate informants for your interviews. Qualitative studies thus tend to rely on a careful process of purposive selection to locate the data sources that are most relevant to the research topic. In these cases, the preliminary use of even a small quantitative study can provide important resources for targeting the most productive or theoretically relevant sources for your qualitative data.

Follow-up Qualitative Extensions to Core Quantitative Research Projects (Chapter 8)

These designs use a qualitative study to follow up on a largely quantitative project (*QUANT → qual*). For example, if you conduct a survey that produces a set of unexpected results, then you could pursue those issues through additional qualitative interviewing. Similarly, if an experimental intervention has more impact at one site than another, then you might use qualitative observations to help clarify the difference. In both of these examples, a follow-up qualitative extension design builds on a core quantitative study, so you can address new questions that cannot be answered within the quantitative data themselves. Investigating these issues with an additional qualitative study is often an effective way to extend your work, particularly in comparison to mounting another full-scale survey or experimental intervention.

Example 1.5   A Qualitative Follow-up Design

Experimental programs that do not achieve their goals are an especially good match to follow-up qualitative extension designs, as illustrated by the efforts to understand the failure of an intervention intended to reduce the rehospitalization of schizophrenic patients (Chinman, Weingarten, Stayner, & Davidson, 2001; Davidson, Stayner, Lambert, Smith, & Sledge, 1997). The project began with an intervention that followed the best available treatment model, using careful monitoring of symptoms to head off rehospitalization. Unfortunately, this intervention had no effect on readmission rates. Rather than simply labeling their experiment a failure, Davidson et al. conducted open-ended interviews with patients who kept returning through the "revolving door" between the community and the psychiatric ward. By asking the patients themselves about their experiences, the research team not only encountered a whole new perspective on why patients came back to the hospital but also discovered a promising way to decrease readmissions.

(Continued)

(Continued)

The qualitative interviews showed that patients were often attracted to life in the hospital—especially in comparison to the lives that they lived in the community. The appealing features of the hospital included "respite, privacy, safety, and, above all, care" (Davidson et al., 1997, p. 777). In contrast, life in the community was often stressful, degrading, and iso-lated. Chinman et al. (2001) then described how the researchers worked with recovering patients to design a program for improving the patients' quality of life in the community so that hospitalization would no longer be as attractive. A key insight involved patients' frequent reports that the hospital was often the only place where people truly cared about their welfare. Hence, the revised intervention brought the former patients together in a regular series of group activities that featured mutual support as well as social opportunities. These group meetings not only assisted with the original goal of carefully monitoring symptoms but also created a community of peers who shared the same experiences and needs. Ultimately, readmission rates did fall in response to these revisions to the original intervention.

The point of the qualitative study in a follow-up qualitative extension design is to learn things that take you beyond the results provided by the quantitative methods that form the core of the project. On the one hand, the results from your quantitative studies may support your original hypothesis, in which case a follow-up qualitative study can help you illustrate the nature of those results. On the other hand, the predetermined questionnaires and protocols may not provide the data you need to investigate new issues that come up during the course of the research. Hence, either expected or unexpected results can create value for even a small qualitative follow-up study.

Follow-up Quantitative Extensions to Core Qualitative Research Projects (Chapter 9)

These designs use a quantitative study to follow up on a largely qualitative project (*QUAL* → *quant*). For example, if you want to know how well the con-clusions from a case study at a single site might apply to other sites, then a small survey can show whether the same processes are at work elsewhere. Similarly, if your open-ended interviews lead you to conclusions about changes that will make a difference in your informants' lives, then a small-scale demonstration program could demonstrate how this intervention would work. As these examples and the extended Example 1.6 show, follow-up quantitative extension designs use a supplementary quantitative study to build on the results from a project that relies on a core set of qualitative methods.

Example 1.6   A Quantitative Follow-up Design

Some of my early research with focus groups used a small quantitative study that followed up on a core qualitative study (Morgan, 1989). The primary goal of the project as a whole was to understand the role of social support networks in the lives of recent widows, and I wanted to do a highly exploratory study of how others affected the widows' adaptation to this stressful life event. Hence, focus group interviews consisted of only one question: "What things have made your life either easier or harder since your husband died?" Note that this question makes no reference to the role of other people so as to address this topic within the larger context of the experience of widowhood. To address issues of social support, I systematically coded for references to other people and things they did they that made life either easier or harder for the focus group participants.

An unexpected result from the qualitative portion of the project was the discovery that although negative interactions with other network members were relatively uncommon, they seemed to have just as much, if not more, impact as positive, supportive interactions. This idea was largely undiscussed in the literature, so I wanted to follow it up with a small survey, whose purpose was to demonstrate that negative aspects of relationships could have strong effects on the lives of older people in general, not just recent widows. The supplementary study contained standard questions about supportive interactions and a new set of questions that asked about parallel versions of negative interactions. I gave this survey to a "convenience sample" of 20 older people who had not experienced a specific stressful life event. Even the small sample in this follow-up study clearly showed how powerful negative relationships were. This served the purpose of enhancing my ability to pursue further research based on more survey measures that demonstrated the ability to apply my insights to a broader, more general set of participants.

The follow-up quantitative study in a follow-up quantitative extension design contributes the ability to enlarge the range of settings and populations that the research project can address. Many qualitative studies are guided by the goal of understanding a particular set of circumstances or "context" in depth and detail. Thus, if you want to demonstrate that the results from a qualitative study apply more broadly or that they can be transferred to other settings, then you might use a follow-up quantitative extension design.

* * *

Taken together, the four designs that make up the sequential priorities model occupy the central portion of this book. Following that section, the chapters in Part 3 (Chapters 10 to 12) take up more specific issues, most of which are extensions of the topics raised in earlier chapters.

CONCLUSIONS

Each of the chapters in Part 1 of the book will conclude with a consideration of the same three basic points, which summarize the basic argument for the book as a whole.

1. *Every successful research project requires two things: a meaningful research question and an appropriate way to answer that question.*

This statement describes the most basic elements that you need before you can begin the process of designing any project. Regardless of whether your research uses qualitative, quantitative, or mixed methods, you need to find appropriate ways to answer meaningful research questions. In particular, you need to match the strengths of your research procedures (i.e., research methods) to your research purposes (i.e., the questions you want to answer). Choosing to do mixed methods research means that you need a wider set of strengths than you can get from either qualitative or quantitative methods alone. The underlying reason you need this combination of different strengths almost always involves the choice to pursue a more complex set of purposes. Thus, the best way to address many of the problems that can arise from the substantial differences between qualitative and quantitative methods is to begin with a strong sense of how your research procedures will accomplish your research purposes.

In terms of future directions for the field of mixed methods research, an emphasis on a pragmatic linkage between purposes and procedures offers a promising direction. This kind of overarching framework is especially important because efforts to integrate qualitative and quantitative research are occurring across such a wide range of disciplines within the social sciences. One way to increase the level of consensus in the field is through a reliance on pragmatism as a conceptual framework. Another way to encourage conversations across disciplines is to develop a concise and comprehensive set of research designs. This book thus pursues both pragmatism at a conceptual level and research design at practical level to provide a common frame of reference for mixed methods research as a field.

2. *Deciding how to do your research depends on a clear understanding of why you are doing the research.*

This second point moves the broad nature of the first point into the realm of the specific decisions you need to make about your research designs. It is often said that your research questions should determine your research methods, and it is research design that creates the essential connection between these two. Effective research design is equally about why you are doing your research and how you will do it. Making decisions about research design thus requires careful attention to both the purposes behind your research and the procedures you use to address those purposes. Hence, the presentations of the designs that make up the core of this book will balance descriptions of how to use a specific design with equivalent discussions of when and why you would use that design.

One of the advantages of mixed methods research is the range of purposes that you can pursue. This flexibility comes at a price, however: the greater complexity of the procedures involved in using a combination of methods. This complexity reinforces the importance of creating explicit and detailed linkages between your purposes for using mixed methods and your procedures for doing so. Thus, the best way to address many of the problems that can arise from the substantial differences between qualitative and quantitative methods is to begin with a strong sense not just of what your research goals and your methods will be but also of how your research procedures will accomplish your research purposes.

3. *Choosing research methods that can accomplish your research goals requires knowing both what your options are and how to evaluate those options.*

Saying that your project requires the different strengths of different methods means that you need to know not only the strengths of those methods but also the specific purposes those strengths can serve. The more you understand what a set of research methods can and cannot do, the easier it is to match those procedures to your purposes. Qualitative and quantitative research already have well-understood sets of assumptions about the strengths of their methods and the purposes that match those strengths. This book moves toward the same level of specificity for the procedures associated with mixed methods research by offering detailed presentations of the four options for research designs, as well as clear guidance for evaluating how well each of those designs matches a specific set of research goals.

In mixed methods research, the need to work with multiple methods complicates the basic idea that you need to choose methods that will answer your questions. In particular, when you collect both qualitative and quantitative data, you need some way to deal with the differences between these procedures. This means you must go beyond selecting each type of method for its specific strengths; in addition, you need to consider your choices according to how you will integrate the different kinds of results that each method produces. This means that choices about research design are even more critical to integrate your research procedures so as to address your research purposes.

* * *

Ultimately, the field of mixed methods research should pursue a path that leads to the same kind of consensus that already characterizes qualitative research and quantitative research. The three parts of this conclusion suggest the broad basis for such a consensus. First, there needs to be a general agreement about the kinds of research questions that are most meaningful to pursue with mixed methods research. Second, there needs to be well-understood statements about the implications those research purposes have for our research procedures. Finally, there needs to be a shared sense of how the specific strengths of different research designs make them well suited for some of these purposes and less appropriate for others. The book cannot promise to address that large an agenda. Still, as the familiar proverb says, a journey of a thousand miles begins with a single step, so it is important to take that step in the right direction.

SUMMARY

Mixed methods research begins with the recognition that different methods have different strengths. Qualitative and quantitative methods can thus make very different contributions to any project that combines the two. These same differences, however, also make it more complex to integrate the results. At the broadest level, pragmatism meets this requirement with a conceptual framework that links research methods and research goals. Next, bringing qualitative and quantitative methods together requires a detailed understanding of their separate strengths, along with research designs that explicitly integrate those strengths. Among three possible approaches to integrating the results from mixed methods research, the current emphasis is on a sequential priorities model. In this model, a supplementary study serves as either an input or a follow-up to a core study, yielding four possible research designs: *qual* → *QUANT, quant* → *QUAL, QUANT* → *qual,* and *QUAL* → *quant.* Taken together, this set of research designs offers a powerful set of possibilities for integrating the results from qualitative and quantitative methods.

DISCUSSION QUESTIONS

The idea that additional methods can contribute additional strengths isn't necessarily the only justification for using mixed methods. What other arguments can you think of for combining qualitative and quantitative methods?

Why is it important to pay attention to the complexities of combining qualitative and quantitative methods? List as many potential problems as you can that might make it difficult to combine these two kinds of research.

ADDITIONAL READINGS

By far the most important resource for learning more is the Handbook of Mixed Methods Research:

Tashakkori, A., & Teddlie, C. (2010). *SAGE handbook of mixed methods research in social & behavioral sciences* (2nd ed.). Thousand Oaks, CA: Sage.

Within that volume, two especially useful orientations to the field as a whole are these:

Creswell, J. W. (2010). Mapping the developing landscapes of mixed methods research. In A. Tashakkori & C. Teddlie (Eds.), *SAGE handbook of mixed methods in social & behavioral sciences* (2nd ed., pp. 45–68). Thousand Oaks, CA: Sage.

Teddlie, C., & Tashakkori, A. (2010). Overview of contemporary issues in mixed methods research. In A. Tashakkori & C. Teddlie (Eds.), *SAGE handbook of mixed methods in social & behavioral sciences* (2nd ed., pp. 1–44). Thousand Oaks, CA: Sage.

CHAPTER 2

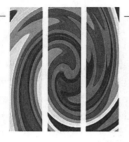

Pragmatism as a Paradigm for Mixed Methods Research

Overview

This chapter provides an overview of pragmatism as a paradigm for research in the social sciences. The first section introduces the core principles of pragmatism, along with the stance that experiences cannot be separated from the social contexts in which they occur. The second section uses the work of John Dewey to develop a more specific approach to pragmatism with a particular emphasis on Dewey's concept of research as a form of inquiry. The chapter concludes with a discussion of pragmatism as a paradigm for mixed methods research, along with a consideration of the alternative paradigm offered by the philosophy of knowledge.

L ike most discussions of paradigms in mixed methods research, this book will rely on pragmatism (e.g., Beista, 2010; Johnson & Onwuegbuzie, 2004; Maxcy, 2003; Morgan, 2007; Patton, 1988; Teddlie & Tashakkori, 2010). Pragmatism as a philosophy originated in the United States in the late nineteenth century. The first detailed summary was the psychologist William James's 1907 book, *Pragmatism* (1995). In addition to James, other major pragmatists include Charles S. Peirce in philosophy; John Dewey in education and philosophy; and George Herbert Mead, whose work served as the basis for symbolic interactionism (for general overviews of pragmatism, see De Waal, 2005; Murphy, 1990; Rescher, 2000).

PRAGMATISM AS A PHILOSOPHICAL SYSTEM

It is important to distinguish pragmatism as a philosophical system from simple notions about what is "pragmatic" (i.e., what works or is efficient in a given situation). Of course, there is an overlap in meaning of the two, based on their origin in the Greek word for "action," which is the central concept in nearly all versions of pragmatism. From a philosophically pragmatic point of view, there is no way that any human action can ever be separated from past experiences and the beliefs that have arisen from those experiences. From childhood on, people take actions according to their likely consequences, and they use the results of those actions to think about what will likely happen if they take similar actions in the future. This leads to a broad definition of pragmatism as a philosophy in which the meaning of actions and beliefs is found in their consequences.

Three other widely shared elements of pragmatism are these:

1. *Actions cannot be separated from the situations and contexts in which they occur.* The idea that actions cannot be separated from situations and contexts corresponds to a pragmatist argument that all action is "action in the world." This world is, in turn, a world of experiences that occur to specific people in specific circumstances. Thus, no objective concept of truth can be assigned to any particular action, because the consequences of any act depend on the situation in which it occurs. Instead of universal truths, pragmatists emphasize *warranted beliefs.* As you repeatedly take actions in similar situations and experience the consequences of those actions, you learn the likely outcomes of acting one way rather than another. These repeated experiences of predictable outcomes produce warranted beliefs.

2. *Actions are linked to consequences in ways that are open to change.* The situational nature of action also means that its consequences can change as situations change. For example, carrying on an otherwise ordinary conversation during a movie demonstrates how the meanings and consequences of the "same" act can vary from situation to situation. More fundamentally, pragmatists believe that it is never possible to experience *exactly* the same situation twice, so any beliefs you have about how to act in a situation are inherently provisional, and you can only act in terms of your warranted beliefs about the *likely* consequences of that line of action. One important implication of this aspect of pragmatism is that the meaning of acts can change over time, whenever the consequences of those acts change. Beliefs are thus continually evolving as a result of ongoing experiences. Figure 2.1 uses the analogy of a spiral to relate changes in actions, experiences, and beliefs.

Figure 2.1	A Pragmatic Perspective on Ongoing Experience

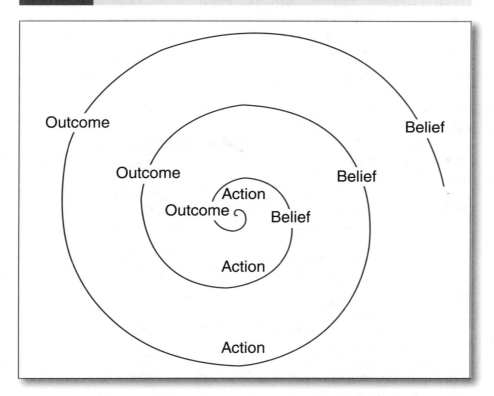

3. *Actions depend on worldviews that are socially shared sets of beliefs.*
Pragmatists treat beliefs as interconnected rather than isolated, and the ultimate
product of experience is a worldview that shapes actions. Because no two people
have identical experiences, no two worldviews are identical. Still, one will find
varying degrees of *shared experience* between any two people, leading to different
degrees of *shared beliefs*. To the extent that two people share the same beliefs
about a particular situation, they are likely to act in similar ways and assign similar meanings to the outcomes of those actions. Worldviews are thus both individually unique at the most detailed level and socially shared at broader levels.

Taken together, these elements of pragmatism demonstrate that it is itself a
unique philosophical worldview. In contrast to philosophies that emphasize the
nature of reality, pragmatists emphasize the nature of experience. In place of
questions about the nature of truth, pragmatists focus on the outcomes of

experience over reality

action. Instead of concentrating on individuals as isolated sources of beliefs, pragmatists examine shared beliefs. Thus, pragmatism as a philosophical stance is quite different from many other philosophical systems—and even more different from the crude summary of pragmatic behavior as "what works."

A PRAGMATIST APPROACH TO RESEARCH

The specific version of pragmatism in this book is based on the work of John Dewey, most notably his book *How We Think* (1933/1986). As a philosopher, Dewey was especially interested in the concept of *inquiry* as a form of experience that helps to resolve uncertainty. Inquiry is thus a conscious response to situations in which how one should act is not immediately clear. When you are faced with such situations, pragmatism asks the key question: What difference would it make to act in one way rather than another? And the only way you can answer this question is by tracing out the likely consequences of different lines of action and ultimately deciding on a way of acting that is likely to resolve the original uncertainty in the situation.

This perspective is quite familiar for researchers in general, and especially those engaged in research design, where the key question is what difference it would make to do a research project one way rather than another. This also points to the importance of warranted beliefs (a concept that originated with Dewey). Research is seldom, if ever, a purely trial-and-error process. Instead, it proceeds from warranted beliefs about the likely consequences of using one research design rather than other. Further, these beliefs are typically shared within a field of research; examples are the worldviews that apply to qualitative, quantitative, or mixed methods research.

Research as Inquiry

Dewey's concept of inquiry links beliefs and actions through a process of decision making. For social science research, this emphasis on decision making matches what Michael Patton (1988) has called a "paradigm of choices." Similarly, Johnson and Onwuegbuzie (2004) recommended a "contingency theory" approach to research design,

> which accepts that quantitative, qualitative, and mixed research *are all superior under different circumstances* and it is the researcher's task to examine the specific contingencies and make the decision about which research approach, or which combination of approaches, should be used in a specific study. (pp. 22–23)

Thus, when you think about what difference it would make to use one method rather than another, you are thinking about the potential consequences of this choice. Moreover, the potential results from your choice can only be evaluated in terms of the goals and purposes behind your original research question. It is important to note, however, that Dewey did not distinguish between research and more everyday forms of inquiry. In both cases, making decisions means evaluating how well the likely outcome of a decision would match your purposes. What distinguishes research is the amount of careful attention and self-conscious decision making it requires. In addition, as a researcher, you are a member of larger research communities, which guide your beliefs about both the kinds of research questions to ask and the kinds of methods that will best address those questions.

Figure 2.2 illustrates Dewey's (1933/1986) general framework for understanding problem solving as a set of five steps. To follow this line of reasoning, you might want to think about an everyday problem that is large enough to require a careful decision-making process (e.g., buying a car). Step 1 involves recognizing a problem, that is, a situation in which your current range of experiences does not supply a line of action that would address the situation; instead, you need to think through the problem and search for a likely solution (step 2). Dewey termed this process of working through the nature of the problem *reflection,* and it is important to note that you can only reflect on the problematic situation by using your existing beliefs. In other words, even though the problem lies outside your existing experience, the only resources that you have for thinking about the problem are your current ideas. (In terms of buying a car, this might mean considering the tradeoff between the higher cost of a new car versus the uncertain reliability of a used car.)

The outcome from reflecting on the nature of the problem, achieved in step 3, is a suggested solution, which consists of a set of actions that seem likely to resolve the problem. The key element in understanding the link between reflecting on the nature of the problem and devising a suggested solution is recognizing that a certain "leap of faith" is involved. You are thus speculating about a possible line of action that would be likely to address the problem. Within pragmatism, this process is known as *abduction*. At its core, abduction consists of generating a kind of if-then formulation, in which your reflection on the nature of the problem leads you to conclude that *if* you act in a particular way, *then* you are likely produce a specific set of outcomes. For example, you might decide that it would be better to buy a used car, as long as you could get a guarantee that would cover necessary repairs.

Rather than moving from a suggested solution to immediate action, step 4 in the inquiry process involves an assessment of that tentative solution. As Figure 2.2 shows, this is once again a process of reflection; for this reason,

Figure 2.2 Dewey's Five-Step Model of Inquiry

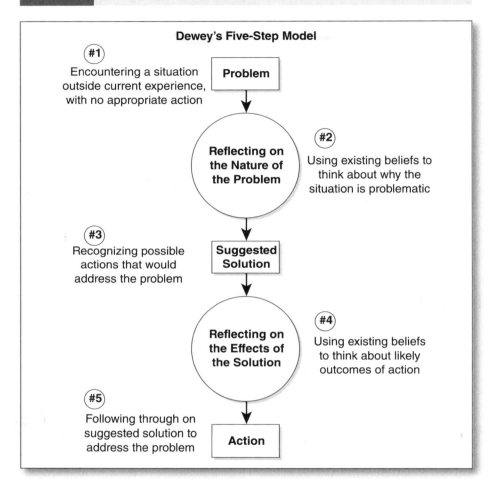

Dewey's explanation of inquiry is sometimes called a "doubly reflective" model. In the same way that step 2 in the model required you to consider the nature of the problem, this stage requires reflection on the nature of the solution. More specifically, you need to consider whether the suggested line of action will not only solve the problem but also avoid producing a new situation that is just as problematic. In the example of buying a car, step 4 might require visiting a number of dealerships to ask about the guarantees they give with used cars.

Step 5 is taking action. Before you act, you have developed a new belief that this kind of action can address this problem. The nature of this belief changes considerably when you experience the actual outcomes of acting. In particular, Dewey (1933/1985) referred to beliefs that arise from the consequences of action as warranted beliefs. The idea that beliefs are warranted distinguishes these beliefs from purely speculative beliefs about what might happen if you acted in a particular way.

What connects this general process of inquiry to research as a specific form of inquiry? Figure 1.1 has already shown the equivalent five-step model as applied to research, and the only difference between that and Figure 2.2 is the labeling of the steps. In other words, the only difference between ordinary problem solving and research is the greater rigor and self-awareness that accompanies the more formal research process. Thus, the start of the process involves the selection of a research question rather than simply "encountering" a problem. Similarly, the form of the suggested solution in research consists of a tentative research design, generated as you evaluate the belief that if you use a given set of methods, you will produce results that directly address your research question. As a final step, you need to take action in the form of collecting and analyzing data and comparing those results to your original goals. If you are satisfied with the conclusions, then you have a warranted belief that this kind of design is indeed an appropriate approach to this kind of research question. Example 2.1 illustrates the operation of this series of steps with regard to an actual research project.

Example 2.1   Applying Dewey's Model of Inquiry

As an example of research as a formal version of inquiry in general, consider a more extended version of the study on Alzheimer's caregiving that I described in Chapter 1. My basic goal in the original project was to understand the difference between family caregivers for someone with dementia who was still living in the community and those caregivers whose family member had moved to a nursing home. From the point of view of the larger research field, there was a widespread interest in how social support networks helped with family caregiving as a stressful life event. Nearly all of the existing work, however, was focused on community-based rather than nursing home–based caregivers. I thus decided to compare the role of social support networks for family

(Continued)

(Continued)

caregivers of Alzheimer's patients in both settings. This choice of a broad research problem amounted to the first step in the process shown in Figure 2.2.

At the next step, my reflections on the nature of this problem pointed to the differences between the goals for studying community-based versus the nursing home–based caregiving. In particular, the greater research base for community-based caregiving pointed toward a quantitative approach that would add to the previous work. In contrast, the less studied topic of family caregiving in nursing homes pointed toward a more exploratory qualitative approach. This need for methods with "different strengths" indicated the value of a mixed methods approach.

Next, the key question for the overall research design was how to collect both of these types of data on a relatively limited budget. I eventually decided on a research design that relied on a combination of qualitative and quantitative data from the same caregivers. Reflecting on this design led to the choice of focus groups with matching surveys as methods. Combining these methods, my research team and I collected data from 200 caregivers.

Expanding Dewey's Model of Inquiry

One notable limitation of the discussion so far is that it seems as if a fixed, step-by-step process connects the detection of a problem to the action that is designed to address it. Actually, there is a set of loops that can lead to more complex paths through the decision-making process. Figure 2.3 shows these alternatives, and Example 2.2 applies them to the same research project as Example 2.1. The two loops on the left are related to each of the reflective processes that occur during inquiry, and the loop at the top opens up the possibility that your reflections may lead you to modify your goals. In this case, thinking about possible ways to address your question may lead you to refine or revise it to better match the range of designs that you can imagine. At the next stage of reflection, the loop indicates that you do not automatically proceed from a choice of design to a choice of methods; instead, considering choices about your methods may lead you to revise your earlier choice of a design. In addition, taking these dual loops together as a set indicates you may go through several rounds of reconsidering both your research question and your research design before you reach a suitable match.

Figure 2.3 Making Revisions Within the Five-Step Model

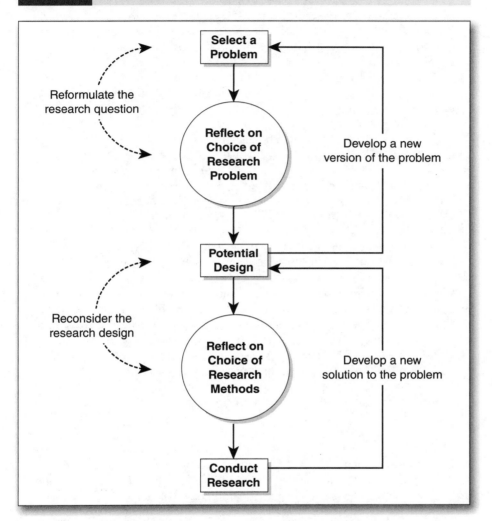

Example 2.2 A Dynamic Application of Dewey's Model of Inquiry

The caregiving study went well until the analysis stage, when I ran into trouble with an important research question: Which mattered more, the caregivers' positive relationships or their negative relationships? The surveys

(Continued)

(Continued)

showed many more mentions of positive relationships within the caregivers' social networks, but the focus groups contained more discussion of negative relationships. In terms of Figure 2.3, this posed a new problem, which required a reformulation of the research question.

This new question also required a reformulation of the research design, because as Chapter 1 emphasized, I didn't start my original work with a clear plan for integrating the qualitative and quantitative data. Now I needed to reflect on the lack of agreement between the two types of data and how to revise the research design accordingly. The most obvious choice was to continue with each of the separate data analyses but to work back and forth between them in a more self-conscious fashion.

At the next step, I chose my specific analysis method by comparing the relative simplicity of working with the survey data and the relative difficulty of recoding the qualitative data. Hence, I reexamined the survey data as a starting point for the further analyses, and those results yielded an important new insight. Comparing the predictive power of the positive and negative relationships showed that even though there were more positive relationships, they had weak effects at best. In contrast, the negative relationships, although rarer, consistently had strong effects across the board. The next question was how to pursue this finding in the qualitative data.

In terms of Figure 2.3, this amounted to a shift to the right-hand side of the diagram and a reconsideration of the research design in terms of a new pattern of results. This led to a revised version of the qualitative results, which showed that the participants were devoting nearly all of their discussion to the negative *effects* of relationships. This would make perfect sense if the negative relationships had strong impacts on their lives while the positive relationships were much less consequential, which is just what the quantitative data indicated.

This new convergence was an interesting way of accounting for the earlier discrepancy. At last, I had an answer to my research question—which meant that I didn't need to follow the final loop of the right-hand side of Figure 2.3 by revising my research goals yet again.

The two feedback processes on the right side of Figure 2.3 connect the more action-oriented aspects of the inquiry process. At the top, once you begin to think about the possible consequences of a specific research design, you may recognize either new problems or new opportunities in the original research question. Similarly, the lower connection recognizes that research is not just one specific action but a complex combination of data collection and analysis; thus, beginning the research process itself may lead you to reconsider your design and possibly even your research question. Example 2.2 demonstrates this kind of reconsideration.

In addition to potentially misunderstanding inquiry as a simplistic step-by-step process rather than a more dynamic system, one may also misinterpret inquiry as a purely individual process rather than a social one. In particular, many of your experiences as a researcher are vicarious rather than personal in that you learn by hearing about the experiences of others. In learning about research, much of the knowledge that you acquire begins in the classroom and proceeds through activities such as working as a research assistant. Thus, your understanding of what difference it makes to do research one way rather than another extends well beyond the realm of your personal experiences.

The social aspects of inquiry are by no means limited to individuals. Research fields as a whole act as "learning communities" (Denscombe, 2008), where interconnected networks of researchers share their experiences. The discussion so far has concentrated on inquiry as an individual process; however, the next section considers inquiry on a community-based level. In particular, it examines pragmatism as a belief system that guides the actions of researchers in mixed methods research as a whole. The goal here is to examine the broader assumptions that lie behind different approaches to research, and questions at this level are typically addressed as paradigm issues.

PARADIGMS AND PRAGMATISM

Understanding what it means to use pragmatism as a paradigm begins with a clear sense of what paradigms are. Thomas Kuhn introduced the concept of paradigms in his book *The Structure of Scientific Revolutions,* which was first published in 1962 (1996). For Kuhn, a paradigm was a belief system that allowed a community of researchers to agree on both the most important questions in their field and the most appropriate ways to answer those questions. Another way to say this is that paradigms make it easy for you to evaluate both whether a proposed research project is worth doing and whether the proposed methods are capable of producing the desired results.

Most of the examples that Kuhn discussed were in the natural sciences. By comparison, the social sciences are "pre-paradigmatic." In other words, fields like education and sociology do not have the kinds of unifying belief systems that guide physics and chemistry. Yet paradigms do exist in the social sciences; instead of occurring at the level of whole disciplines, these paradigms operate within smaller subfields (see Kuhn, 1962/1996, pp. 174–210). There is thus a considerable difference between the consensus in a broad field such as physics and the smaller, more specific paradigms that exist within the social sciences. For example, if you were putting together a thesis committee, working within a shared paradigm would mean working with professors who were all knowledgeable about both your key topics and the typical methods in your research area. Example 2.3 describes one such research area.

Example 2.3	Stress, Coping, and Social Support as an Example of a Paradigm

The ongoing example in this chapter comes from a field known as "stress, coping, and social support," and this research area developed a coherent paradigm during the late 1970s. The shared sets of problems that guide this area examine how stress is related to outcomes such as depression and well-being. In particular, researchers share an interest in the ways that coping and social support may reduce the negative consequences of increased stress.

At a conceptual level, the field often examines stress in terms of a series of life events, which can be summarized in inventories that assign the most stressful life events higher weights. Coping can be separated into cognitive and behavioral domains, with cognitive coping emphasizing ways of thinking that can reduce the impact of potentially stressful events and behavioral coping consisting of actions that reduce the impacts of life events. For social support, individuals' networks are treated as resources that can help minimize the impacts of life events.

These conceptual variables are typically measured through questionnaires that use self-reports to capture each of the three core topics, and a general consensus exists about a number of specific scales that can be used for data collection and analysis. Analysis of these data is typically conducted through regression, with the straightforward prediction that stressful life events will have negative effects on well-being while coping and social support will have positive impacts. In addition, there are more complex hypotheses about various specific combinations of the three key variables.

Like most well-developed paradigms, this one sounds very straightforward, yet just before the emergence of this paradigm, careful research on concepts such as stressful life events, coping mechanisms, and social support did not exist. Indeed, the idea of social support has become so commonplace that it has entered our general vocabulary, even though it began as a theoretical concept within this paradigm.

Based on the definition above, a paradigm for *social science research methods* would define the important questions to pursue with regard to research methods, as well as the appropriate ways to address those questions. In essence, this treats research methods as a specialized subfield within the social sciences. Another name for this field is *research methodology,* which literally means the "study of methods." Note that this concept of methodology is quite different from simply specializing in one type of method or another (e.g., surveys or participant observation, statistics or narrative analysis, etc.). Instead, this version of methodology concentrates on the broader study of social science methods as a whole. At most a few hundred researchers are actively involved in asking and answering questions about research methodology in the social sciences. The current argument is that pragmatism provides a paradigm for studying social science research in general and mixed methods research in particular.

An Alternative Approach to Paradigms: Realism and Constructivism

Although Kuhn's earlier work was responsible for the popularity of paradigms, he also felt the need to admit the looseness of his original use of the term *paradigm* in later editions of his book. It is thus not surprising that different fields have attached rather different meanings to the concept of paradigms. Within social science methodology, the most prominent version of paradigms is based on abstract system borrowed from the philosophy of knowledge. Ironically, Kuhn explicitly downplayed this version of paradigms in an important postscript to his book's later editions (1962/1996). Nonetheless, it is the version of paradigms that you are most likely to encounter within the discussion of social science methodology, and it is important to distinguish it from the pragmatic view above.

This version of paradigms was developed by Lincoln and Guba (1985; Guba, 1990; Guba & Lincoln, 2005) using a fundamental triad of concepts from the philosophy of knowledge: ontology, epistemology, and methodology. In this version of paradigms, these three concepts are unified sets of assumptions about the nature of the reality (ontology), what can be known about that reality (epistemology), and how to go about producing such knowledge (methodology). The clearest examples of this kind of paradigm are realism and constructivism, as summarized in Box 2.1; the realist paradigm provides the assumptions that are typically associated with quantitative research, while constructivism provides the typical assumptions for qualitative research.

BOX 2.1   Realism and Constructivism

Realism

Realism begins by assuming there is a "real world" that is external to the experiences of any particular person, and it posits that the goal of research is to understand that world.

Ontology There is a single reality that exists apart from our perceptions or interpretations of that real world.

Epistemology Our knowledge about the world can be subject to error, so what we know today may be replaced by future knowledge.

Methodology Researchers test evidence according to its ability to explain events in the world, and they revise their theories in response to that evidence.

Constructivism

Constructivism begins by assuming that everyone has unique experiences and beliefs, and it posits that no reality exists outside of those perceptions.

Ontology There are multiple realities that reflect the different experiences and beliefs of different people.

Epistemology Each individual possesses a unique perspective on reality and thus his or her own individual conception of "truth."

Methodology Researchers can learn about the experiences and beliefs of others, and they provide interpretations of these data in the form of theories.

Using this version of paradigms, you would begin your research with a set of beliefs about the nature of reality and what it means to have knowledge of that reality. Then you would select a set of research questions and methods that match those assumptions. This approach is based on a version of the philosophy of knowledge that would be termed *metaphysical* because of its emphasis on the nature of reality and what can be known about that reality (Hacking, 1983). These metaphysical issues are especially evident in how the realist and constructivist paradigms handle the concept of *truth*. Following Box 2.1, most **realists** would pursue truth by collecting and testing evidence about the nature of the "real world." Most constructivists, however, would deny the possibility of any such universal notion of truth, since different people have different understandings of the world and what is true for one person might not be true for another.

Pragmatism as a Paradigm

Those who follow the metaphysical version of paradigms argue that approaches to research based on realism and constructivism are inherently incompatible (or, following Kuhn, "incommensurate"). In contrast, pragmatism takes what amounts to a middle road through these assumptions. First, with regard to reality, pragmatists such as Dewey would argue that, even though there is a reality that exists apart from human experience, it can only be encountered through human experience. In other words, all knowledge of the world is socially constructed, but some versions of that construction are more likely to match individuals' experiences. You are thus free to believe anything that you want, but some beliefs are more likely than others to meet your goals and needs. Another way to say this is that the world has an "obdurate" quality (Blumer, 1969), which furthers some lines of actions and resists others.

With regard to epistemology, pragmatism argues that all knowledge of the world is based on experience. This is in sharp contrast to the philosophy of knowledge approach, which emphasizes the concept of truth. Combined with the belief that the world is both real and socially constructed, pragmatists also believe that all knowledge is social knowledge. In particular, every individual is born into a world that has already been experienced and interpreted by previous generations. This means that all of your perceptions of that world are the product of your social experiences since infancy, so any knowledge is inescapably social knowledge. Pragmatists thus acknowledge that each individual's knowledge is unique because it is based on individual experience, while also asserting that much of this knowledge is socially shared because it comes from socially shared experiences.

At the level of methodology, these philosophical assumptions are devoted to questions about why you would want to do research one way rather than another—or produce one form of knowledge rather than another—rather than questions about the nature of research methods themselves. In particular, the assumptions associated with realism and constructivism do not have a *direct connection* to questions about combining qualitative and quantitative methods (e.g., Lincoln & Guba, 1985; Smith & Heshusius, 1986). Thus, you do not need to believe in the existence of an external reality to do surveys, nor do you need to deny the existence of truth if you choose to do participant observation. Instead, it is *more likely* that quantitative researchers will rely on realist assumptions and qualitative researchers will rely on constructivist assumptions.

What would a pragmatist make of the distinction between realism and constructivism? Essentially, these are two different belief systems. In particular, each would not only pose its own set of problems and questions but also have its own preferred ways of addressing those issues. In other words, each meets the Kuhnian definition of paradigms by generating a distinctive consensus about both the purposes of research and the appropriate procedures for pursuing those purposes. At the same time, the results from these two "paradigms" for social science research need not be "incommensurate," because each operates in the same socially shared world. On the one hand, if those who follow these two paradigms do not believe in the mutual relevance of the knowledge they produce, then there will be relatively few situations in which they would produce shared knowledge. On the other hand, those who believe in the mutual relevance of the results from these two approaches are likely to find useful points of complementarity between the knowledge that they produce. Any attempt to integrate qualitative and quantitative research is obviously based on this assumption of mutual relevance.

It is important to note, however, that pragmatism was not included in most discussions of social science research paradigms until quite recently (e.g., Creswell, 2008). One likely reason for this omission is pragmatism's lack of attention to the metaphysical concerns that are central to philosophy of knowledge version of paradigms, as summarized in Box 2.1. In particular, questions about the nature of reality and truth are less central to pragmatism, which concentrates instead on whether knowledge is *useful* (i.e., whether it can be used to guide behavior that produces anticipated outcomes). William James (1907/1995) summarized this as an emphasis, not on whether a thing is true in some metaphysical sense, but on what difference it makes to believe that something is true and act accordingly. Pragmatism thus sidesteps issues such as the nature of reality and truth in favor of emphasizing action as the basis for knowledge.

In addition, by following Kuhn's preferred conception of paradigms, pragmatism argues that concepts such as realism, constructivism, and, indeed, pragmatism itself are human creations that are continually reshaped as they are used. This is quite different from the assumption that all approaches to social science not only *can* be but *should* be conceived and compared in terms of their metaphysical assumptions. Too often, the philosophy of knowledge, with its emphasis on ontology, epistemology, and methodology, is treated as having an external reality that gives it a privileged position for judging social science research. Instead, pragmatism treats it as just one of many possible ways of thinking about social research and suggests that each should be judged by the range of actions that it makes possible.

CONCLUSIONS

As does each of the chapters in Part 1, this chapter concludes by addressing the three basic issues highlighted at the end of Chapter 1.

1. *Every successful research project requires two things: a meaningful research question and an appropriate way to answer that question.*

Within pragmatism, all experience begins with a problem to be addressed or a question to be answered. Next, those purposes need to be connected with a set of procedures that can address the original issue. Ultimately, this combination of purposes and procedures produces action and consequences. This pragmatic approach to inquiry creates a process of planning that starts with your research question, leading to a research design, followed by a choice among available methods. In addition, inquiry within the pragmatist paradigm generates a cycle by which the results of any research project will update the understanding of both future research questions and the strengths of methods for addressing those questions. Pragmatism thus treats research as a process that actively unites purposes and procedures, where neither can be considered in the absence of the other.

For mixed methods research, this choice of pragmatism as a paradigm points to an inquiry process that is built around combining the different strengths of qualitative and quantitative methods. However, simply using different methods with different strengths is not enough. In addition, a clear link must exist between any set of methods and a research question that truly benefits from combining the strengths of those methods. More specifically, there needs to be a plan for *integrating* the results of different methods. Thus, from a pragmatic perspective, both the purposes and the procedures in mixed methods research need to focus on integration as the goal that drives the inquiry processes.

2. *Deciding how to do your research depends on a clear understanding of why you are doing the research.*

The pragmatic system of inquiry puts the beginning of research directly in the determination of the research question, which then motivates the rest of the research process. This corresponds to the essential advice that your research question must guide your choice of research methods, which reflects a thoroughly pragmatic view of the research process. The pragmatic system thus leads to two forms of reflection: first on the nature of the problem and its potential solutions, then on the nature of the potential solution and likely actions. On the one hand, this process of reflection connects the design process to the core research question; on the other hand, it connects design concerns to the choice of specific methods. The pragmatist perspective on inquiry is especially useful in tracing the ways that research designs look both "upward" toward research purposes and "downward" toward research procedures. Pragmatism thus places research design in a crucial role that bridges the gap between research questions and research methods.

From the standpoint of mixed methods research, the centrality of research design points to the unavoidable complexity of combining qualitative and quantitative methods. This matches pragmatism's emphasis on decisions about research design as the core of research-based inquiry. Seen in this light, it becomes clear why pragmatism as a paradigm for social research has arisen with mixed methods research. In particular, the need for innovative insights about complex decision-making in mixed methods research provides a natural connection to the emphasis on reflective decision-making in pragmatism. Thus, the choice of pragmatism as a paradigm in mixed methods research mirrors the larger inquiry process by reflecting on the available alternatives and selecting an approach to research that is built around precisely the needs of mixed methods research as a field.

3. *Choosing research methods that can accomplish your research goals requires knowing both what your options are and how to evaluate those options.*

All research designs reach the point where it is necessary to select methods for collecting and analyzing data. Pragmatism explicitly includes these choices in the broader sequence of decision making that leads from problem selection to the outcomes from these research methods. In particular, inquiry as a process emphasizes reflecting on the fit between potential solutions and likely outcomes. This captures pragmatism's emphasis on decision making: These decisions are treated as potential actions that need to be evaluated in terms of their likely consequences. This amounts to asking the basic pragmatist question: What difference would it make to do things one way rather than another? More specifically, what difference would it make for you to address this particular research question by collecting and analyzing these data in this particular way? Ultimately, you need to be able to justify your choice of research methods, and this evaluation can only be done within the context of the research questions those methods are designed to answer.

In mixed methods research, complex decisions require evaluating not just the separate strengths of the relevant qualitative and quantitative methods but also the combined strengths of a set of methods. In addition, these decisions have to be made in terms of an integrated set of strengths, not just a combination of separate strengths. These strengths are not, however, abstract properties of the methods themselves. Instead, because pragmatism treats inquiry as a process in which reflection unites research questions and research methods, the strengths of research methods can only be considered in terms of the ultimate research goals. For mixed methods research, this points to the priority of producing research designs that explicitly match the needs of specific types of research questions with the strengths of different combinations of methods.

* * *

This chapter has described pragmatism as a paradigm that is directly linked to the needs of mixed methods research. The relevance of pragmatism to inquiry-based decision making is by no means limited to mixed methods research, however. Instead, it applies equally well to both qualitative research and quantitative research. What these approaches have in common is a goal of matching the strengths of methods to the needs that arise from a given research question. Despite this shared need to pair research questions and research methods, the newness of mixed methods research puts it in a unique position. As the next chapter will demonstrate, qualitative and quantitative researchers can benefit from generations of experience in matching their preferred types of research questions to familiar categories of research methods. By comparison, mixed methods researchers are still creating research designs that combine well-understood sets of strengths that address well-defined research questions.

SUMMARY

A number of mixed methods researchers argue in favor of pragmatism as a paradigm for this field. From a pragmatist point of view, research is a form of action to meet goals that are framed in terms of research questions. Among several forms of pragmatism, John Dewey's emphasis on inquiry is especially useful because it provides a direct link to issues of research design. For Dewey, inquiry in both everyday life and research begins with a problematic situation that needs to be addressed through action. The process of addressing a problem requires careful reflection on both the nature of the problem and the range of possible solutions. This kind of pragmatic inquiry centers on the question, What difference would it make to act one way rather than another? This decision-making process ultimately leads to action and consequences, which need to be evaluated in terms of how well they address the original problem. The most common alternative to pragmatism concentrates on realism and constructivism as two alternate ways to understand the world and what it would mean to have knowledge of that world. From a pragmatic point of view, however, questions about the nature of reality are less important than questions about what it means to act and experience the consequences of those actions.

DISCUSSION QUESTIONS

Dewey's model of inquiry states that ordinary inquiry and scientific inquiry are essentially the same, with the major difference being the amount of care that goes into scientific inquiry.

Is the process of answering research questions really the same as ordinary problem solving? In particular, does anything distinguish the scientific method from everyday inquiry?

Pragmatism tends to ignore the connection between realism and constructivism and either qualitative or quantitative research. How important do you think the distinction is between realism and constructivism as fundamental approaches to social science research?

ADDITIONAL READINGS

For introductions to pragmatism, see the following:

De Waal, C. (2005). *On pragmatism.* Belmont, CA: Thomson Wadsworth.
Murphy, J. P. (1990). *Pragmatism: From Peirce to Davidson.* Boulder, CO: Westview.
Rescher, N. (2000). *Realistic pragmatism: An introduction to pragmatic philosophy.* Albany: State University of New York Press.

For discussions of the older, more metaphysical paradigm based on the philosophy of knowledge, see the following:

Guba, E. G., & Lincoln, Y. S. (2005). Paradigmatic controversies, contradictions, and emerging confluences. In N. K. Denzin & Y. S. Lincoln (Eds.), *The SAGE handbook of qualitative research* (3rd ed., pp. 191–215). Thousand Oaks, CA: Sage.
Morgan, D. L. (2007). Paradigms lost and pragmatism regained: Methodological implications of combining qualitative and quantitative methods. *Journal of Mixed Methods Research, 1,* 48–76.

CHAPTER 3

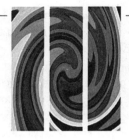

Research Design and Research Methods

Overview

This chapter uses an emphasis on research design to discuss qualitative, quantitative, and mixed methods research as three major approaches to research in the social sciences. The first major section considers the role of research methods in each of these approaches. This discussion then provides a basis for comparing qualitative and quantitative research as the two traditional alternatives in social science research. The third section examines the specific strengths of various qualitative and quantitative methods and illustrates how these strengths can be used in mixed methods research. The final section considers the situation of mixed methods research as a newer and thus less fully developed approach to doing social science research.

I n social science research, one of the most basic choices you are likely to face is between using qualitative methods and quantitative methods, or some combination of the two. But is this really just a question about *methods,* or does some larger distinction among *qualitative research, quantitative research,* and *mixed methods research* need to be made? In large part, the answer depends on what the difference is between "qualitative" and "quantitative" approaches to research.

Although the use of words versus numbers as data may seem like an obvious way to distinguish whether a piece of research is qualitative or quantitative, there is a broad consensus that this is not an effective way to make the distinction (e.g., Hammersley, 1992). In particular, you can use content analysis to convert the texts produced by qualitative methods into numbers for quantitative analysis (Neuendorf, 2002; Weber, 1990); alternatively, you can also convert quantitative data into cases for qualitative analysis (e.g., Onwuegbuzie, Slate, Leech, & Collins, 2007, 2009; Thoits, 1995). Further, although this book concentrates on studies that collect *both* qualitative and quantitative data, some authors define mixed methods research as including also a single data set that is either collected qualitatively and analyzed quantitatively or vice versa (e.g., Teddlie & Tashakkori, 2009, 2010). Thus, there are issues concerning not only the type of data you collect but also how you analyze the data.

Once you recognize that different kinds of research involve more than the format of the data, it is only a short step to realizing that the terms *qualitative* and *quantitative* involve more than the kinds of methods you use. Although it is common to speak of participant observation and open-ended interviewing as "qualitative methods" and survey interviewing and experimental interventions as "quantitative methods," the real distinction is in the way that these methods are used. As Lincoln and Guba (1985) noted, methods are not intrinsically associated with one kind of research or another, so the key concern is not which methods are used to generate data but how they are used and for what purposes.

Rather than thinking of methods as the key features that distinguish different approaches to research, it is more helpful to think of methods as tools that provide a set of strengths that you can use to accomplish a range of goals. In other words, there is more to doing "qualitative research" than merely using qualitative methods, and the same is true for the link between "quantitative research" and quantitative methods. Consequently the remainder of this chapter will use the capitalized terms *Qualitative Research* and *Quantitative Research* to avoid confusion with the specific methods that are associated with them; likewise, the term *Mixed Methods Research* will be capitalized going forward in this chapter. (For similar arguments on the limited role that methods play in defining the difference between Qualitative and Quantitative Research, see Hammersley, 1992; Smith & Heshusius, 1986.)

Thus, to think about the differences between Qualitative and Quantitative Research, as well as where Mixed Methods Research fits into this picture, you need to consider both the more theory-driven set of procedures associated with the level of "research," as well as the more technical set of procedures associated with "methods." The next section will examine how decisions about research design link your purposes to the broader, more theoretical aspects of procedures for conducting Qualitative, Quantitative, and Mixed Methods Research, while the following section will examine decisions about research methods as a narrower, more technical aspect of procedures.

COMPARING QUALITATIVE AND QUANTITATIVE RESEARCH

This section begins with a systematic comparison of Qualitative and Quantitative Research, withholding the comparison to Mixed Methods Research until the end of the section. One reason for starting with these two long-standing approaches to social science research is that understanding their separate strengths is crucial for understanding the Mixed Methods approaches of combining those strengths. Another reason for beginning with Qualitative and Quantitative Research is that this comparison is such a well-known topic in textbooks on research methods. In contrast, there is currently less consensus about the various purposes and procedures involved in combining qualitative and quantitative methods. The first part of this section thus paves the way for the comparison of research design procedures in Qualitative and Quantitative Research.

By tradition, introductory textbooks on social science research compare Qualitative and Quantitative Research through side-by-side comparisons of a number of key features in these two approaches (see Reichardt & Cook, 1979, for an early and influential version of such a comparison). Table 3.1 compares these two forms of research according to three basic distinctions: Qualitative Research is typically inductive, subjective, and contextual, while Quantitative Research is typically deductive, objective, and general. Although most other efforts to compare Qualitative and Quantitative Research contain several more dimensions than the three shown here, those lists often contain a mixture of both broad research *purposes* and specific research *procedures*. In contrast, Table 3.1 brings together both purposes and procedures in a more compact list of essential features.

3 Basic Distinctions

Induction and Deduction

Qual / Quan — Fundamental Difference

The distinction between induction and deduction is a fundamental difference between Qualitative and Quantitative Research. In particular, the inductive purposes associated with Qualitative Research typically start with observations, which you then use to create theory or generate hypotheses. This inductive

Induction

Qual: Create theory – Generate Hypo   *Quan: test theory*

[handwritten margin note: Purposes & Procedures]

Table 3.1	Comparing Qualitative and Quantitative Research
Qualitative Research	**Quantitative Research**
Induction	**Deduction**
Purposes	Purposes
• Generates theory from observations. • Oriented to discovery, exploration.	• Tests theory through observations. • Oriented to cause and effect.
Procedures	Procedures
• Emergent design. • Merges data collection and analysis.	• Predetermined design. • Separates data collection and analysis.
Subjectivity	**Objectivity**
Purposes	Purposes
• Emphasizes meanings, interpretation. • Tries to understand others' perspectives.	• Emphasizes things that can be measured. • Results do not depend on beliefs.
Procedures	Procedures
• Researcher is involved, close to the data. • Researcher is the "research instrument."	• Researcher is detached, distant from the data. • Relies on standardized protocols.
Context	**Generality**
Purposes	Purposes
• Emphasizes specific depth and detail. • Analyzes holistic systems.	• Emphasizes generalization and replication. • Analyzes variables.
Procedures	Procedures
• Uses a naturalistic approach. • Relies on a few purposively chosen cases.	• Uses experimental and statistical controls. • Works across a larger number of cases.

process of beginning with observations leads to goals such as discovery and exploration. In contrast, the deductive purposes in Quantitative Research typically begin with theories and hypotheses, which you evaluate through observations. This deductive process of moving from theory to observations is also associated with goals such as linking causes to effects.

This distinction between inductive and deductive purposes also has a procedural dimension. Inductive purposes aimed at theory generation and discovery correspond to an "emergent" approach to research design. In particular, the ongoing, open-ended observations that are the hallmark of induction can lead to shifts in both your data collection and analysis strategies. For example, your decisions about what to do next in a qualitative study often emerge from

[handwritten margin notes: Deduction — test theory; Procedural Dimension — emergent or predetermined]

your earlier observations and interviews. This approach calls for a flexible merger of data collection and analysis, since it is impossible to know when your observations will become analytic insights. The procedures associated with deduction are, necessarily, quite different. In particular, theory testing requires you to rely on predetermined designs that first collect and then analyze data. For example, only severe problems would justify the alteration of either a survey questionnaire or an experimental intervention once the data collection was under way.

Thus, the emphasis on induction in Qualitative Research is related to theory creation and discovery through flexible, emergent research designs. In comparison, the emphasis on deduction in Quantitative Research is related to theory testing through explicit, predetermined research designs.

Subjectivity and Objectivity

Qualitative Research captures a set of purposes associated with meaning and interpretation. This emphasis on subjectivity applies to both how you do your research and what you study—acknowledging your own interpretive actions as a researcher as well as the importance of meanings in the lives of the people you study. In contrast, Quantitative Research pursues a set of purposes associated with objectivity. This emphasis on objectivity typically leads to a concern with detached measurement and a goal of minimizing your own impact.

There is also a procedural dimension to the distinction between subjectivity and objectivity. In Qualitative Research, the subjective purposes aimed at meaning and interpretation also involve close, personal contacts that use the researcher as the "instrument" for recording observations. For example, as you conduct your qualitative observations and interviews, your own beliefs and experiences will affect not only how you collect data but also the conclusions that you draw from what you see and hear. Objective procedures reverse this, emphasizing instead standardized measurement protocols. For example, when you set up your procedures in a survey project or an intervention, you want to be sure that other researchers who use similar procedures will reach similar results.

Thus, the subjective purposes that characterize Qualitative Research are related to meaning and interpretation, based on close contacts between researchers and the people they study. In comparison, the purposes that characterize Quantitative Research are related to measurement and detachment, based on a careful separation between researchers and the people they study.

Context and Generality — *Qan*

The third set of purposes and procedures in Table 3.1 distinguishes the context-oriented purposes of Qualitative Research from Quantitative Research's emphasis on greater generality. Qualitative Research typically examines specific situations or sets of people in depth and detail. In addition, this approach often relies on a holistic approach that examines as many of the relevant elements as possible. Alternatively, Quantitative Research typically tries to understand larger numbers of people in ways that apply to a wider range of settings. This emphasis on generality also leads to the expression of research questions in terms of variables that often act as elements in abstract models.

Procedurally, the attention that Qualitative Research gives to the holistic understanding of specific contexts is paired with studying behavior as it occurs naturally, with a minimum of intrusion by the researcher. When combined with an emphasis on depth and detail, this necessarily leads to studying relatively few, carefully chosen cases. In participant observation, for example, you would often concentrate on understanding as much as possible about a single, well-chosen setting. Similarly, in-depth interviewing often leads you to study a wide range of factors that influence your research topic, an approach that often produces a large amount of data on a small number of people who meet some specific set of criteria. In contrast, the emphasis on generality associated with Quantitative Research leads to efforts at controlling "extraneous" factors so that the research can apply to a wide range of people or settings. For example, in a survey, you would rely on well-defined samples and carefully constructed variables so your results will represent equivalent variables in larger populations. Similarly, in experiments and program interventions, you want to concentrate on the factors that interest you most so your results will relate to a wider range of people and settings.

Thus, the emphasis on context in Qualitative Research generates detailed understandings of holistic systems through naturalistic studies with relatively small numbers of cases. In comparison, the emphasis on generality in Quantitative Research produces broadly applicable information through well-controlled procedures with larger numbers of cases.

* * *

This conceptual framework makes it easier to understand what Qualitative Research and Quantitative Research are all about. On the one hand, Qualitative

Research consists of purposes and procedures that integrate inductive, subjective, and contextual approaches. On the other hand, Quantitative Research integrates purposes and procedures that are deductive, objective, and generalized. The next section moves from this relatively abstract discussion of Qualitative and Quantitative Research to the more concrete realm of qualitative and quantitative methods.

THE STRENGTHS OF QUALITATIVE AND QUANTITATIVE METHODS

Because Mixed Methods Research combines the strengths of qualitative and quantitative methods, one must know what it means to say that a method is either qualitative or quantitative. Participant observation and open-ended interviewing are the common forms of qualitative methods, and what makes them "qualitative" is a set of strengths that are well suited to the purposes associated with Qualitative Research (see Box 3.1). In terms of the previous section, this amounts to saying that when your research goals emphasize the inductive-subjective-contextual purposes associated with Qualitative Research, then methods such as participant observation and open-ended interviewing are likely to provide the strengths you require. Equivalently, if your purposes emphasize the deductive-objective-generalized purposes associated with Quantitative Research, then you are likely to find the strengths you need in quantitative methods such as survey interviewing and experimental interventions.

BOX 3.1   Strengths of Qualitative and Quantitative Methods

Qualitative Methods

Participant Observation

- Starts with observations as a basis for generating theory. (Induction)
- Concentrates on meaning of observations. (Subjectivity)
- Studies events as they occur in naturalistic settings. (Context)

Qualitative Interviewing

- Allows interview topics to emerge during conversation. (Induction)
- Listens to others' interpretations and perspectives. (Subjectivity)
- Can collect depth and detail on a range of factors related to a topic. (Context)

(Continued)

(Continued)

Quantitative Methods

Survey Interviewing

- Can test hypotheses across a wide variety of variables. (Deduction)
- Uses standardized procedures for questions and answers. (Objectivity)
- Can apply results to a wider range of people or settings. (Generality)

Experimental Interventions

- Creates preplanned changes and tests outcomes. (Deduction)
- Relies on procedures that can be reproduced by other researchers. (Objectivity)
- Concentrates on key variables by "controlling" other factors. (Generality)

As Box 3.1 shows, each of these methods has strengths that correspond to the broader purposes and procedures associated with either Qualitative Research or Quantitative Research. This does *not,* however, imply that any use of qualitative (or quantitative) methods means you are automatically doing Qualitative (or Quantitative) Research. Recall, in this regard, the argument from the beginning of this chapter that what matters most is not *what* methods you use but *how* you use them and *why* you use them that way (i.e., your purposes and procedures). For the two qualitative methods mentioned above, participant observation and open-ended interviews, this section examines how the strengths of those methods match the inductive-subjective-contextual purposes and procedures that characterize Qualitative Research. Similarly, the strengths of survey interviews and experimental interventions are examined in terms of their match to the deductive-objective-generalized purposes and procedures in Quantitative Research.

In addition, the strengths of each method will be considered in terms of their potential role in Mixed Methods Research. To illustrate these possibilities, each method will be paired with one of four sequential contributions designs described in Chapter 1 (which are also the subject of Chapters 6–9).

Participant Observation

The inductive goals of Qualitative Research are particularly well suited to the strengths of participant observation, since this method continually asks the researcher to encounter and make sense of unfamiliar events and settings. In essence, each day of participant observation gives you the opportunity to discover new things by exploring the research setting. Ultimately, however, the goal of participant observation is to build these observations into a broader account that not only describes the research site but also provides an understanding of why things are the way they are. This progression from observation to theory is the heart of the inductive approach.

Subjectivity is also a strength of participant observation, both in terms of your interpretation of others' perspectives and your own efforts to create meaning. Observing others' lives allows you to immerse yourself in their world in an attempt to understand what that world means to them. At the same time, being close to what you are trying to understand lets you pursue your own emerging interpretations. Participant observation thus makes it possible for you to probe the subjective understandings of the people you study at the same time as you engage in a subjective effort to give meaning to your observations.

The ability to investigate context is another clear strength of participant observation. In particular, any event that you observe is connected to both the setting in which it occurs and the participants who are involved. This allows you to describe things in depth and detail while also using your observations to create a more holistic understanding of why things happen the way they do. Of course, participant observation always involves a choice to pay more attention to some things and less to others, but it also forces you to recognize that anything you observe is connected to everything else and nothing is context-free.

Overall, it should be obvious why social scientists classify participant observation as a "qualitative method," since its strengths are so well suited to the goals of Qualitative Research. This does not mean, however, that these strengths have to be used solely for Qualitative Research. Indeed, the ability to observe behavior in naturalistic settings can be of value for a great many research purposes. For example, consider what Chapter 1 termed preliminary qualitative designs (*qual* → *QUANT*). If your ultimate goal is to design an effective intervention program, then it could be helpful to begin by observing how similar programs are currently operating. In a preliminary qualitative design, the strengths of participant observation help you get close enough to the situation to discover how the things that interest you operate in their natural context, and this information allows you to improve the effectiveness of the quantitative portion of the project. Thus, the close match between the strengths of participant observation and the purposes of Qualitative Research does not in any way prohibit other kinds of research from using those same strengths for other purposes.

Qualitative Interviewing

The most obvious strength that open-ended interviewing brings to inductive research is the ability to pursue topics that emerge during the course of the conversation. Thus, the typical semi-structured interview includes both the topics of interest to you as a researcher and the additional interests and insights that the research participant raises. You can then use later interviews to pursue things that you heard earlier. In particular, as you develop tentative conclusions from your earlier work, you can challenge, refine, and extend those ideas in your further conversations. Once again, the data collection process facilitates the essential inductive movement from observations to theoretical summaries.

Open-ended interviewing also provides strengths with regard to the dual subjectivity in Qualitative Research. In particular, you must make sense of what the research participant is telling you to increase your understanding of that person's perspective on your research topic. This kind of interview inevitably emphasizes not only the research participant's beliefs and interpretations but also the researcher's subjective processes. This is a major strength of qualitative interviewing because it gives the researcher an opportunity to learn more about others' beliefs and meanings—including the subjective preferences and expectations that underlie their outwardly observable behaviors.

The concentration on context that occurs in open-ended interviewing is not limited to the immediate situation or setting in which the interview occurs. In addition, this interview format gives you the ability to ask about an exceptionally wide range of factors that may be relevant and to pursue the connections among those factors. For example, this kind of qualitative interviewing often takes a life history approach, which asks participants to construct narratives that connect your research topics to as much of their personal experience as possible. Thus, each person's experiences and beliefs are treated as occurring within a specific context that consists of their whole life as well as the larger cultural and social forces that shaped their life.

Overall, the strengths that open-ended interviewing offers are well suited to the inductive-subjective-contextual purposes associated with Qualitative Research. Yet, these same strengths can also be used for a variety of other purposes. For example, in a follow-up qualitative study (*QUANT → qual*), you might begin with a survey and then pursue in-depth interviews to help you understand unanticipated results from your quantitative analyses. If your goal is to interpret the quantitative findings, then qualitative interviews can help you explore the specific experiences and perspectives of the survey respondents themselves. Once again, it is the strengths of the method that determine when and how you use it.

Survey Interviewing

As a "quantitative method," surveys are well suited to deductive hypothesis testing, because they can measure a relatively large number of variables and investigate the relationships among them. For example, if a theory discusses differences between men and women, then a survey can ask questions that test whether these predictions match the data. For this purpose, the content of the survey is defined according to the needs of the survey, and the resulting data are used to assess the adequacy of theory.

Surveys have a particular strength with regard to objectivity because of the use of easily examined and reproduced questionnaires to generate data. In principle, the results from any survey should be the same (within specifiable statistical limits) whenever the same questions are asked of equivalent samples of research participants. Procedurally, this emphasis on objectivity corresponds to asking each respondent a standardized set of questions and recording his or her answers in a fixed set of response categories. It is thus no accident that these questionnaires are often referred to as survey "instruments," thereby capturing the sense that anyone who uses this tool appropriately will obtain an equivalent indication of the data.

In terms of producing generalized results, the overall set of strengths that surveys offer in this regard should not be confused with the more specific goal of *generalizability*. Generalizability depends on statistical procedures for drawing the sample of survey respondents in a way that specifies the likelihood that the sample represents the properties of the larger population. This ability to represent populations from samples may be the ultimate in generality, but the basic process of survey interviewing is also "generalized" in the sense of treating every respondent in a context-free fashion, regardless of the sampling procedures used. Rather than treating respondents as unique individuals, survey data summarizes each case as a set of values for a collection of variables, producing results that can be stated in general terms as relationships among these variables.

Overall, surveys have obvious strengths for providing the deductive-objective-generalized data that are associated with Quantitative Research. Yet this does not limit surveys to research that fits within this particular configuration of purposes and procedures. For example, in a preliminary quantitative design (*quant* → *QUAL*), highly comparable data and relatively large samples from survey data can be very useful as a preliminary step in locating potential participants for a qualitative study. If your goal is to interview a theoretically interesting but relatively rare category of research participants, then you might be able to locate these informants with a systematic search through a standardized set of data that was available on everyone in a large sample. Thus, even though the standardized procedures of survey methods are typically more suited to Quantitative rather than Qualitative Research, they may still play a useful role in the latter.

Experimental Interventions

Experiments have a notable set of strengths for meeting the deductive goals associated with Quantitative Research. In particular, experiments are designed to provide clearly observable links between experimentally manipulated causes and well-defined outcomes that serve as effects. With experiments, you can intervene in the world and determine whether the intervention, or "treatment," changes the world in the ways that you predicted. With the exception of social psychology, in which research often occurs in "labs," most experimental research in the social sciences takes the form of program interventions. For example, you might modify the services that an organization delivers and then determine whether that organization's clients either use more services or receive greater benefits from those revised services.

Objectivity is a good fit to the standard of replicability, which is one of the key features of experimental methods. This emphasis on objectivity is also evident in the fixed, predetermined procedures that are essential to well-conducted experiments. Hence, you should be able to reproduce other researchers' experimental results as long as you follow exactly the same procedures they used. While laboratories with standardized instrumentation offer the ultimate in terms of objectivity, program interventions follow the same logic by establishing experimental protocols that guide both the treatment of each research participant and the measurement of the outcomes from those treatments.

Experimental methods are also well known for their strengths in producing results that apply to generalized processes rather than to specific individuals or settings. In particular, experimental designs attempt to control for other potentially relevant factors so you can examine the clearest possible version of the relationship between the variables of interest. Program interventions and other quasi-experimental methods also seek to control or eliminate nonexperimental influences to generate greater confidence that the intervention can be applied to other organizations that share the same basic characteristics.

Overall, experimental interventions definitely deliver a set of strengths that are well matched to purposes and procedures of Quantitative Research. Once again, however, these same strengths can also contribute to studies that are largely qualitative in nature. For example, in a follow-up quantitative design

(*QUAL→quant*), it might be desirable to extend an in-depth case study with a small demonstration program. If your goal is to demonstrate that the insights from your qualitative work can be transferred to other settings, then an experiment can demonstrate your ability to convert those ideas into standardized program activities that produce the predicted results in other settings. Of course, the vast majority of Qualitative Research studies will have little need for this particular kind of follow-up study, but there certainly are circumstances in which the additional strengths of an experimental study could make a notable contribution to your larger purposes.

* * *

The key message from this section is that the distinctions among Qualitative Research, Quantitative Research, and Mixed Methods Research depend less on which methods you use and more on the ways that you use them. Thus, the same strengths that make methods useful in either the inductive-subjective-contextual package of Qualitative Research or the deductive-objective-general package of Quantitative Research can also serve other purposes. In particular, the illustrations from the four designs associated with sequential contributions show how the strengths from one type of method can contribute either preliminary inputs or follow-up extensions that enhance the performance of a different method.

THE STATUS OF QUALITATIVE, QUANTITATIVE, AND MIXED METHODS RESEARCH

Qualitative Research, Quantitative Research, and Mixed Methods Research each represent different approaches to producing knowledge in the social sciences. As the two best-known and most fully developed approaches, Qualitative and Quantitative Research offer the clearest packages of purposes and procedures, and one or the other will often be the best choice for a research project. One obvious advantage of these two traditional approaches is that each provides a well-understood basis for linking purposes and procedures. As a result, working within either the Qualitative or Quantitative Research tradition simplifies the process of describing both what you are doing (i.e., your research purposes) and why you are doing it the way you are (i.e., your research procedures).

Qualitative and Quantitative Research are not the only alternatives, however. Mixed Methods Research makes it possible to do things that would be more difficult or even impossible to accomplish by operating solely within either the inductive-subjective-contextual or the deductive-objective-general packages that characterize the two more traditional approaches. This flexibility, however, comes at the cost of greater uncertainty about the purposes and procedures associated with Mixed Methods Research. The lack of a set of established traditions for Mixed Methods Research can make it more difficult to convince others of either the value of your research or the appropriateness of your research procedures.

With regard to your research goals, the fact that Mixed Methods Research projects pursue combinations of purposes that do not fit neatly within the traditional boundaries of Qualitative or Quantitative Research makes this approach more likely to require direct discussions about why you are doing this kind of research. The mere recognition that different methods have different strengths is not enough to support a decision to do Mixed Methods Research. Instead, you need to demonstrate how this approach allows you to accomplish purposes that would be more difficult to achieve with either Qualitative or Quantitative Research alone. Thus, one of the challenges that you will face in doing Mixed Methods Research is a requirement for more explicit arguments to convince others that your research goals are indeed worthwhile.

Once you can clearly state the purposes that guide your research, then you must design a set of procedures that will meet those purposes. The choice of which methods to use and how to apply those methods is, again, more straightforward within the well-developed traditions of Qualitative and Quantitative Research. The range of design options—and the reasons for selecting one option over another—are continually evolving within both Qualitative and Quantitative Research; however, these new developments are based on a well-known foundation of prior practices. For Mixed Methods Research, even when you can clearly state a set of meaningful purposes, the lack of established traditions can still make it difficult to justify your claims about the appropriate procedures for accomplishing those purposes.

Because Mixed Methods Research projects use a combination of the strengths that are traditionally associated with either qualitative or quantitative methods, you have to provide justifications that go beyond asserting the value of each separate method. In particular, you need to demonstrate how your research design *integrates* a specific combination of strengths that can do a better job of meeting your research goals than you could do with either qualitative or quantitative methods alone. At present, however, Mixed Methods Research provides less practice-based guidance about either the design options that are available to you or the criteria you would use to evaluate these options. This lack of ready-made, taken-for-granted justifications means that you will often need to produce explicit arguments about the appropriateness of using a given set of procedures to accomplish a particular set of purposes.

Ultimately, Mixed Methods Research may also develop into a well-understood tradition that is implicitly associated with a set of clearly understood purposes and procedures. Until that time, you are much more likely to receive requests for explicit justifications related to your research goals and procedures when you do Mixed Methods Research rather than Qualitative or Quantitative Research. Hence, one of the major goals of this book is to create not only a better understanding of the purposes and procedures associated with Mixed Methods Research but also a better sense of how they can be integrated within a Mixed Methods Research design.

CONCLUSIONS

1. *Every successful research project requires two things: a meaningful research question and an appropriate way to answer that question.*

All the other choices that you make during your research flow from your initial choice of a research question. In particular, you need to decide if you will use Qualitative, Quantitative, or Mixed Methods Research. Each of these approaches offers different ways to make decisions about both the broad purposes that guide your research and the specific procedures you use. These choices are easier within both Qualitative and Quantitative Research, because these well-established traditions offer consensual understandings about the types of questions they ask and the types of methods they use to answer those questions. In contrast, Mixed Methods Research is still working on these issues. The differences between Mixed Methods Research and the two more traditional approaches are even greater with regard to how they use the different strengths of different methods. In particular, Mixed Methods Research sees the strengths of methods as distinct from the routine ways that those methods are used within either Qualitative or Quantitative Research. Hence, the best way to answer your research question may be to use one strength from what is typically considered a qualitative method and a different strength from a quantitative method.

From a pragmatic perspective, it is important to reemphasize the earlier point that it is not qualitative and quantitative methods that define the difference between Qualitative and Quantitative Research; instead, it is the way those methods are *used*. Concentrating on how methods are used means that they are best understood as tools with different strengths, but these strengths need to be defined according to the research questions they address. In particular, any given Mixed Methods Research project needs to consider the strengths of qualitative and quantitative methods within the context of a specific research question. The pragmatic link between beliefs and consequences thus means that, without the tools to put beliefs about purposes and procedures into action, those beliefs become detached from the practice of research.

2. *Deciding how to do your research depends on a clear understanding of why you are doing the research.*

Qualitative Research and Quantitative Research represent well-understood options for linking an understanding of why you want to do your research and decisions about how to do your research. Qualitative Research emphasizes connections between purposes and procedures that are inductive, subjective, and contextual, while Quantitative Research equivalently matches purposes and procedures that are deductive, objective, and generalized. Consequently, these two approaches offer well-established guidelines for reasoning back and forth among your research questions, your research design, and your research methods. This consensus about both research purposes and procedures provides a framework in which well-developed justifications for research designs connect the strengths of specific methods to those broader purposes and procedures. In contrast, Mixed Methods Research is still developing this kind of consensus about both research purposes and the justifications that link those purposes to research designs. Once again, this book places responsibility on research design as the fundamental process for connecting specific research procedures ("how to") with broad research purposes ("why to"). In particular, the next chapter will present three broad sets of purposes for combining qualitative and quantitative methods.

Pragmatism's emphasis on the linkage between beliefs and their consequences corresponds to the connection between the broader purposes in each research tradition and the conduct of research in those traditions. In particular, research designs connect beliefs about meaningful research questions ("why to") with appropriate methods for answering those questions ("how to"). From a pragmatic point of view, this need to connect purposes and procedures with research is equally important in Qualitative, Quantitative, and Mixed Methods Research. The difference between Mixed Methods Research and the other approaches is the higher degree of consensus about how to connect purposes and procedures in Qualitative and Quantitative Research, as opposed to the relatively low degree of consensus about such connections within Mixed Methods Research.

3. *Choosing research methods that can accomplish your research goals requires knowing both what your options are and how to evaluate those options.*

Qualitative methods, quantitative methods, and mixed methods represent three different sources of techniques for answering research questions. In some cases, the choice may be straightforward. This is certainly the case when you choose Qualitative Research as a way to match purposes and procedures that are inductive, subjective, and contextual with methods such as participant observation and open-ended interviewing. Similarly, deductive, objective, and generalized purposes are well matched to quantitative methods such as experimental interventions and survey interviewing. In contrast, Mixed Methods Research requires a conscious decision about which strengths you need from specific qualitative and quantitative methods. Even then, it is one thing to describe the combination of qualitative and quantitative methods that you want you use and quite another to specify a strategy for integrating the different results that those methods produce.

Because pragmatism emphasizes the different consequences that can arise from making different decisions, it corresponds naturally to making choices about how to do your research. For a developing field like Mixed Methods Research, this translates into the need to develop the kinds of consensual beliefs about purposes and procedures that will provide solid guidance for choices among different research methods. According to pragmatism, such guidance is crucial because it provides you with ways to trace the connections between your beliefs and the likely consequences of doing your research one way rather than another. The outcomes of your research will depend on your decisions about which methods to use as well as your more detailed decisions about how to use those methods and integrate their results. Consequently, the bulk of this book will concentrate on presenting a series of practical research designs that demonstrate both a range of options and a set of rationales for using your research goals to choose among these options.

* * *

Although this book provides one set of answers about the connection between meaningful research questions and appropriate ways to answer those questions, it is important to recognize that there are other possible answers. Consequently, the next chapter will present three broad sets of purposes for combining qualitative and quantitative methods, while Chapters 6 through 9 present four specific research designs for integrating qualitative and quantitative methods. Differences over the specifics of Mixed Methods Research are less important, however, than the need for a consensual framework about purposes and procedures, which can also provide clear guidance about the most effective ways to bring together the different strengths of different methods. This book provides one such framework.

SUMMARY

It is important to distinguish between the larger purposes served by Qualitative and Quantitative Research and the specific methods that are used to collect and analyze either qualitative or quantitative data. There are three basic ways to compare Qualitative and Quantitative Research. First, induction and deduction compare the way that qualitative approaches work from observations up to theories (induction) with the way that quantitative approaches work from theories down to observations (deduction). Second, subjectivity and objectivity compare Qualitative Research, which emphasizes getting close to research participants to understand meaning (subjectivity), to Quantitative Research, which tries to minimize the impact of researchers as they attempt to understand things through measurement (objectivity). Finally, context and generality compare qualitative approaches that concentrate on research results in their specific, local circumstances (context) with quantitative approaches that try to place research results into a broader realm (generality). Qualitative and quantitative methods are designed to meet these objectives: Qualitative methods produce data by emphasizing induction, subjectivity, and context, while quantitative methods produce data using deduction, objectivity, and generality. For Mixed Methods Research, however, these three dimensions represent different strengths that can be met by qualitative and quantitative methods. Hence, a Mixed Methods project might combine a qualitative method that is used primarily for induction and a quantitative method that is used primarily for deduction, and so on.

DISCUSSION QUESTIONS

How important is the distinction between Qualitative and Quantitative Research and qualitative and quantitative methods? If Mixed Methods Research is primarily about combining methods, then how important is it to consider the two broader approaches to research?

Mixed Methods Research argues that it is possible to separate qualitative and quantitative methods from the original justifications for those methods. This means induction, subjectivity, context, and so forth do not have to work together in guiding research. Is this separation so simple, or is it difficult to separate methods from the purposes they were originally designed to serve?

ADDITIONAL READINGS

For more information about participant observation, see the following:

Fetterman, D. M. (2009). *Ethnography: Step-by-step* (3rd ed.). Thousand Oaks, CA: Sage.

For more information about qualitative interviewing, see the following:

Rubin, H. J., & Rubin I. S. (2004). *Qualitative interviewing: The art of hearing data* (2nd ed.). Thousand Oaks, CA: Sage.

For more information about program interventions, see the following:

Shadish, W. R., Cook, T. D., & Campbell, D. T. (2002). *Experimental and quasi-experimental designs for generalized causal inference.* Boston, MA: Houghton Mifflin.

For more information about survey research, see the following:

Fowler, F. J. (2008). *Survey research methods* (4th ed.). Thousand Oaks, CA: Sage.

CHAPTER 4

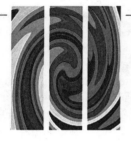

Motivations for Using Mixed Methods Research

Overview

The first section of this chapter lays out a typology for three basic purposes for integrating qualitative and quantitative methods: convergent findings, additional coverage, and sequential contributions. The core of the chapter consists of three sections that describe these motivations, with an emphasis on the work involved in *integrating* qualitative and quantitative methods for each of these three basic purposes. Even though this book concentrates on sequential contributions, it is important to understand where this particular purpose fits within the broader range of reasons that lead researchers to combine different methods. Further, because there is no claim that sequential contributions is the only or even the best reason for combining qualitative and quantitative methods, it is important to consider a range of other purposes for doing mixed methods research.

Although there are a wide variety of motivations for integrating qualitative and quantitative methods, there is little consensus about how to summarize these different purposes. The result is a wide range of poorly understood options, with little information about how to choose among them. This led Hammersley and Atkinson (1995) to criticize what they called "methodological eclecticism"—an anything-goes approach to research design. This kind of unstructured inquiry is rare in mixed methods research, but it is matched by what has become a central problem: how to integrate the results of qualitative and quantitative methods (e.g., Bazeley, 2012; Bazeley & Kemp, 2012; Medlinger & Cwikel, 2008; Moran-Ellis et al., 2006; Plano Clark, Garrett, & Leslie-Pelecky, 2010; Yin, 2006). Given that qualitative and quantitative methods produce such different data, and that analyses typically produce results that come in different formats, how can you bring them together in an effective fashion?

Within mixed methods research, the primary response to this issue has been to generate a series of "typologies" that distinguish various purposes for combining qualitative and quantitative methods. Over the years, researchers from a number of fields have created any number of systems to describe the motivations for using mixed methods research, to the point where such typologies have become a central feature of the field as a whole (Teddlie & Tashakkori, 2010). Early versions of these typologies mostly collected relatively isolated examples of research that combined qualitative and quantitative methods (e.g., Brannen, 1992; Bryman, 1988; Rossman & Wilson, 1985; but see Sieber, 1973, for an alternative approach). An important turning point was the work of Greene, Caracelli, and Graham (1989), who analyzed 57 studies that combined qualitative and quantitative methods to generate a five-category typology. Since then, a variety of other typologies for integrating different methods have appeared (e.g., Creswell & Plano Clark, 2011; Greene & Caracelli, 1997; Morse, 1991; Morse & Niehaus, 2009; Teddlie & Tashakkori, 2009, 2010).

One problem with even the most recent typologies, however, is that they rely almost entirely on *theories* about how researchers might go about combining methods rather than the *purposes* for combining them. Historically, the work of Greene et al. (1989) is an important exception. More recently, Bryman (2006) pursued the same strategy by collecting studies from the mixed methods research literature and classifying them according to the authors' reasons for combining methods. According to Bryman's typology, there are as many as 17 reasons why researchers choose to use both qualitative and quantitative methods.

The current approach emphasizes a pragmatic, purpose-driven perspective on combining methods, but it fits those purposes into a compact typology. This summary of purposes should help you recognize the range of reasons why researchers have been motivated to combine qualitative and quantitative methods. In addition, this typology demonstrates how these different purposes for combining methods are typically matched with different procedures and research designs. In particular, it should help you understand your basic options for doing mixed methods research while also helping you match your own research purposes to one of these three motivations.

A NOTATION SYSTEM FOR COMBINING
QUALITATIVE AND QUANTITATIVE METHODS

To describe the basic options that are available for combining qualitative and quantitative methods, Figure 4.1 expands on the notation that was briefly introduced in Chapter 1. This notation originated in the work of Janice Morse (1991, 2003). The top half of Figure 4.1 shows that you can assign different levels of priority to each study within a project that uses different methods. In particular, a method can play a supplementary role (symbolized as *qual* or *quant*), where the data collected might not stand on their own in a separate study but still make a notable contribution to a larger project that relies on other methods. Supplementary methods are generally paired with core methods (symbolized as *QUAL* or *QUANT*), which determine the uses of the supplementary method. The difference between capital and small letters also indicates that the core methods will almost always be able to stand alone as complete studies in their own right, whereas supplementary studies may or may not be able to stand alone because their designs are dependent on the needs of the core study.

The bottom half of Figure 4.1 shows three ways of connecting the data produced by different methods. First, *convergence* examines the extent to which different methods produce equivalent results and is symbolized by the use of an

Figure 4.1   A Notation System for Combining Different Methods

qual or quant	Supplementary Methods add to an overall project but their results may not be able to stand on their own. Supplementary methods are marked with the use of all small letters
QUAL or QUANT	Core Methods are strong enough to stand on their own, and they may drive the use of supplementary methods within a project. Core Methods are marked with the use of all capital letters.
=	Convergence investigates the same question with multiple methods, to determine whether they produce similar results. Convergence is shown with an equal sign.
+	Addition assigns different methods to different purposes, so that each makes a distinct contribution to the overall results. Addition is shown with an addition sign.
→	Sequencing links the results from separate methods, so that what is learned from one method influences how another is used. Sequence is shown with an arrow sign.

equal sign. Second, *addition* brings together methods that each serve a separate purpose, as symbolized by the plus sign. Finally, in *sequencing,* the results of one method influence how a subsequent method is used; hence, the use of an arrow as the symbol of this linkage.

There is, however, one notable difference between this present version and Morse's original formulation. Where Morse (1991, 2003) used the plus sign to indicate that the data were collected at the same time and the arrow to indicate that the data were collected in sequential studies, the current emphasis is on *how the data are used* rather than *when they are collected.* Thus, studies linked by a plus sign in the present model might have been collected at different times or even as parts of different projects. In that case, the plus sign simply indicates that you *use* both kinds of data simultaneously, regardless of when they were collected.

Similarly, two data sets linked by an arrow might be collected simultaneously but used sequentially. For example, if you collected open-ended qualitative items within a survey, you might analyze the quantitative data first and then use the qualitative data to interpret those results. Simply because the data originated at the same time does not affect your ability to use them sequentially. (For an illustration of a sequential design that collected survey and open-ended interviews at the same time, see Example 8.7.)

In addition, both qualitative and quantitative data are often collected at the same time but are then used sequentially within what are known as *embedded designs* (Creswell & Plano Clark, 2011). Embedded designs typically involve qualitative studies that are conducted as part of larger quantitative intervention programs, such as random controlled trials. More often than not, these qualitative studies follow up on findings from the intervention. So, with regard to the literal timing of the two components in the overall project, portions of the qualitative study do occur simultaneously with portions of the quantitative study, but *when the studies occurred is less important than how the studies were used.* It is the use of the qualitative study as a follow-up to findings from the quantitative study that makes this a sequential design. (For an illustration of a sequential design that occurred within the context of a larger intervention, see Example 8.4.)

THREE BASIC MOTIVATIONS FOR COMBINING QUALITATIVE AND QUANTITATIVE METHODS

These three ways of linking different methods—convergence, addition, and sequencing—correspond to the three basic purposes that are the core of this chapter, which were illustrated in Figure 1.1 in Chapter 1. Here, Figure 4.2 presents a more detailed version of the earlier diagram to summarize those

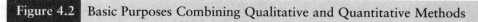

Figure 4.2   Basic Purposes Combining Qualitative and Quantitative Methods

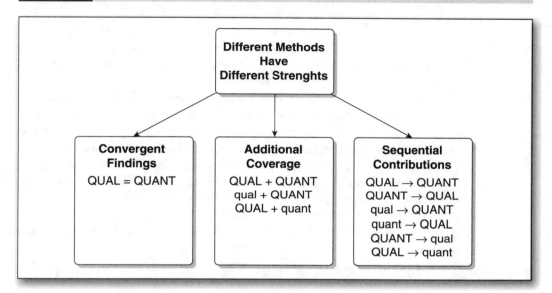

three purposes. The left side of the diagram starts with the earliest reason for combining methods, *convergent findings,* which uses qualitative and quantitative methods to address the same research question. You are most likely to rely on convergent findings when you need to produce greater certainty in your results by showing that methods with different strengths lead to similar conclusions. There is only one basic design for such projects, *Qual = Quant,* because each separate study must produce results that stand on their own, with neither method taking priority over the other.

In the middle of Figure 4.2, *additional coverage* assigns the different strengths of different methods to different goals within the overall project. This motivation relies on a division of labor that matches each method's strengths to a separate goal within the overall research project. You are most likely to pursue additional coverage as a purpose when each method can provide a distinctively different kind of data for the project as a whole. The three subtypes of additional coverage suggest either that each method could make an equal and substantial contribution to the overall project or that either the qualitative or the quantitative method could supplement the coverage that a core method provided.

Finally, projects that are motivated by *sequential contributions* link methods so that one enhances the effectiveness of another. The point of linking the methods is to use what you learn from one method to inform how you will use another method. You are most likely to rely on sequential contributions as a purpose when the strengths of one method can serve as an input to or follow-up on another method, thus allowing you to accomplish more than if you had used either method in isolation. Studies guided by this basic purpose can have considerable flexibility in both the sequence and priority of the methods, yielding designs such as *qual* → *QUANT* or *QUAL* → *quant*.

The differences among these three basic purposes for integrating qualitative and quantitative methods make it clear why the simple assertion that "different methods have different strengths" is only a broad starting point for mixed methods research. All three of these basic purposes arise from that one fundamental insight, but they each pursue it in their own way. In convergent findings, the goal is to locate similar results through methods with different strengths. In additional coverage, the goal is to pursue different tasks, which are assigned to methods with different strengths. In sequential contributions, the goal is to use the strengths of one method to contribute to or build on the different strengths of another method. The distinctive purposes that characterize these separate motivations also lead to different procedures for collecting and analyzing data. Thus, even though all three of these purposes originate from the same basic principle, they each require their own specific research designs.

CONVERGENT FINDINGS

Among the three reasons for integrating qualitative and quantitative methods that are shown in Figure 4.2, comparing the degree of agreement between different methods has the longest and most prominent history. Like many of the ideas that have influenced social science methodology over the past several decades, the idea of seeking convergent results from different methods stemmed from the work of Donald Campbell and his colleagues (Campbell & Fiske, 1959; Webb, Campbell, Schwartz, & Sechrest, 2000). Campbell originated the term *triangulation* to refer to the search for convergent findings as a purpose for combining methods, but that word has since been popularized to include any use of different methods (see the discussion below).

Campbell based the idea of triangulation on procedures in navigation and surveying, as illustrated in Figure 4.3 (see Blaikie, 1991, for an extended discussion of triangulation as an analogy). When you see an object from only one point of view, the most you can do is to lay out a straight line from your current position in the direction of the object. Adding a second sighting on the same object from a different position generates two intersecting lines with the object

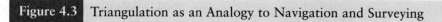

Figure 4.3 Triangulation as an Analogy to Navigation and Surveying

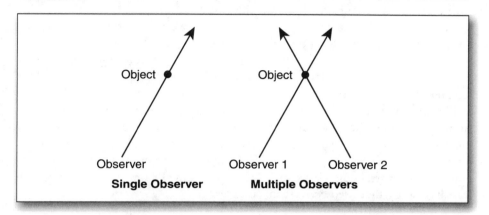

located at the point of intersection, which is the tip of the triangle. By analogy, if you use only one method, you may be limited in your ability to observe a phenomenon. If, however, you also use a different method and still produce similar observations, that convergence can increase your confidence in your conclusions. When a qualitative and a quantitative method agree, you will have more faith in the results that you have "located."

One other important feature of designs that use convergent findings is that the two methods must be used independently of each other. More specifically, the results of one method cannot have any influence on the results of the other method. This separation is necessary so that you can compare two completely separate sets of results to assess their degree of convergence. For example, in Campbell's own early work (Campbell, 1956), he assisted the US Navy in assessing the performance of a set of submarines. On the one hand, Campbell collected quantitative ratings of performance from the Navy's records; on the other hand, he collected a separate set of qualitative ratings from the ships' crew members.

The prominent recognition of convergent findings as a basic purpose for doing mixed methods research is only indirectly due to the work of Campbell and his co-authors, however. Instead, it was Norman Denzin's use of these ideas in his textbook *The Research Act* (1970), whose explicit expansion of Campbell's work brought the concept of triangulation to the fore. Unfortunately, the very popularity of that label created problems. Over time, the term *triangulation* was used so broadly that it became, for all practical purposes, a synonym for any project that used different methods. In particular, when Greene et al.

(1989) compiled their series of studies that combined methods, they found that researchers frequently claimed to be pursuing triangulation even when their work made no attempt to compare the results from different methods. This confusion over the meaning of *triangulation* is the reason for relying on the label *convergent findings* in the present discussion.

In general, you are mostly likely to be motivated by convergent findings to use both qualitative and quantitative methods when you need to produce greater faith in your research results. The search for convergent findings is especially well suited to situations in which you need to rule out the possibility that something about the methods themselves produced the results. Whenever you need to show that the results of your research are not dependent on the strengths of one particular method, there will be value in showing that other methods with different strengths lead to similar conclusions. Example 4.1 presents one research study that used convergent findings.

Example 4.1   Convergent Findings

Kenaszchuk et al. (2012) assessed the degree of consensus between qualitative and quantitative studies regarding the extent to which doctors and nurses collaborated in their work at hospitals. In the qualitative portion of their project, the researchers did ethnographic fieldwork to observe professional collaboration in the general internal medicine wards at seven hospitals. To collect the quantitative data, they had the nurses from these same wards use several survey scales to generate ratings on their collaborative relationships with doctors.

To compare the two studies, they produced rank orderings of the seven hospitals in terms of the degree of collaboration, with separate rankings for the fieldwork and for each quantitative measure. They then used statistical tests to determine the degree of agreement between the fieldwork rankings and the rank ordering for each of the quantitative scales. Overall, they found that the relationships between the qualitative and quantitative ratings indicated moderate to large degrees of agreement. The authors thus concluded that there was a substantial degree of convergence between the qualitative and quantitative data.

Issues Related to Integration

Convergent findings has a longer history than the other two basic purposes considered here, which has both sharpened its purposes and revealed its problems. One particularly troublesome problem arises whenever studies motivated by convergent findings produce results that fail to converge. Although Campbell and Fiske (1959) commented briefly on the concerns raised by divergent results, they treated this primarily as a logical issue. Thus, when two sets of results fail to converge, it is common to conclude that the divergence must be due to problems with one method or the other, but when you have only two sources of data, it is logically impossible for a simple comparison to say which source is responsible for the difference. A common response to divergent results is attempting to resolve the discrepancy through either additional analyses of the original data sets or the collection of new data. Unfortunately, nothing within the convergent findings approach itself gives guidance about how to use additional analyses and new data as a strategy for resolving divergent results. More often than not, the authors of these studies end up with doubts about whether the two methods actually did study the same thing, as in Example 4.2.

Example 4.2   Divergence Rather Than Convergence

School systems are generally seen as an important mechanism for the integration of young immigrants into their new social settings. This poses an important question about the degree to which schools meet the distinct needs of immigrant children. Slonim-Nevo and Nevo (2009) investigated this issue in Israel, starting with a longitudinal study of adolescents who were having difficulty adjusting. Based on this quantitative data, they identified a set of students who had improved the most during the school year and another set of students whose scores had deteriorated the most. The goal for the qualitative portion of the project was to understand both the factors that encouraged success and the barriers that prevented it. Pursuing this goal, however, required a substantial degree of agreement between the qualitative and quantitative data in terms of whether these students had indeed improved or deteriorated.

In several of the qualitative interviews, the students themselves disagreed with the categories to which they were assigned by the quantitative analysis. Thus, some of the students who were classified as success cases felt that they had done worse over the course of the year, and some of the students labeled as least successful felt that they had made substantial progress. The authors then considered three possible sources for the discrepancies between their qualitative and quantitative data: problems with the quantitative data, problems with the qualitative data, and differences in the kinds of things that the two studies targeted. Ultimately, they argued for the third option, namely, that the two results tend to focus on different aspects of the students' experiences. Thus, though the two studies fail to converge, each adds something to the other.

A further set of issues that convergent findings raises with regard to integration involves practical problems in comparing the results of qualitative and quantitative methods. Campbell and his colleagues (Webb et al., 2000) recognized the tradeoff between the greater value and the great difficulty of comparing the results from very different methods. On the one hand, it is relatively easy to compare the results from two similar methods; however, this produces a weak form of convergence, because methods with similar strengths would be expected to produce similar results. On the other hand, the more meaningful comparison between methods with different strengths comes at the expense of greater difficulty in collecting and comparing data. For example, it can take a considerable amount of effort to demonstrate convergence between the results of studies that involve participant observation and experimental intervention.

This problem is complicated by the need to pursue the two studies as independently as possible. Because whatever you learn in one study cannot influence anything you do in the other study, you cannot compare the studies until the results are available. In practice, the most common way to bridge the distance between the qualitative and quantitative data is to do a content analysis of the qualitative data so that it can be reduced to counts. This allows for a relatively direct comparison of the two types of data, but it comes at the expense of sacrificing much of the inductive-subjective-contextual approach that goes with full-scale qualitative research.

Up to this point, the issues presented have dealt with difficulties in accomplishing the integration of qualitative and quantitative methods. In contrast, another problem concerns the value of the results that convergent findings produces, even when it does work. In particular, comparing two independent studies to increase your certainty about the results essentially requires you to study the same thing twice in hope of producing the same results. In some circumstances this would indeed be a reasonable choice. For example, if you were conducting research that could have major policy impacts, then convergent findings from methods with different strengths would provide reassurance about policy makers' ability to make decisions based on those results. In many other situations, however, you would be wise to question the value of doubling the amount of effort and resources you devote to your work just to learn the same thing twice.

In terms of future directions, the ideas associated with convergent findings do provide a specific, although limited, motivation for combining qualitative and quantitative methods. The early impact of the concept of triangulation went well beyond this specific purpose, however. Since the heyday of triangulation in the 1970s and early 1980s, it has become clear that the search for convergent findings is only one of several possible purposes for doing mixed methods research. In addition, the relatively long history of this motivation has revealed a series of issues about both the means for accomplishing this form of integration and the value of the results it produces. Despite the decreasing popularity of convergent findings as a broad motivation for combining methods, it still serves the important purpose of using the strengths of different methods to minimize the limitations of any one method.

ADDITIONAL COVERAGE

Additional coverage assigns different methods to different purposes, allowing the overall project to pursue a wider range of research goals than would be possible with any single method. The key defining feature of additional coverage is a *division of labor* that assigns each method to a separate purpose that matches the strength of that particular method. One common analogy is that this approach amounts to assembling "many pieces of a complex puzzle into a coherent whole" (Jick, 1979, p. 608). Alternatively, Lawrenz and Huffman (2002) have described this approach as making connections between islands of data that are grouped into "archipelagos," while Bazeley and Kemp (2012) spoke of "mosaics." In addition, Creswell, Plano Clark, Gutmann, and Hanson (2003) used the terms *nested* and *embedded designs* to refer to the case where one method performs a specific and limited role within a project that primarily relies on another method (i.e., *QUAL + quant* or *QUANT + qual*). The present use of the label *additional coverage* makes it clear that the goal in this use of different methods is to add to the range of results for the project as a whole, as shown in Example 4.3.

Example 4.3   Additional Coverage to Clarify Results

Plano Clark et al. (2010) conducted a survey to evaluate a program in which graduate students spent part of their time teaching in K–12 schools. In one major component of that work, the researchers' goal was "to develop a more complete picture by presenting two complementary sets of results" (p. 161). In particular, they wanted to understand how large an impact the program had on the students' progress toward completing their graduate degrees, as well as the sources of this impact. On the quantitative side, Plano Clark and colleagues had students' numerical ratings of the positive and negative effects that the program had on completing their degrees. On the qualitative side, they had open-ended responses from the same survey.

(Continued)

(Continued)

Somewhat surprisingly, a majority of these students rated participating in the program as having positive effects on completing their graduate degree, despite the time and effort required. Examining the qualitative data showed a variety of advantages for program participation, including social factors such as increased motivation and the development of relevant skills. For example, the qualitative data showed a number of students indicated a positive value for increasing their oral communication skills, and further examination of the quantitative data confirmed this pattern, finding high ratings on improvement in communication skills.

Overall, this study showed a successful "division of labor" through a process of examining both qualitative and quantitative data. The result was a more complete understanding of both the nature of the program's effects on the participants and the sources of those effects than could have been achieved by one type of data alone.

Historically, additional coverage arose at least partly in response to convergent findings as a purpose for combining methods. Indeed, several qualitative researchers explicitly favored this motivation as an alternative to the validity-oriented purposes associated with convergent findings. Thus, Fielding and Fielding (1986) argued for combining methods "with the intention of adding breadth or depth to our analysis" (p. 33). Ultimately, Denzin (1989) himself joined this camp, noting that different types of data will "reveal different aspects of what is being studied" (p. 245). Similarly, additional coverage promotes the goal of integrating the findings from different methods into a more "holistic" understanding.

From a practical point of view, the simplest implementation of additional coverage is a strict division of labor, such that each method plays a separate, relatively self-contained role within a larger project. This situation is especially likely to occur in complex, multifaceted projects that must accomplish several purposes, as demonstrated by Example 4.4.

Example 4.4   Additional Coverage in a Project With Multiple Goals

The welfare reforms that the US government enacted in 1996 had widespread effects on millions of lives, so it is hardly surprising that this project (Winston et al., 1999) combined three methods to understand how this major change in federal policy affected low-income families. The first component was a longitudinal survey to follow more than 2,000 families for several years. This was paired with a developmental study of 700 children, which used qualitative observations and interviews. Finally, ethnographic methods were used to study 200 families who lived in the same neighborhoods.

The longitudinal survey was designed to collect three waves of interviews over a 4-year period. Like the rest of the project, this sample came from three cities selected for their regional and ethnic diversity: Boston, Chicago, and San Antonio, Texas. The sample in each city was drawn from inner-city neighborhoods with high proportions of poor and near-poor families. Within each household, the survey targeted one focal child and his or her primary female caregiver. The 2-hour interview was evenly divided between questions related to the child's development and the adult respondent's experiences.

The second component of the project collected qualitative data on 700 families with a child aged 2 to 4 years; these families were drawn from the initial survey. In particular, this study of each child's development included observations at the child's primary child care setting, as well as a second visit to each family's home for an extended interview with the mother and a videotaped interaction session between the mother and child.

The ethnographic research used a separate sample drawn from the same neighborhoods and using the same eligibility criteria as the survey. The ethnographic study targeted a more detailed description of how welfare policies affect the day-to-day lives of low-income families by observing not only the home life of these families but also their experiences in welfare offices and other social service agencies. In addition, the ethnographic study emphasized observations of the local neighborhood to help the researchers understand the influence of the immediate social context in which these families lived. The goal for this combination of qualitative and quantitative methods was to produce a more comprehensive account than would be possible with any one method alone.

In general, additional coverage is most likely to motivate combining qualitative and quantitative methods in research projects that include diverse or complex goals. In particular, the need to achieve a variety of goals benefits from a division of labor that matches different methods to those goals, which is the heart of additional coverage. Alternatively, understanding multiple aspects of a complex phenomenon may benefit from the different perspectives that a combination of methods can offer. Either way, the ultimate goal is to use the different strengths of different methods to generate a broader variety of data than just one method could.

Issues Related to Integration

The briefer history of additional coverage means that there has been less time to develop specific approaches to integrating qualitative and quantitative methods for this purpose, let alone to resolve the problems that have been detected. Most of these arise, once again, from questions about how to compare and combine the results from different methods.

This issue of *whether* to compare results is less problematic in additional coverage than in convergent findings, because there is no requirement to keep the two processes independent. The question of *how* to integrate the results remains problematic, however. For example, in his revised assessment of triangulation, Denzin (1989) essentially shifted from a convergent findings to an additional coverage position, stating that the real value of using different methods is to "broaden, thicken, and deepen the interpretive base of any study" (p. 247). Unfortunately, he did not provide any guidance about how to accomplish this goal.

The issue of comparing results arises because social phenomena seldom provide a sharp separation between purposes that can be assigned exclusively to different methods. Hence, there are likely to be areas of overlap in the results from the different methods, leading to questions about the similarities and differences in the findings. Logically, one strategy for implementing additional coverage might be to rely on a strict division of labor that not only assigns a separate, self-contained role to each method but also treats the results as equally separable. This option minimizes your need to compare the results, but it does so by essentially ignoring the issue of how to integrate the different sets of results. Although you could treat the studies as if they were completely independent, and even publish the results of each method separately without any attempt to integrate them, this strategy leaves it as an "exercise for the reader" to make sense of your overall results.

It may seem that addressing the issues of comparison and integration could be accomplished by having a strong design right from the start. The most common design for implementing additional coverage as a purpose is, however, notably weak in this regard. In this design, commonly known as *parallel strands* (Leech & Onwuegbuzie, 2009), the collection and often the analysis of the qualitative and quantitative data proceed along separate tracks. This version of additional coverage relies on conducting studies that run in parallel, which can create questions about when and how integration occurs. Hence, articles that report on projects with parallel strands often present two separate results sections, one for the qualitative data and one for the quantitative, with only a minimum of integration.

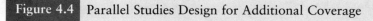

Figure 4.4   Parallel Studies Design for Additional Coverage

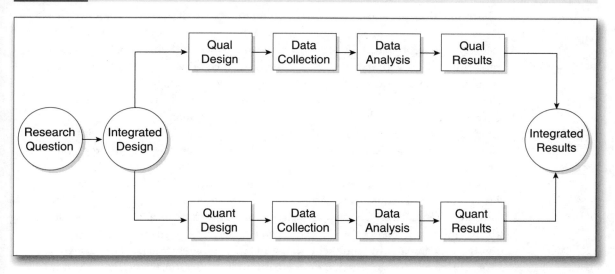

To understand why parallelism is such a common design in studies that pursue additional coverage, it is important to consider the logistical differences that underlie the basic mechanics of collecting qualitative and quantitative data. Most notably, surveys and experimental designs require that the measurement tools and procedures not only be in place at the start of the data collection but also remain the same throughout the data collection. Thus, as Figure 4.4 shows, there is little possibility for any meaningful contact between the two procedures between the design and analysis stages. If the data turn out to be difficult to compare or if the results tend to diverge, then ultimate integration will be problematic. This lack of full integration in projects that use parallel strands often leads to reports of the research that have two separate results sections, one for the qualitative data and one for the quantitative.

In terms of future directions, both the practical and theoretical challenges associated with comparing and integrating different methods in additional coverage may be a reflection of its relative newness as an explicit motivation for mixed methods research. If so, then the next step will be to develop clearer statements about how issues of comparison and integration fit into both the purposes and procedures associated with this motivation. For the moment, however, questions about the ways that qualitative and quantitative methods can or cannot be compared and integrated within additional coverage have yet to be resolved.

SEQUENTIAL CONTRIBUTIONS

The remaining purpose, sequential contributions, is the central topic of this book. Probably the most common other name for this motivation is *development* (e.g., Greene et al., 1989; Sandelowski, 2000), but that label conveys a more limited sense than the range of uses described here. In studies that pursue sequential contributions, the goal is to use the *results* of one method to enhance the performance of another. The results from the overall project are strengthened because the results from one method allow another method to do more than it could have by itself. Studies that are motivated by sequential contributions thus use the different strengths of different methods for different purposes, with one method contributing to the other in a preplanned fashion.

The history of sequential contributions differs from that of the two previous basic purposes, because the concept of triangulation played little role. Although several statements related to sequential contributions were available at a relatively early date (Sieber, 1973), this purpose never received much attention in discussions devoted to triangulation. Even so, practicing researchers have consistently found uses for sequential contributions, as demonstrated by the examples in Chapter 1. More recently, methodological interest has grown in the idea of using one method to increase the capacities of another (Morgan, 1998; Morse, 2003; Sandelowski, 2000).

In comparison to convergent findings, in which different methods are designed to answer the same research question, studies motivated by sequential contributions use different methods for separate but related purposes. In addition, the logic of convergent findings requires you to conduct independent studies with the goal of comparing the similarity of their results. In contrast, pursuing sequential contributions requires an explicit linkage between the studies that make up the overall project; the goal is to use what you learn with one method to enhance your use of another method. Clearly, these differences in purposes lead to differences in the research designs you will use to meet these goals.

In comparison to studies motivated by additional coverage, which emphasizes each method's ability to perform a separate role within the overall project, studies motivated by sequential contributions require explicit linkages between methods. Both of these basic purposes rely on a division of labor that assigns different methods to different purposes; however, when you follow sequential contributions as a purpose, this division of labor is based on more explicit and preplanned linkages between the methods. In contrast, additional coverage emphasizes the separate purposes that you assign to each method. Once again, these differences in purposes have distinct implications for research design.

In general, sequential contributions is most likely to motivate combinations of methods in projects that can be structured as a sequence of related studies, where the results from one method will have direct relevance for how you use another method. With a sequence of linked studies, what you learn from the first study in the series can provide inputs that enhance the performance of later methods. Alternatively, you may use the later methods to extend what you learned from the earlier studies. Either way, a key feature of the sequential contributions approach is that you design one set of methods to contribute to the capacities of another method.

Issues Related to Integration

Just like the other basic purposes discussed above, sequential contributions raises issues related to integrating methods, but these issues do not involve comparisons between the results from different methods. Instead, the most important problems associated with sequential contributions are difficulties in creating effective *linkages* between the methods. This means you must pay careful attention to maximizing the likelihood that the results you produce with one method match the needs of the other method. The practical issues involved in effectively linking different methods are summarized in the next chapter, which considers sequential contributions in more detail. In addition, Chapters 6 through 9 describe the potential problems associated with each of the four specific research designs that make up Part 2 of this book.

At the theoretical level, studies motivated by sequential contributions mark a major departure from the underlying logic of convergent findings and additional coverage, because this approach requires far less attention to comparisons between the results from qualitative and quantitative methods. Instead, the two methods are integrated through the goal of using the strengths of one method to produce data that can guide the design and implementation of another method, regardless of whether you begin with a qualitative or a quantitative method. Hence, the integration of qualitative and quantitative methods is based on the ways that one method can make use of the results from another rather than on a direct comparison of the results from the two methods.

In terms of future directions, sequential contributions is of particular interest because it addresses distinctive purposes that set it apart from the other two motivations in this chapter. Its current state of development is also quite different. Convergent findings represents an older purpose that is increasingly understood as having both a range of practical problems and a relatively narrow set of applications. Additional coverage is a newer motivation whose accepted procedures and purposes are still under debate. In contrast, research based on sequential contributions—as the next chapter argues—is both new enough to show substantial unexplored potential and familiar enough to offer workable procedures for pursuing these opportunities.

COMPARING THE THREE MOTIVATIONS

Table 4.1 provides a general overview of the three basic motivations, starting with division of labor between the qualitative and quantitative methods. In convergent findings, there is no division of labor, because each study is a self-contained effort to answer the same research question. In contrast, assigning different roles to each method is one of the defining characteristics of additional coverage so that each set of results brings something unique to the overall project. Sequential contributions also relies on a division of labor so that the results from one method can enhance the performance of the other.

In terms of the relationship between the methods, within the overall research design, convergent findings uses the two methods in a completely independent fashion so that neither can influence the results of the other. For additional coverage, the tendency to pursue the qualitative and quantitative methods in a parallel fashion reflects both the need to assign separate purposes to each method and the logistical difficulties in connecting the results of one method to the ongoing research activities in the other. For sequential contributions, connecting the two methods is essential so that one set of results can increase the effectiveness of the other.

Table 4.1	Summary of Motivations for Mixed Methods Research: Convergent Findings, Additional Coverage, and Sequential Contributions			
	Division of Labor	Relationship Between Methods	Point of Integration	Ease of Integration
Convergent Findings	None	Independent	Conclusion of studies	Problematic
Additional Coverage	Clear-cut	Typically parallel	Typically at analysis	Can be problematic
Sequential Contributions	Clear-cut	Linked	Between studies	Relatively straightforward

In terms of the point of integration between the qualitative and quantitative studies, the results from convergent findings cannot be compared until both studies are completed. Integration in additional coverage typically occurs during analysis, when the results of the qualitative and quantitative studies need to be compared to create the overall, composite picture. The point of integration in sequential contributions occurs at the dividing point between the two methods, where the results from the first study help define the design and procedures for the second study.

Finally, with regard to how easy or difficult it is to integrate the results from the two studies, this is most problematic for convergent findings, both because of the very different form of qualitative and quantitative data and because of the potential difficulty posed by divergent results. Working with two different data sets in additional coverage can pose the same issues with regard to the different forms of the data and their potential divergence, and such problems are particularly likely to arise when the two studies proceed in parallel until a final integration of the results.

Overall, the three motivations represent different stages of development and their ability to serve as the source of effective designs for mixed methods research. Convergent findings is both the most mature and the most problematic of these motivations. The goal of directly comparing the two sets of results is well understood, but the means for producing this comparison have not progressed much since its introduction over 40 years ago. Additional coverage represents an intermediate case with regard to both its state of development and its potential for generating new directions. The main obstacle to using this motivation is the difficulty of specifying, first, how to give the two methods separate roles and, then, how to integrate their different results. In contrast to the other two motivations, sequential contributions has the immediate potential for both more mature development and the creation of effective research designs. Taken together, this combination of maturity and effectiveness points to the capacity of sequential contributions designs for not only combining qualitative and quantitative methods but also integrating their results.

CONCLUSIONS

1. *Every successful research project requires two things: a meaningful research question and an appropriate way to answer that question.*

Convergent findings, additional coverage, and sequential contributions each ask different kinds of questions that, in turn, lead to different approaches to mixed methods research. Labeling these approaches "motivations" emphasizes the different purposes they serve. In research that pursues convergent findings, the attempt to produce similar results from methods with different strengths serves the larger purpose of increasing faith in the results. In additional coverage, matching separate goals to methods with different strengths adds to the range of relevant information that can be generated. In sequential contributions, linking the strengths of one method to the use of another method enhances the overall performance of both methods. Thus, although each of these purposes relies on the underlying logic that "different methods have different strengths," they use that fundamental insight to pursue three very different kinds of research goals.

For each of these three basic motivations for combining methods, pragmatism highlights the importance of inquiry as a process that connects purposes and procedures. In particular, all three point to different conceptions of the most meaningful research questions you should pursue and the most appropriate means for addressing those questions. Each of these three purposes thus defines its own set of desired consequences, whether that is more credible results, coverage of a wider range of topics, or increased effectiveness of methods. In turn, each of these three sets of beliefs about meaningful goals leads to a different set of beliefs about the appropriate procedures for accomplishing those goals.

2. *Deciding how to do your research depends on a clear understanding of why you are doing the research.*

If convergent findings, additional coverage, and sequential contributions are three different reasons why you might do mixed methods research, then it should come as no surprise that they also point to three different answers about how to do your research. The available knowledge about how to pursue each of these approaches to mixed methods research is strongly influenced by the overall level of experience that social scientists have with each motivation. For convergent findings, the level of experience is high enough to reveal not only problems in the implementation of this motivation but also limitations in its practical value. For additional coverage, there seem to be sound arguments for the practical value of the results it can produce, but the level of experience is still too low to provide either solid procedures for implementing this motivation or theoretical clarity about when it is most appropriate. For sequential contributions, the current argument is that the level of experience with this motivation is sufficient to support a much broader range of applications.

An essential element of pragmatic inquiry is the process of reflecting on the connection between decisions and their likely consequences. For research, this means choosing research designs according to both their ability to meet basic purposes and their likelihood of producing predictable results. As basic purposes for doing mixed methods research, convergent findings, additional coverage, and sequential contributions each provide their own context for connecting research goals and research procedures. Hence, these three purposes represent separate paths for inquiry in mixed methods research. In particular, each of these purposes matches a set of research questions to well-justified procedures for meeting those goals. Once you sort your research into one of these categories, it is an important step toward answering the pragmatic question about why you would choose one set of actions rather than another.

3. *Choosing research methods that can accomplish your research goals requires knowing both what your options are and how to evaluate those options.*

This chapter emphasizes the importance of understanding your purposes for using mixed methods research so you can select a combination of methods that will actually serve your purposes; however, matching your choice of methods to your underlying purposes can be quite a challenge. Convergent findings, additional coverage, and sequential contributions amount to three options for doing mixed methods research that each lead to different standards for evaluating the different strengths of different methods. In a perfect world, there would be a simple set of rules that produced an exact match between any given research purpose and a set of options for research design, and these would give strong guidance about evaluating different strategies for combining methods. The real world is, of course, more complicated. One way to reduce that complexity is to concentrate on only a subset of the choices available, and this is the strategy behind this book's emphasis on sequential contributions.

From a pragmatic perspective, the decision about which research methods to use is the action that produces consequences from a line of inquiry. In terms of conducting a research project, the choice of a research design can only take you so far. Beyond that, you need not only decide which methods to use within a given design but also make more detailed decisions about the practical implementation of those methods in the field. For a pragmatist, those decisions all arise from a set of beliefs about how research works. Yet, the fundamental principle in pragmatism is that the meaning of your beliefs comes from considering the likely outcomes of acting on those beliefs. Hence, the true test of your beliefs about the research process comes at the point when you put your methods into practice.

* * *

Ultimately, it is up to you to justify why your chosen combination of methods matches the purposes that motivated your research. In particular, it should be obvious by now that this book does not claim that there is any one "right way" to combine qualitative and quantitative methods. Even though studies motivated by sequential contributions are the core topic of this book, that is just one of several reasons for doing mixed methods research. The key point is that social science researchers have developed a range of reasons for doing mixed methods research, and no single approach to combining qualitative and quantitative methods is ever likely to serve all these purposes. Hence, Part 1 of this book describes the theoretical justification and practical value of pursuing this motivation, while Part 2 presents a series of research designs that demonstrate how to implement studies based on sequential contributions.

SUMMARY

Mixed methods research offers three basic options for integrating the results from qualitative and quantitative methods. First, convergent findings compares the results of different methods that attempt to answer the same research question, but this approach to integration can be especially problematic when the two studies produce diverging rather than converging results. Second, additional coverage assigns the different methods to different goals, but projects that use this approach often collect the separate sets of results in parallel tracks that can be difficult to integrate. Finally, sequential contributions uses what is learned through one method as either an input to or a follow-up on a second method. Because sequential contributions offers the most successful approach to integrating the results from qualitative and quantitative studies, it is the primary topic for the remainder of this book.

DISCUSSION QUESTIONS

Some people argue that exploring the divergence between two methods that study the same question should be considered another reason for combining methods. How would you compare convergence and divergence as motivations for doing mixed methods research?

This chapter is pessimistic about the current ability to integrate qualitative and quantitative methods using additional coverage. Do you think this pessimism is justified? What alternatives would you suggest for integrating methods using additional coverage?

ADDITIONAL READINGS

There are any number of alternative typologies for categorizing the motivations for using mixed methods research. For an approach based on an extensive review of studies that use mixed methods research, see the following:

Bryman, A. (2006). Integrating quantitative and qualitative research: How is it done? *Qualitative Research, 6,* 97–113.

For a more theory-based approach, see the following:

Leech, N. L., & Onwuegbuzie, A. J. (2009). A typology of mixed methods research designs. *Quality & Quantity, 43,* 265–275.

CHAPTER 5

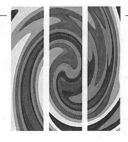

The Sequential Priorities Model

Overview

This chapter provides a transition between the basic issues in Part 1 of the book and the specific designs in Part 2 by introducing four research designs associated with the sequential contributions motivation for doing mixed methods research. The first section discusses the decision to concentrate on sequential priorities as a basic purpose for combining methods, and the second section summarizes sequencing and prioritizing as two practical principles that create a series of research designs for implementing the goals associated with sequential priorities. The third section gives an overview of the four designs that make up this model, and the final section gives an overview of the decision-making process that guides not only this chapter but also the others in Part 1 of the book.

If, as the previous chapter argued, sequential connection designs are only one of several basic purposes for mixed methods research, then why emphasize this particular approach to integrating qualitative and quantitative methods? The answer lies in the essential practicality of research based on sequential contributions. In particular, this approach leads to research designs for combining the strengths of qualitative and quantitative methods that are both *accessible* and *dependable*.

The accessibility of the present approach to sequential contributions means that this kind of research does not require a great deal of additional training. In particular, this book emphasizes four research designs that allow you to rely on methods you already know, while adding a targeted set of additional skills. Of course, asserting that this approach to integrating qualitative and quantitative methods is relatively accessible is hardly the same as saying that anyone and everyone can do this kind of research. Still, projects that rely on sequential priorities are likely to be highly accessible to a wide range of researchers.

The dependability of sequential contributions means that this kind of research operates in reasonably predictable ways. This dependability results from the fact that many of these research designs are already widely used—if less widely recognized—in the social sciences. Because a number of examples of this kind of work are already available in the literature, you can get a good sense of both what these designs require from you and what they are likely to deliver. Of course, asserting that these designs are relatively dependable is not the same as saying that they will work for everyone every time. Even so, projects that rely on sequential contributions are nearly as dependable as complex studies that involve only a single method.

Because research based on sequential contributions is both relatively accessible and dependable, it also is not especially innovative. This decision to concentrate on a relatively straightforward approach reflects a belief that the biggest problem in the field of mixed methods is a limited practical ability to integrate the results from qualitative and quantitative methods. Practicality alone is only a limited virtue, however. To be truly useful, any approach to research must link practical applications to a coherent set of purposes. The previous chapter laid out a broad summary of the purposes associated with sequential priorities as a reason for combining qualitative and quantitative methods. The remainder of this chapter outlines a set of procedures for implementing sequential priorities, while also paying careful attention to the linkage between the purposes and procedures associated with this basic purpose.

SEQUENCING AND PRIORITIZING

As a motivation for doing mixed methods research, sequential contributions can lead to a number of different research designs, and Chapter 10 will present more complex designs that pursue this purpose. For now, however, it will help to concentrate on two fundamental principles that lead to a straightforward and powerful set of designs: sequencing and prioritizing. In particular, connecting qualitative and quantitative methods through both sequencing and prioritizing generates the four research designs in the *sequential priorities model,* as shown in Table 5.1.

Table 5.1	Sequential Priorities Designs for Integrating Qualitative and Quantitative Methods

		Priority	
		Core Method Is *Quantitative*	Core Method Is *Qualitative*
Sequence	Supplementary Method Is *Preliminary*	**Preliminary Qualitative Input** • *qual* → QUANT Purposes: Preliminary qualitative study is a basis for collecting and interpreting the quantitative data. Can generate hypotheses, develop content for questionnaires and interventions, assist in pretesting other methods, and so on.	**Preliminary Quantitative Input** • *quant* → QUAL Purposes: Preliminary quantitative study is a basis for collecting and interpreting the qualitative data. Can locate major differences between subgroups, guide purposive sampling, establish results to pursue, and so on.
	Supplementary Method Is *Follow-up*	**Follow-up Qualitative Extension** • QUANT → *qual* Purposes: Follow-up qualitative study helps extend what was learned from the core quantitative study. Can demonstrate bases for results, examine reasons for failed hypotheses, explore the theoretical significance of outliers, and so on.	**Follow-up Quantitative Extension** • QUAL → *quant* Purposes: Follow-up quantitative study helps extend what was learned from the core qualitative study. Can develop measures of key concepts, compare concepts and relationships across different samples, test associations, and so on.

Sequencing calls for designs that use the supplementary method either in a preliminary position, as an input to the core method, or in a follow-up position, as an extension of the core method. As the rows in Table 5.1 show, a sequence that begins with a qualitative method will be followed by a quantitative method, while a sequence that begins with a quantitative method will be followed by a qualitative method. *Prioritizing* calls for designs that combine a core method with a supplementary method, in which the latter explicitly serves the purpose of contributing to the core method. As the columns in Table 5.1 show, the core method can be either qualitative or quantitative. When the core method is qualitative, the supplementary method will be quantitative, and vice versa.

It is important not to confuse the *priority* you give to a method with the sheer *size* of that study. Priority is a matter of the relative importance of each study within the current project, which is a function of the *purposes* that the core and supplementary methods serve. Specifically, a study that collects a large amount of data may play only a supplementary role within the particular combination of methods that you are using. For example, if you were using a preliminary quantitative input design (i.e., *quant → QUAL*), you might start by using the existing data from a large survey as a way to locate a much smaller number of informants for in-depth interviews; regardless of that size difference, your core priority for *this* project would still be the qualitative interviews. Hence, the priorities you assign to the methods within a sequential priorities design are a function of the purposes that each method serves within the overall project.

Just as it is important not to confuse the priority you assign to a method with the sheer size of that study, it is also important not to confuse the *sequence* in which you use two methods with the *order* in which you collect the data. Sequencing is based on the order in which the data are *used* rather than the order in which they are collected. For example, one useful strategy in design that uses qualitative methods for follow-up purposes (i.e., *QUANT → qual*) is to ask open-ended questions as part of a larger survey so that qualitative data can either illustrate or extend the quantitative results. In that design, both kinds of data are collected at the same time, but the core goals are met by the quantitative results, followed by carefully targeted analyses of the qualitative data to supplement those quantitative findings.

The fact that the arrow (→) serves as the symbol for linking methods in sequential priorities demonstrates the central importance of sequencing for this purpose. Indeed, the defining characteristic for sequential priorities is the sequential use of the results from one method as a contribution to the other. Yet, decisions about sequencing are often easier to make when you begin by giving different priorities to a core and a supplementary method. Ironically, it turns out that giving both methods the same level of priority leads to more complex design decisions; these equal priority designs will be discussed later in this chapter.

Deciding on Priorities for Core and Supplementary Research Methods

Selecting one of the sequential priorities designs almost always begins with concentrating on the priorities for your core method, because this method is central to meeting the overall purposes of your research project. Hence, this discussion of making decisions about priorities will include most of the content on designing sequential priorities, while the following section will address the specific issues associated with sequencing.

Establishing priorities within the sequential priorities model creates a design cycle that connects the needs of the core method with the strengths of the supplementary method, as shown in Figure 5.1. This design cycle begins by defining the needs of the core method. Starting with the needs of the core method allows you to consider how a supplementary method could contribute additional strengths that could enhance that core method. The first step is to select a core method with the strengths that are most crucial for your overall project. For example, if your most important goal is to generate in-depth knowledge about a specific setting, then you might well rely on participant observation as your core method. Or, if your most important goal is to produce generalizable data about a larger population, then you would probably rely on a survey.

Step 1 in Figure 5.1 connects the design of the supplementary study to the needs of the core study, and the direction of the arrow shows that the needs of the core method come first and determine the design of the supplementary

Figure 5.1   Research Cycle for Sequential Priority Designs

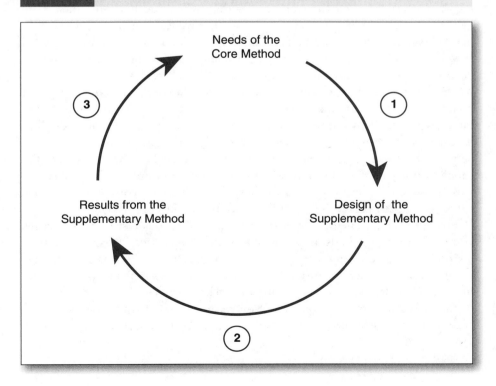

study. This cycle emphasizes the practical value of deciding on the core method as the starting point, because the needs of the core method drive the design for both the core method itself and the supplementary method. In addition, communication is crucial to creating a design that will integrate qualitative and quantitative methods in ways that match the goals of the project as a whole. Unless you are conducting the entire project by yourself, communication and coordination will require careful attention. Chapter 11, on teamwork, will discuss these issues in detail, but it should be clear that you need to pay attention to partnership and communication at each step in the design cycle.

In step 2, you follow through on the design for the supplementary study and collect the data. By now, it is implicit that this stage must make an appropriate contribution to core method, but that assumption needs to remain central, even when it is in the background. In particular, one problem that can arise at this stage is the conversion of what should be a supplementary study into a full-fledged study of its own. Typically, supplementary studies are not designed to stand alone; instead, they serve more limited and specific purposes that are driven by the core method. For example, in a preliminary qualitative input design (*qual* → *QUANT*), in which you are using focus groups to create items for a survey, you might use only a handful of highly targeted groups and stop collecting data when the survey is ready rather than when you have met the classic qualitative standard of data "saturation." Alternatively, if you are doing a preliminary survey to locate a specific set of participants for a core set of focus groups (*quant* → *QUAL*), you may well rely on a small, nonrandom sample that is well designed for this purpose but inadequate for most full-scale survey research.

Once the results from the supplementary study are available, you can match them to the original needs of the core study. In this final step 3, you integrate the results from the supplementary study into the core methods. This is where the strengths of sequential priorities designs are most apparent. Specifically, if you have linked the needs of the core method to the design of the supplementary method and followed through with appropriate data collection and analysis, then it is highly likely that the results from your supplementary study will indeed be a good fit with the needs of your core study.

Overall, using sequential priorities for mixed methods research encourages you to prioritize methods as one way to create connections between multiple methods. In this case, the key question is whether the project as a whole has needs that can be met by pairing a core method with a supplementary method. In particular, decisions about prioritizing ask you whether a supplementary method will add strengths to enhance the performance of your core method so you can accomplish things that would be difficult with the core method alone.

Deciding on a Sequence for Core and
Supplementary Research Methods

A supplementary method can contribute to the core method in two ways. One option is to use the supplementary method as an input in the preliminary stages of the project, thus providing information that will improve the subsequent performance of the core method. The other option is to use the supplementary method as a follow-up study to extend the results from the core method, thus generating additional information that builds on what the core method provided. These choices clearly reflect different purposes, which lead to different designs to match those purposes. In particular, using supplementary methods as inputs that contribute to your core method is not the same as following up on the results that you already have from a core method.

Overall, sequencing is a defining element of any study motivated by sequential priorities. For designs that pursue sequential priorities, the key question is whether the project as a whole has needs that can be met by using a supplementary method that serves as either an input or a follow-up to a core method. In particular, the sequence decision asks how you can use a supplementary method to enhance the performance of the core method in ways that go beyond what the core method could accomplish alone.

OVERVIEW OF THE FOUR SEQUENTIAL PRIORITIES DESIGNS

As part of the transition to a more detailed presentation of specific research designs for pursuing sequential priorities, it is important to emphasize that these designs are descriptive statements about how research can be done and has been done, *not* prescriptive statements about how research should be done. The four designs in Table 5.1 thus amount to a set of options, and the key task for any researcher is to evaluate whether one of these options might suit the purposes of a particular research project.

The approach described here produces what are a set of four generic research designs that have potential applications across a wide variety of research settings. Hence, there is a value to terms like *qualitative (or quantitative) input designs* and *follow-up qualitative (or quantitative) designs,* because they describe a set of well-understood options for both thinking about and describing research. This echoes the point made earlier, that the field of mixed methods research needs a clearer sense of the practical options that are routinely available for combining qualitative and quantitative methods.

Of course, any actual research project will vary in the extent to which it relies on one and only one of these four combinations, so it is best to think of the four options within the sequential priorities model as "generic designs." These designs are generic in the sense that they provide general models that can be employed for a variety of related research questions. Thus, each of these designs brings together a coherent set of research questions and a strategy for combining qualitative and quantitative models.

From this standpoint, these four designs provide basic building blocks for thinking about and describing some of the most practical ways to integrate qualitative and quantitative methods. When one of these designs fits your purposes, this framework can provide a convenient way of communicating with your colleagues about what you did and why you did it that way. It is also important to remember that mixed methods research can be more complex than the two-step sequences in this particular model. For example, Chapter 10 will consider the extension into three-step designs, such as *qual → QUANT → qual*. Starting with the four basic building blocks from this chapter, the four detailed chapters in Part 2 will simplify the task of explaining those more complex designs.

Designs Based on Preliminary Inputs

In every research project, there is an obvious value to starting out right. The top row in Table 5.1 consists of two designs that create sequential priorities through supplementary studies that serve as inputs to a core method. In these designs, you begin by identifying the *basic needs* that can improve the performance of the core method. Of course, in many circumstances, the core method can function self-sufficiently without the need for any additional inputs. Hence, the decision to use inputs from a preliminary study should be based on a strong argument that the supplementary method will improve the subsequent performance of the core method.

Qualitative Input Designs. In projects where a supplementary qualitative method serves as an input (*qual → QUANT*), the initial qualitative method contributes a set of inductive, subjective, and contextual strengths (see Chapter 3) that are useful as a starting point for a core quantitative method. Most designs based on inputs from qualitative methods begin with the recognition that quantitative methods are highly dependent on the use of standardized, predetermined measures and procedures. This tradeoff between the openness of the preliminary, qualitative study and the fixed procedures in the core, quantitative method is often a key feature of these designs. Hence, preliminary qualitative input designs emphasize the ways that supplementary qualitative methods can contribute to the measures and procedures in the core quantitative portion of the project. For example, whenever you lack a set of ready-made measures and procedures that suit the purposes of the core quantitative method, you may well benefit from preliminary studies that use exploratory qualitative research (i.e., induction) in an attempt to interpret (i.e., subjectivity) issues related to the specific topics and groups (contexts) you are about to study.

Quantitative Input Designs. In projects where a supplementary quantitative method serves as an input (*quant* → *QUAL*), the strengths of quantitative methods in producing deductive, objective, and generalized information serve as a first step that can enhance the performance of the core qualitative method. Preliminary quantitative input designs are typically based on the recognition that qualitative methods emphasize the in-depth examination of data from relatively few people or cases. This tradeoff between the breadth of the preliminary, quantitative method and the depth of the core, qualitative method is often a key feature in these designs. Anything that helps in the selection of appropriate data sources can make a valuable contribution to the effectiveness of a core qualitative method. In particular, if you do not already have a set of well-chosen cases that suits the purposes of the core qualitative method, then you may well benefit from a preliminary study that uses predetermined criteria (i.e., deduction) to do a systematic search (i.e., objectivity) through a larger database (generality) of potential cases.

Designs Based on Follow-up Extensions

Many studies can benefit from additional research that extends the initial findings. The two remaining designs in Table 5.1 each use a supplementary method to follow up on information obtained from a core method. In these designs, the core method provides a set of results that you want to take a step further. First, you identify a set of *additional strengths* that could improve the results you already have from the core method; then you match those strengths to an appropriate supplementary method. Of course, in many circumstances, the core method itself will be sufficient without the need for any additional follow-up. Hence, use of these follow-up designs should be based on a strong argument that the supplementary method will improve the performance of the core method.

Follow-up Qualitative Designs. In projects where a supplementary qualitative method serves as a follow-up (*QUANT* → *qual*), the question is how the existing information from a core quantitative method might be enhanced through the strengths that qualitative methods have in serving inductive, subjective, and contextual purposes. One common use for this design occurs when a quantitative method produces unexpected results. Because quantitative methods rely so heavily on measuring theoretically determined variables with standardized procedures, they may not provide the resources necessary to pursue unanticipated results. Qualitative methods, however, are well suited to this kind of exploratory work. Hence, these designs follow up on the core quantitative method with a supplementary qualitative method to give you new information that enhances the value of your overall set of results. In particular, whenever the data from your quantitative methods alone are not sufficient for pursuing an unexpected set of results, a follow-up qualitative extension design may provide new insights (i.e., induction) that help you interpret (i.e., subjectivity) the responses of specific groups with regard to specific topics (context).

Follow-up Quantitative Designs. In projects where a supplementary quantitative method serves as a follow-up (*QUAL → quant*), the strengths of quantitative methods in serving deductive, objective, and generalized purposes enhance the results from a core qualitative method. Because qualitative methods rely on emergent interpretations to produce in-depth data about a limited number of cases, it may be difficult to determine the extent to which the conclusions are transferable to other groups or other settings. Quantitative methods, however, are well suited to determining whether your key results apply to a wider set of cases. Hence, these designs contribute to the value of the core method's results by demonstrating ways that your conclusions have relevance beyond one researcher's interpretations of a particular group or place. For example, if your original qualitative study can say little about how well your conclusions will apply elsewhere, then you may benefit from a follow-up quantitative extension design that produces similar results (i.e., deduction) by systematically examining (i.e., objectivity) a larger set of cases (generality). Of course, many qualitative studies are not interested in this kind of transferability, but when that is an important goal, this type of design has much to offer.

EQUAL PRIORITY DESIGNS

As noted earlier, the four designs in the sequential priorities model do not exhaust the possible ways to implement sequential contributions as a broader motivation for combining qualitative and quantitative methods. In particular, there are two "equal priority" designs:

$$QUAL \rightarrow QUANT$$

$$QUANT \rightarrow QUAL$$

Although the two equal priority designs, $QUAL \rightarrow QUANT$ and $QUANT \rightarrow QUAL$, seem straightforward, they actually present difficulties that the sequential priorities model avoids. In particular, because there is no single core method, there is no obvious need to specify how the needs of one study affect the design of the other. With reference to the design cycle in Figure 5.1, there is no clear starting point because both studies can serve as core methods: Should the first method serve as an input to the first, or should the second method serve as a follow-up? When it is not clear which method creates the need for the other, determining how the strengths of one method contribute to the needs of the other is difficult.

An alternative goal is to have each study stand on its own at the same time, as one study also explicitly serves as either an input or a follow-up to the other. Unfortunately, this approach is also problematic. Consider a $QUAL \rightarrow QUANT$ study in which the $QUAL$ study both stands alone and provides the preliminary inputs associated with a $qual \rightarrow QUANT$ design. Alternatively, the $QUANT$ portion might be intended to be both a stand-alone study and a $QUAL \rightarrow quant$ follow-up component. In the first case, the qualitative study serves as complete piece of research that can stand on its own, but it also serves a supplementary role that is driven by a core quantitative study. The second case poses an equivalent inconsistency. As Example 5.1 demonstrates, this can lead to a distinct conflict of interest between these two priorities.

> **Example 5.1   Equal Priorities as Conflicting Priorities**
>
> An illustration of the problems that can arise with equal priority designs comes from a study of how family members share the management of their finances. The difficulties in this project arose because the qualitative study served two separate purposes: to aid in the development of the survey questions and to serve as "a stand-alone piece of qualitative research designed to explore and increase our understanding of the dynamics of relationships between household members and the complex processes involved in the distribution of resources between them" (Laurie & Sullivan, 1991, p. 115). This created a $QUAL \rightarrow QUANT$ design in which the initial qualitative study was designed to follow its own priorities at the same time that it provided inputs for the design of the quantitative component.
>
> Creating the survey questions was a particular source of tension, and it highlights the difference between writing standardized questions that must apply to a large population and understanding the unique experiences
>
> *(Continued)*

(Continued)

and perspectives of individual families. For its qualitative purposes, the study collected data from 9 focus groups with 80 people, separate interviews with both partners in 19 couples, and all the members in 6 three-generation households. While that amount of data might be reasonable for a stand-alone qualitative study, it is far more than most preliminary qualitative input studies would ever need. As a result, "at times, consensus could not be achieved and the research process was a constant exchange of competing views" (Laurie, 1992, p. 150).

Much of the tension between the two teams on this project centered on the level of depth and detail in the qualitative data as opposed to the limited survey coverage that was available for the same topics. Thus, even though the qualitative study consistently indicated the complexity of household financial arrangements, the survey items had to fit within a 5-minute time limit. There was thus an unavoidable discrepancy between the "wealth of information on the often subtle and complex negotiations between household members" and what could be captured in a small number of survey questions (Laurie & O'Sullivan, 1991, p. 116).

However, in one important way equal priority designs can work smoothly—when each study is conducted separately so that the second study builds on what you learned in the first. In other words, if you do two different studies in a sequence, then the products of the first study will unquestionably be available to the second. This situation can be considered a *research program*, in which you link different projects across time. This kind of mixed methods research is very important, and it will be considered in Chapter 10 on more advanced designs. What makes research programs different from the kinds of research designs covered here is that the qualitative and quantitative methods are not integrated within a single project. Instead, you begin a research program with one autonomous project and then follow up with another stand-alone project. In a research program, the potential contributions of the first study only become apparent after that study is complete; similarly, you cannot define the goals of the second study until you know the results from the first study.

The message here is that equal priority designs are difficult but by no means impossible. To the extent that the two portions of the project function more like the two separate studies in a research program, there will be fewer problems in creating a design that begins determining how either study will contribute to the needs of the other. Of course, this separation comes at price, because its "wait-and-see" quality makes it harder to ensure that results of the first study will be well integrated with the goals of the study.

THE SEQUENTIAL PRIORITIES MODEL AS
A FINAL STEP IN DECISION MAKING

Decision making has been a central theme throughout Part 1 of this book. In particular, Chapter 2 emphasized the importance of decision making in a pragmatic approach to mixed methods research. Chapter 3 considered the fundamental decision to combine the different strengths of qualitative and quantitative methods. Next, Chapter 4 distinguished three motivations for doing mixed methods research. Finally, this chapter used the sequential priorities model to lay out the choices among a set of specific research designs.

Figure 5.2 places these choices in a different context by laying out the full series of decisions that go into designing a particular integrated research project. The diagram starts at the top, with the decision to do integrated research, and then moves to the choice of which motivation to pursue. Assuming that your goals match the purposes associated with connected contributions, the next decision concerns which of the four priority sequence designs you will use. Finally, at the bottom left in the diagram, you still need to make all of the more specific decisions that are necessary to implement a particular study. At each decision point, the real question is whether the choices you make meet the purposes you are pursuing.

It is important to start with the initial choice about whether to do integrated research at all, as this approach only makes sense when the strengths of an additional method can take you beyond what you might accomplish with any one method. Consequently, there is always the question of how much is added by the use of multiple methods in comparison to using a single, well-chosen method that provides whatever strengths are most important for your purposes. This book thus avoids any claim that using multiple methods is inherently superior to using only one method. Instead, the process of research design begins with a choice of whether to do qualitative research, quantitative research, or mixed methods research, and that choice should be based on how well each approach suits your purposes.

At the next level, the motivations from Chapter 4—convergent findings, additional coverage, and connected contributions—represent three basic choices about why to do integrated research, and the challenge is to select the one that best fits your research goals. Although the remainder of this book concentrates on research motivated by connected contributions, it is important to reinforce the point that other reasons for doing integrated research may well lead to choices that are different from the ones described here.

Moving to more specific decisions, the next step in Figure 5.2 offers a choice among the four designs that make up the sequential priorities model. Any design

Figure 5.2   Steps in the Decision to Use a Sequential Priorities Model

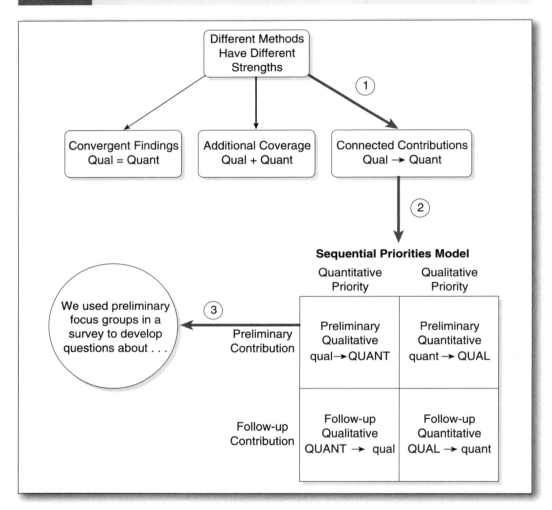

based on this model actually requires a pair of decisions: one about the priority you assign to qualitative and quantitative methods (i.e., which will serve as your core method, and which will play a supplementary role) and one about the sequence that connects the two methods (i.e., whether the supplementary method will serve as a preliminary input to or a follow-up extension of the core method). The chapters in the next section lay out these four options, along with a sense of what each can accomplish.

Within any of the sequential priorities designs are a number of options about how to implement each design, and these options are represented by the final level of specificity in Figure 5.2. For purposes of illustration, Figure 5.2 uses an example of a design based on preliminary qualitative inputs. In this case, the implementation of that design is tied to the choice of using a preliminary set of focus groups to assist in developing the content for a survey instrument. Of course, you would need to accompany this choice with a solid justification for why your particular research goals benefit from this specific combination of qualitative and quantitative methods.

Ultimately, using focus groups as an input to the development of a survey is only one example of several reasons why you might pursue a preliminary qualitative input design. Similarly, that design is only one of four options with the sequential priorities model, just as connected contributions is only one option among several motivations for pursuing integrated research, and integrated research itself is a choice with qualitative research and quantitative research as other alternatives. Each of these levels offers a set of alternatives, and your challenge is to evaluate those options and make choices that are well suited to your research goals. Of course, this decision making will be more complex in cases that involve less familiar goals and less certainty with regard to the appropriate design. Still, regardless of how commonplace or unusual the specific issues are, the fundamental process of decision making will be the same.

CONCLUSIONS

1. *Every successful research project requires two things: a meaningful research question and an appropriate way to answer that question.*

In considering the sequential priorities model, it is important to recognize that each cell in this model consists of not only a different design but also a different basis for justifying a particular combination of qualitative and quantitative methods. Using a qualitative or quantitative method as a preliminary input is quite different from using either of them as a supplementary follow-up. Setting up these four options as "generic designs" creates a series of matches between packages of related research questions and specific strategies for combining qualitative and quantitative methods. Each of these designs brings together a coherent set of research questions with a design that integrates the needs of one method with the contributions from another method.

From a pragmatic point of view, reaching the level of specificity associated with selecting one of the four sequential priorities designs means that you have both made a decision about the research design you will use and gained an understanding about why it makes sense to do things that way. The next step is to convince others that your decisions about the match between your research questions and research methods are indeed the appropriate choices. This process of justification highlights the pragmatic assumption that all decisions are made within a social context. One notable value of expressing the sequential priorities model as a set of generic designs is that it increases your ability to communicate with others about your research. In that regard, the overall logic behind the sequential priorities model provides a useful way to explain why you matched your research question to one of these specific designs. The key point here is that communicating with others requires an underlying set of shared assumptions about the appropriate ways of matching your research questions and your research methods.

2. *Deciding how to do your research depends on a clear understanding of why you are doing the research.*

The sequential priorities model is especially useful for guiding decisions about research design. In this case, you use the data in a sequential order so that the results from one method are available to contribute to the other method. By assigning priorities to the methods, you identify a set of plans for integrating the results of the supplementary method with the needs of the core method. This process relies on a design cycle that ensures that the results from a supplementary method enhance the effectiveness of a core method. This design process starts with the needs of a core method and then proceeds through a sequence of steps to design a supplementary study that can meet those needs. The cycle is completed by integrating the results of the supplementary method with the purposes behind the core method. The needs of the core method are thus the source of both your reasons for using the supplementary method and your decisions about how to use that method.

From the standpoint of pragmatism, research designs do not have value in and of themselves; instead, they define procedures that serve a given set of purposes. In addition, you need to be able to justify your choices about research design issues. On the one hand, this means explaining how your research design matches your research question; on the other hand, it means explaining the connections between your overall research design and the specific methods you will use. For mixed methods research, you also have to go a step further, demonstrating how your research design will integrate qualitative and quantitative methods. At a practical level, the sequential priorities model supplies a basis for your own choices about how to integrate different methods. At a larger level, it also provides a basis for talking with others about why you made the decisions you did. This model thus serves as a tool for both making decisions and communicating about those decisions.

3. *Choosing research methods that can accomplish your research goals requires knowing both what your options are and how to evaluate those options.*

Collecting and analyzing data from qualitative and quantitative data has to be considered with regard to integrating the results from these methods. The sequential priorities model provides a framework for making decisions about how you will use your methods.

Will you use a qualitative or a quantitative method as your core method? Will you use your supplementary method as a preliminary input or as a follow-up extension? Making those two decisions takes you a long way toward defining the methods that you will need for your research design. The next step is to move beyond the generic designs in Part 1 of this book to examine how they can be implemented using methods such as participant observation, open-ended interviewing, experimental interventions, and survey research. The key point is that integrating the results from these methods will be much more straightforward when that integration is conducted within a well-organized system like the sequential priorities model.

In terms of the pragmatic emphasis on the social context for decision making, consensus is especially important for choices about research methods. In particular, your choice of specific research methods provides the most concrete statement about what difference doing your research one way rather than another will make. Reaching consensus requires a discussion that goes well beyond broad statements about the overall strengths of research methods. Instead, any given research project requires an explicit set of decisions about how to use a given set of research procedures to address a corresponding set of research purposes. This makes it even more important to create a setting in which your audience shares your sense of both the available options and the standards for evaluating those options. The sequential priorities model provides a basis for exactly this kind of discussion.

* * *

The chapters in Part 1 put forth an increasingly specific view of decision making in mixed methods research, starting with the general value of combining the different strengths of different methods, then laying out a clear set of basic purposes for using both qualitative and quantitative data, and finally generating a powerful set of research designs for implementing the most promising of these purposes. Part 2 continues this theme by providing guidance on both the reasons for using each of the sequential priorities designs as well as practical information about implementing each of those designs. In particular, each of these four designs represents another level of specificity, in which increasingly well-defined research questions are paired with increasingly detailed combinations of methods.

SUMMARY

There are four research designs that apply sequential contributions as a motivation for doing mixed methods research. These are derived using a combination of two kinds of sequencing (so that one method is either an input or a follow-up to the other) and two levels of priority (so that one method drives overall design and the other supplements the needs of the core method). Qualitative input designs use a supplementary qualitative method prior to a core quantitative method (*qual* → *QUANT*); for example, one might use preliminary focus groups to generate items for a survey research project. Quantitative input designs begin with a supplementary quantitative method that serves the needs of a core qualitative method (*quant* → *QUAL*); for example, one might use survey respondents to locate specific categories of participants for an interview study. Qualitative follow-up designs use supplementary qualitative methods to investigate the results of a core quantitative study (*QUANT* → *qual*), such as by completing a set of case studies to explore the findings from a program intervention study. Finally, quantitative follow-up designs use supplementary quantitative methods to move beyond what is available from a core qualitative study (*QUAL* → *quant*), such as by conducting a set of surveys to show that the results from a qualitative study apply more generally.

DISCUSSION QUESTIONS

Are all four of the sequential priorities designs likely to see the same level of usage, or do you think that some will be more "popular" than others?

Are equal priority designs really more complex than designs that use a core method and a supplementary design? Some authors go so far as to claim that almost all mixed methods studies use some degree of prioritizing because it is very difficult to maintain equal priorities when one uses different methods that pursue different goals. What do you think?

ADDITIONAL READINGS

For an additional summary of the sequential priorities model, see the following:

Morgan, D. L. (2006). "Connected contributions" as a motivation for combining qualitative and quantitative methods. In L. Curry, R. S. Shield, & T. T. Wetle (Eds.), *Improving aging and public health research: Qualitative and mixed methods* (pp. 53–63). Washington, DC: American Public Health Association.

Part 2

Four Basic Designs

CHAPTER 6

Preliminary Qualitative Inputs to Core Quantitative Research Projects

Overview

This chapter examines preliminary qualitative input designs, in which the quantitative portion of the study is the core priority and the supplementary, qualitative study begins the sequence by gathering data that will serve as an input to that core method. The goal is to enhance the effectiveness of a predominantly quantitative piece of work by connecting it with inputs from a preliminary qualitative study. Hence, the decision to use a preliminary qualitative input design means collecting relatively limited amounts of observational or open-ended interview data, whose most common purpose is to assist in developing the content for either a survey or an experimental intervention.

Like all the chapters in this section, this chapter begins with a discussion of the basic uses for the design under discussion. The body of the chapter presents detailed demonstrations of research designs that match these uses, in this case, through discussions of qualitative inputs to survey research and program interventions. The next section of the chapter provides a set of additional uses for preliminary qualitative input designs, and the chapter concludes with a discussion of how the specific issues in this chapter fit into the broader sequential priorities model.

Preliminary qualitative input designs occupy the first cell in the broader sequential priorities model because they have received the most attention. The popularity of qualitative input designs does not mean that they are in any way superior to the other three designs in the model; rather, they are simply the ones that previous researchers have explored most thoroughly. Hence, this category of designs makes an instructive starting point for describing the work involved in using connected contributions as an approach to integrating qualitative and quantitative methods.

As in each of the designs in the sequential priorities model, the fundamental dynamic driving preliminary qualitative input designs is that you give priority to the core, quantitative portion of the project, even though the supplementary qualitative study typical happens first. In practice, the first step is to design the core quantitative study and only then design and execute the preliminary qualitative study. Put another way, designing the preliminary qualitative study to meet the needs of the quantitative methods means that you must begin by clarifying those needs.

By far the most common reason for using a qualitative input design is to generate content for a survey or program that you want to put into the field. Thus, whenever you need to learn more about the people who are going to be the respondents in a survey or the participants in a program intervention, the strengths of qualitative methods are well suited to producing that information. Of course, many surveys rely almost entirely on well-proven sets of existing questions, and many programs are based on extensions of proven interventions. Alternatively, when you are working with new topic areas or new groups of research participants, you may not have the resources that you need to design the content for your core quantitative study—and that is when preliminary qualitative input designs can make an important contribution.

THREE BASIC USES FOR PRELIMINARY QUALITATIVE INPUT DESIGNS

Fortunately, the large volume of prior work on qualitative input designs points to a series of well-defined uses for preliminary qualitative methods. This existing knowledge base thus makes it possible to go beyond the general strength of qualitative methods in generating content for surveys and programs. In particular, this chapter presents three specific justifications for using qualitative methods as inputs to quantitative methods.

1. In *discovery-oriented uses* of qualitative input designs, the supplementary, qualitative study is largely exploratory. The goal is to reveal things that may have an impact on the quantitative portion of your project.

2. In *development-oriented uses,* the qualitative study examines a prespeci-fied set of issues that are essential to the success of the larger quantitative study. The goal is to increase your understanding of those substantive topics.

3. In *definition-oriented uses,* the qualitative study supplies detailed infor-mation to improve the performance of the quantitative methods. The goal is to specify the actual, operational content for your key research topics.

Moving from discovery through development to definition amounts to pro-ducing increasingly specific information from the preliminary qualitative study.

These three versions of qualitative input designs each rely on different strengths from qualitative methods. Although many preliminary qualitative studies emphasize the exploratory capabilities of qualitative methods, discovery-oriented applications explicitly rely on this inductive strength. In contrast, development-oriented applications often emphasize the strengths of qualitative methods for subjective purposes by helping you understand things from a par-ticipant's point of view. Finally, definition-oriented applications rely on quali-tative methods to provide the kind of depth and detail that comes from examining issues within a specific context. Thus, when you choose a discovery-, development-, or definition-oriented qualitative input design, you need to con-sider the specific strengths that the qualitative study will contribute to the overall project.

This points to a distinction between two decisions. First, when should you use a qualitative input design at all? Second, when should you use a particular version of this type of design? Although these two questions apply to all four of the sequential priorities designs covered in this book, the greater experience researchers have with qualitative input designs translates into a greater ability to address specific issues—such as an emphasis on discovery, development, or definition. Hence, this chapter's description of qualitative input designs will be more detailed than the equivalent discussions in the next three chapters, where this level of specificity is not as fully developed.

This distinction among discovery, development, and definition as three dif-ferent uses for qualitative input designs is most useful for descriptive or "heu-ristic" purposes. Once again, these distinctions amount to "ideal types" that can help guide your thinking. In practice, many projects will pursue more than one of these purposes. For example, if you are in the earliest stages of an interven-tion project, in which you are trying to discover the target behaviors for a program, you would still be interested in factors that might affect the eventual development and definition of that program. Alternatively, if you are further along on a survey project, and your basic goal is to define question wording, then you could be foolish to ignore information that would help you develop new questions or discover new topics to include in your project. Therefore, the uses for preliminary qualitative methods in any real-world research project will typically include some mix of discovery, development, and definition.

Distinguishing among these three uses for qualitative input design does, however, provide a valuable conceptual framework. In particular, the procedures that you use to design and implement a qualitative input study will depend on whether you are using the preliminary qualitative methods for discovery, development, or definition. Hence, understanding these distinctions can assist in several vital functions, including clarifying your goals in conducting preliminary qualitative research; designing the qualitative study itself; and linking the preliminary qualitative study to the core, quantitative portion of the project. The examples in the next two sections illustrate how these issues operate in qualitative input designs that involve both survey research and experimental interventions.

QUALITATIVE INPUT DESIGNS TO SURVEY RESEARCH

This section begins with an extended example of a preliminary qualitative study within a larger project devoted to survey research. The remainder of the section uses a conceptual framework based on discovery, development, and definition to describe the range of uses that survey researchers have found for qualitative input designs.

As noted in the example for preliminary qualitative projects in Chapter 1, Krause (2002) used several forms of qualitative interviewing to generate an extensive series of survey items concerning the place of religion in the lives of older Americans. The overall goal for this project was to go beyond the relatively simple measures that already existed in the study of religion while also learning more about the role of religion for this particular age group. This goal arose from an increasing interest in the connection between the health of the elderly and their religious beliefs and practices—an area that could not be investigated without better measures of religious beliefs and practices among older people.

Krause's qualitative work began with focus groups, moved on to open-ended individual interviews, and ended with a specialized set of cognitive interviews (Willis, 2004). At each stage, the participants were selected to be typical rather than unusual examples. In addition, all the studies included both whites and blacks to ensure that the final set of survey items would be equally applicable to both of these groups. The overall project concluded with a national sample of 1,500 survey interviews.

This project involved much more preliminary qualitative research than would be typical for generating survey content, reflecting the additional methodological goal of comparing several different qualitative techniques as inputs to survey items. Thus, Krause's (2002) work is an especially useful example because it included studies that match all three of the specific purposes associated with preliminary qualitative designs—discovery, development, and definition. With regard to discovery, an initial set of focus groups began with very general, open-ended questions, for example, "What is the most important part of living a religious life?" (Krause, p. 266). The goal at this point was to discover the broadest possible range of topics that connected these older participants to religion. As the focus groups proceeded, the interview guide evolved to target more clearly specified domains within the broader areas that were uncovered in the earlier discussions. One example concerned church-based sources of social support: "Some people say that the help and guidance they get from people at church is important. What do you think? What are some of the ways people in your church may help each other?" (Krause, p. 266).

The value of developing questions through qualitative work was illustrated by information gathered from the portion of the project that relied on individual interviews. This stage of the project involved 131 one-on-one, tape-recorded conversations that were conducted in the participants' homes. This unusually large number of interviews was useful because "the content domain of religion is so vast" (Krause, 2002, p. 267). In particular, the individual interviews were designed to pursue the wide range of topics that had appeared in the analysis of the focus groups.

Although the principal goal in these interviews was to learn more about participants' perspectives on topics that had been uncovered in the earlier focus groups, Krause (2002) was also interested in examining additional topics that were of theoretical interest but that had received little attention in the group discussion. This goal meant shifting to a more directive interviewing style that placed more emphasis on the researcher's interests and less on the participants' self-reported perspectives. These questions occurred near the end of the interview to ensure that it was not overly influenced by researcher-introduced topics. For example, although the topic of forgiveness had received a great deal of attention in the literature on individual experience of religion, it seldom arose during the relatively exploratory focus group discussions. Nonetheless, when Krause asked directly about forgiveness in the individual interviews, the topic produced some of the most interesting and "emotionally charged" responses in the entire study. These responses indicated that it was indeed an important part of the participants' perspectives on the role of religion in their lives.

In the final stage of the overall project, a series of cognitive interviews constituted a thorough effort to define the content of survey items. Cognitive interviewing (Presser et al., 2004) involves a variety of essentially qualitative approaches that investigate how potential survey respondents understand the questions they are asked. In this case, the interviewers first asked a question and then followed up with a series of relatively targeted probes that investigated the specific elements of each question. For example, after hearing a draft version of a question about whether they would be able to "forgive and forget" someone who had hurt them, the participants were asked, "What does the phrase 'forgive and forget' mean to you? If you were to ask a friend about this, how would you do it—what words would you use to see if they can forgive and forget?" (Krause, 2002, p. 271). Once again, the interview participants were evenly divided between blacks and whites to maximize the likelihood that both sets of participants shared similar understandings of the question content.

Krause's (2002) work is valuable for showcasing a series of qualitative methods that progressively discover, develop, and define a set of survey items. Ultimately, this effort produced 175 questions covering 14 domains that captured the role of religion in the lives of older Americans. One point that needs to be made clear, however, is that the choice of discovery-oriented focus groups and development-oriented individual interviews was determined by specific aspects of this particular project; either of these methods can be used for any of the three purposes associated with preliminary qualitative designs. (In contrast, cognitive interviews are a more specific tool that has been purposely created for fine-tuning survey items at the final stage of their definition.) It should also be clear that there is no need to conduct three separate qualitative studies to develop survey content. Instead, most projects will pursue more limited goals—both methodologically and substantively—than was the case here.

Overall, this example is noteworthy because it not only illustrates a careful application of a preliminary qualitative design but also gives a detailed summary of the work involved at each stage of discovery, development, and definition.

Discovery as a Purpose for Qualitative Inputs in Surveys

In quantitative projects that use preliminary qualitative methods for discovery or exploration, your goal is to uncover things that are essentially unknown at the start of the project. These designs emphasize the inductive strengths of qualitative methods, thus helping you understand unfamiliar topics and situations. Too often, preliminary qualitative work in survey research is stereotyped as dealing almost entirely with issues of question wording; however, when you are operating in an explicitly discovery-oriented mode, the key goal is to learn what you should ask about prior to worrying how you should phrase the questions. Krause's work on religion, for example, began with relatively unstructured focus groups to locate the set of basic topics that he then pursued in more depth.

Exploratory versions of qualitative input designs are especially valuable when you need to know more about either the topic of your survey or the respondents you will be interviewing. A classic example of using preliminary qualitative methods when entering an almost entirely new field of study comes from early social science research on AIDS/HIV. Although the need for epidemiological data led these projects to rely on large-scale surveys, the researchers recognized that they knew very little about the lives of the people who were at highest risk. Hence, several of these projects (e.g., Joseph et al., 1987) began with focus groups and other open-ended interviewing techniques as a way to learn more about the range of issues that the survey should cover. Discovery-oriented approaches can also be useful when you want to reconceptualize measures in a well-studied example.

One of the key advantages of discovery-oriented designs is to improve the specification of the models that you will test. Situations in which you have limited knowledge about the lives of the people you will be interviewing pose the serious danger that your survey will omit some crucial topic. By doing discovery-oriented work, you can uncover topics or "domains" that should be included in the survey. It is important to understand that leaving out factors that are part of the process you want to study is not just a matter of missed opportunities but is a source of potentially serious statistical bias in your results. The technical term for omitting variables that should be part of your model is *specification error* (e.g., Berry & Feldman, 1985). If you are familiar with regression analysis, then you know that leaving an important variable out of the analysis will affect the values of all the coefficients that you do estimate. There is no statistical solution for specification error, so if you are uncertain about whether your survey includes a wide enough range of relevant variables, then preliminary, discovery-oriented, qualitative studies may well improve the quality of your numerical estimates.

Development as a Purpose for Qualitative Inputs in Surveys

In projects that rely on preliminary qualitative methods for development, your goal is to increase your understanding about how a set of predetermined issues operate in the lives of the people you wish to study. Often this amounts to locating questions that will operationalize a theoretical concept. These designs emphasize the subjective strengths of qualitative methods so that you can learn about others' perspectives on the things that interest you.

Development-oriented versions of survey research typically attempt to locate a set of questions that adequately cover a well-defined topic or domain. Typically, the goal is to create a multi-item scale that will capture a broad, underlying concept, and qualitative methods let you can hear respondents' perspectives on the topic area you want to capture. Using preliminary qualitative methods to operationalize the concepts you want to measure puts you in touch with the behaviors and opinions that people associate with your research topics. This can be especially useful when you are trying to create a set of questions that apply equally well to several categories of respondents, such as men and women, different ethnic or age groups, and so on. Krause's (2002) study is a good example because of its collection of qualitative inputs from both European Americans and African Americans. By conducting preliminary, qualitative work with each of the major categories of respondents that you hope to compare, you increase the likelihood that the questions you develop will be equally meaningful to all the people you interview.

Finding out which questions are meaningful to your future survey respondents can have several benefits. The most obvious attraction of this approach is its ability to increase validity. If you want to find out whether the questions that you have in mind mean the same thing to both you and your respondents, then you should experience their point of view, and this is a major purpose for development-oriented versions of qualitative input designs. In an extreme case, you may find that a set of theoretically generated constructs have very little relevance to the lives of your respondents. For example, creating survey items that operationalize a particular theory may lead you astray if that theory does not accurately capture the thoughts or experiences of the respondents.

Of course, you do not want to make the opposite mistake by overlooking potentially important theoretical inputs merely because they did not appear spontaneously in preliminary qualitative work. Instead, if you want to know how an issue affects the lives of the people you intend to survey, then the obvious thing to do is to talk to them about it. Investigating the relevance of theoretical concepts is a particularly important goal for development-oriented designs, as illustrated earlier by Krause's (2002) work on "forgiveness."

In addition to validity, the reliability of a survey instrument can also benefit from preliminary developmental work. This is especially true for checklists and attitude scales, which require multiple items that all effectively target the same underlying phenomenon. Thus, by generating a sufficient number of survey items that effectively capture what your topic means to the survey respondents, development-oriented qualitative input designs can improve both the reliability and validity of survey measures.

Definition as a Purpose for Qualitative Inputs in Surveys

In projects whose purpose for preliminary qualitative methods is definition, your goal is to determine the content of the survey instrument. These designs emphasize the contextual strengths of qualitative methods for studying social life, either in detail or as applied to specific circumstances.

The primary reason for beginning a survey research project with a definition-oriented qualitative study is to assist in creating the item wording for the questionnaire. Regardless of the theoretical or practical concerns that motivate your interest in a research topic, asking effective survey questions requires knowledge of how the survey respondents think and talk about these topics. Understanding the respondents' language allows you to craft questions that are meaningful to them. Since the quality of the data in a survey depends directly on the questions you ask, it is not enough just to ask about the right things (discovery) with questions that meaningfully capture your interests (development). Beyond those essential goals, you also have to write the questions in language that participants can easily understand (definition).

Beyond question wording, any number of other "mechanical" aspects of survey work can be defined through qualitative work. For example, you can determine "skip patterns" to be sure that the right people get asked the right questions. Another operational benefit from preliminary qualitative work is the prior creation of coding systems for open-ended items so you can code and enter the open-ended items at the same time as the rest of the data. (This is particularly useful when you are doing computer-assisted interviews.)

Finally, one especially noteworthy problem can come up with qualitative methods, not only when they are used in the definition of survey content but also when they serve discovery and development applications: Avoid the temptation to substitute the insights from your qualitative work for pretesting. Because the data in a qualitative input study are collected in a very different format and context than the survey data that will be collected later, there is no guarantee that what people say or do in the qualitative portion of the study will directly correspond to what they say and do in the survey. The only way to learn whether survey questions work in the way that you intend is to try them out—which is what pretesting is all about (Presser et al., 2004). If your preliminary qualitative work was successful, then your pretesting for the survey should be more straightforward than it would have been without a qualitative input design.

QUALITATIVE INPUT DESIGNS TO PROGRAM INTERVENTIONS

Preliminary, developmental qualitative studies have a variety of uses in program interventions. Many versions of participatory and action research (e.g., McIntyre, 2008) use qualitative methods to increase contact between program users and program managers or designers. Other researchers rely on preliminary qualitative methods for the largely technical purpose of increasing a program's effectiveness and efficiency. Like the previous section, this one also begins with an extended example and then moves on to consider the uses of preliminary qualitative methods for discovery, development, and definition in intervention programs.

My colleague Peter Collier and I used two rounds of focus groups to help design the content for his Students First Mentoring Program (Collier & Fellows, 2009). The target population for this intervention was incoming "first-generation students" at a large, urban public university. At the same time that these students proudly described themselves as the first person in their family to go to college, they also encountered many barriers due to their lack of familiarity with what it takes to be a successful university student. The core goal of this project was to create a mentoring program that would help these students make the transition to the university experience; before we could do that, however, we had to understand more about their needs and possible ways to meet those needs.

Our first focus groups were oriented toward a combination of discovery and development. In particular, we needed to know more about the specific kinds of problems that first-generation students encountered, as well as how they responded to those experiences. We also conducted groups with students from more highly educated backgrounds to make sure the problems we heard from first-generation students were not generic issues that most students experienced. More importantly, we also interviewed faculty members to hear their perspectives on whether first-generation students had a unique set of difficulties. Those faculty members consistently shared a perception that first-generation students were poorly prepared, but not in the sense of academic or subject-matter deficiencies. Instead, faculty members emphasized a general lack of understanding of the expectations associated with being a college student, which was made even worse by students' poor decision making when they did have problems. As one instructor put it, "These students aren't failing my class—they're failing college altogether."

For the first round of groups, we chose to interview students who successfully continued past their freshman year so we could hear about strategies that helped them overcome any initial problems they had. Students from more highly educated backgrounds not only reported very few problems in making the transition to university but even had difficulty providing personal examples of the problems that the faculty had targeted. In contrast, first-generation students were quite vocal about their problems with determining what faculty members wanted from them. These continuing students still expressed considerable frustration with how hard it was to understand their instructors' expectations. They produced repeated examples of how hard they had studied for a test or worked on an assignment only to get a poor grade because they did not understand what the professor wanted them to do.

These groups helped confirm that first-generation students did have a special set of difficulties in adjusting to their role as college students. To create the intervention, our analyses led us to conduct a second round of focus groups that concentrated on the following areas: understanding professors' expectations, understanding syllabi, appropriate ways to communicate with professors; campus resources to receive assistance, and effective time-management strategies.

This second round of groups combined goals related to the development and definition of the service delivery program. In particular, although the first groups had helped us uncover a clear set of problem areas, we still needed a better understanding of the strategies that students used to cope with these issues. Thus, at the level of development, our questions on each issue asked the students to tell stories about both the problems they had encountered and the ways they had dealt with those problems. At the level of definition, the earlier groups, by sharing strategies from "successful" first-generation students, had suggested a means for both locating and delivering the specific content in the program materials. Thus, we limited the participants in this second round of groups to first-generation students who had successfully completed their first year at the university, and we made notes about which participants had stories that could serve as useful sources of advice.

The final result from these two rounds of preliminary qualitative work was a set of videos, one for each of the problem areas discovered in the first round of focus groups. These videos featured the voices of actual first-generation students. For example, the videos included scenes that showed students at a table discussing their experiences as new students at the university. Although these conversations look quite natural in the videos, they were actually rehearsed and staged by reminding each student of specific things that he or she or others had mentioned in the focus groups and then prompting the students to take turns introducing these topics in their filmed exchange.

Each video concentrated on topics related to both the nature of the problem and the range of solutions that we had developed from the two sets of groups. In addition, the personal stories and statements from the first-generation students who participated in those groups defined the actual program content. Ultimately, the value of this program material came from its ability to speak to first-generation students who are entering the university—showing that they are not alone in this experience and providing a set of successful strategies for dealing with the kinds of problems they are likely to encounter.

Overall, this extended example of preliminary qualitative inputs for a program intervention follows the same pattern as the earlier example for survey research: It provides a detailed illustration of the work involved in discovery, development, and definition of the content for the program.

Discovery as a Purpose for Qualitative Inputs in Interventions

The primary reason for beginning an experimental intervention program with a preliminary, discovery-oriented qualitative study is to learn more about the people who will participate in the program. The less you know about either the type of program you will be delivering or the people who will be participating in the program, the more you can benefit from the inductive strengths of a preliminary, discovery-oriented study. In some cases, a preliminary qualitative study will be your first encounter with the people who will be using the program. This kind of exploratory learning is especially important when there are cultural differences between those who are in charge of a program and those who will use it.

In practical applications, discovery-oriented needs assessment can help you understand others' experiences with and thoughts about the concerns that the program is designed to address. This kind of work is most useful when you are trying to select appropriate goals for your project. For example, consider a minority cultural group that is currently "underserved" with regard to the services that the program will provide. What do members of this group think their needs are? Are they even aware of the kind of programs that are currently available? How would they usually meet the needs that your program would cover? By investigating these kinds of questions, discovery-oriented qualitative studies help you set goals that match the needs of the people an intervention program intends to serve.

Development as a Purpose for Qualitative Inputs in Interventions

Preliminary, development-oriented qualitative studies can increase the effectiveness of your intervention program by incorporating participants' perspectives into the implementation and operation of the program. Even when you are relatively familiar with both the kind of program you want to deliver and your target audience, the subjective strengths of developmental work can still help ensure that the program operates in ways that match the needs and preferences of the people it is supposed to serve. Often, preliminary qualitative work on an intervention program can bridge gaps between the program's creators and its consumers. By learning more about the perspectives of those who will be using the program, you can develop a version of the program that avoids an externally imposed "one size fits all" approach.

Developmental qualitative studies are most useful after you have determined the program's goals and when you are planning the implementation stage. At this point, the crucial questions often focus on how to organize and deliver services. Continuing the previous example of an underserved community group, you can use qualitative methods to investigate questions such as these: Could you reach this community through the kinds of programs that you already deliver, or is a more innovative approach needed? Assuming that you can reach community members through your traditional programming, would they come to your existing programs, or should you open a new site specifically for this community? Are your existing staff members prepared to work with this community, or will you need to do substantial retraining and new hiring? Good planning can increase a program's effectiveness, and developmental qualitative work can help match the programs you deliver to the needs and preferences of the people who are supposed to benefit from those programs.

Definition as a Purpose for Qualitative Inputs in Interventions

A preliminary, definition-oriented, qualitative study helps ensure the on-the-ground, day-to-day effectiveness of an intervention program. It may not be enough to just have appropriate goals or good plans. Ultimately, success or failure depends on understanding the actual context in which your program operates.

Definition-oriented preliminary studies can target refinements in both the content of your program and how it is delivered. Preliminary qualitative work that pays careful attention to detail and context can locate the barriers to implementation and facilitators that make or break a program. Typical questions at this stage include these: What specific tactics will you use to locate and attract the desired participants for your program? What will people experience when they first encounter your program site or personnel? How can you ensure comfortable and effective communication between your staff members and the program's participants? What kinds of follow-up procedures with clients will boost your program's performance? In doing this kind of definitional work, you should remember that how things are said is often just as important as what is said: Qualitative research can help you learn about the "messages" that your program is sending.

Finally, as with the previous warning that qualitative input designs cannot replace pretesting in surveys, it is just as true that preliminary qualitative research is no substitute for the well-tested procedures that researchers use to assess the likely impact of intervention programs. For instance, just because people say that they need a particular service is no guarantee that they will actually use such a program. Even when you use qualitative interviews or focus groups as inputs to the design of a program intervention, you are still only hearing about attitudes and preferences—which may not translate into actual behavior once you deliver the program. Hence, it is best to think of the input from preliminary qualitative work as improving the content of programs, rather than ensuring their success. Even so, discovering more about the people who will use your program is almost always better than merely making assumptions about what they want.

ADDITIONAL BENEFITS OF QUALITATIVE INPUT DESIGNS

So far, this discussion has concentrated on a relatively straightforward set of contributions of preliminary qualitative studies to largely quantitative projects, but the benefits of qualitative input designs are not limited to discovering, developing, and defining the content of surveys and experiments. Two additional important uses that researchers have found for the use of preliminary qualitative studies are in generating hypotheses and working with research participants, as illustrated in Box 6.1.

> ## Example 6.1   Additional Uses for Qualitative Inputs
>
> O'Brien (1993) described a number of ways that she used focus groups in the early stages of a larger survey about personal relationships and safer sex practices among gay and bisexual men at risk for AIDS. For the questionnaire itself, she used this qualitative data to locate new variables that expanded the survey (discovery), gain a better understanding of the men's experiences surrounding the project's core concepts (development), and learn the language this set of men used to discuss these issues (definition). In addition, the focus groups contributed to the larger study by generating hypotheses for later testing and by building relationships that helped her develop the sample for her subsequent survey.
>
> One area where O'Brien's (1993) preliminary qualitative research led to new hypotheses concerned communication strategies in negotiating safer sex. In particular, several of the men suggested that practicing safer sex did not necessarily depend on talking about it. This led her to write survey items that allowed her to examine other ways of negotiating safer sex, including nonverbal communication.
>
> In terms of working with research participants, O'Brien learned that an ongoing connection to the community would be vital to her ability to recruit the sample for her survey. Creating a meaningful sample of gay and bisexual men is a demanding task, and like many other researchers in this area, O'Brien sought a diverse sample that was not skewed toward any particular group. This required access to the widest possible range of participants within a community in which some members were intensely concerned about their privacy. Through both the discussions in the focus groups and her experiences in recruiting the participants for the preliminary study, she learned that her personal credibility would be a key factor in her ability to work in this community. This encouraged her to develop a network of relationships that emphasized her continuing commitment to this community as well her trustworthiness and accessibility.

Generating Hypotheses

Quantitative researchers seldom undertake a qualitative study solely for the purpose of generating hypotheses, since an interest in a quantitative research implies that a set of research questions is already in place. Yet, the hypotheses you generate may be the most valuable result from a qualitative input design. Despite the long-standing tradition of deducing hypotheses from theory, it makes just as much sense to generate hypotheses inductively, and this is precisely what good qualitative research does.

As noted in the earlier discussions of discovery as a goal in qualitative input studies, one of the most common reasons for hypothesis generation is the realization that additional variables need to be investigated. For survey researchers, this often means expanding the models you will assess in your analyses. Those tests may ultimately reject the hypotheses from the qualitative study, but finding that you can safely ignore a variable is far better than omitting something that may influence the specification of your entire model. For experimental interventions, hypothesis generation often consists of discovering additional factors that may affect the program's chances of success. As with surveys, there is a cost-benefit issue: The damage from ignoring a factor may be far greater than the cost of incorporating it into the design for your program.

Often, quantitative researchers start work on a qualitative input design with relatively limited purposes, such as defining the wording of survey questions or program materials, and then are surprised to come away from the qualitative study with a whole new set of ideas. If, however, you consciously begin with the recognition that qualitative input designs can generate new hypotheses, you will increase the likelihood that your qualitative study will generate new insights.

Working With Research Participants

Another common benefit from preliminary qualitative work is the ability to build relationships with the people who will be responding to your surveys or participating in the programs you deliver. This is especially valuable in applied research settings. While general-population surveys and theory-testing experiments typically require only the briefest of relationships with research participants, applied work often involves sustained contacts between researchers and those who provide you with information. Whenever your preliminary qualitative work creates ongoing relationships with the residents of a community or the members of an organization, it not only helps you learn more about those people but also gives them a chance to get to know you.

Building relationships in the early stages of a project can be especially helpful in your subsequent recruitment efforts. For survey work, many textbook accounts of generating survey samples are limited to general impersonal sources, such as household addresses, mailing lists, telephone books, or random-digit dialing. Yet some surveys require a good deal more contact between the researchers and the respondent population to develop a successful sampling strategy. This is particularly true for what are known as "hidden populations" (Schensul, LeCompte, Trotter, Cromly, & Singer, 1999), whose members have good reasons to hide their membership in a particular group or category. In those cases, preliminary qualitative work can be an important step toward both locating sources for your sample and encouraging the cooperation of the people you find (see Box 6.1).

The idea of learning about research participants and building relationships with them is often even more important in intervention programs. In surveys, the typical goal is to get someone to spend an hour or so answering your questions, but intervention programs often ask much for more than that from clients. Even though programs usually offer clients more benefits than they would get from being in a survey, communicating the desirability of participating in a program requires a degree of mutual understanding that may not exist without an ongoing relationship. Further, if trust is an important element for participation in your program, then preliminary qualitative research can provide insights into appropriate steps for creating that trust.

* * *

Overall, both generating hypotheses and working with research participants demonstrate the additional benefits that can result from closer contacts between those who design research projects and those who participate in them. In many projects, it helps to get closer to the research participants to explore the issues that matter in their lives, learn their perspectives on things, and understand the context in which the larger research project will operate. These are precisely the kinds of strengths that qualitative methods can offer, so it is hardly surprising that preliminary qualitative studies have benefits that extend well beyond generating content for surveys and programs.

CONCLUSIONS

In many ways, this chapter sets the pattern for the three that follow. In each of these discussions of the four sequential priority designs, the goal is to examine not only the specific purposes and procedures associated with that design but also the potential problems in applying it. These chapters are thus focused on practical concerns and real-world examples.

There is, however, one major difference between the current chapter and the others in this part of the book. Because designs based on qualitative inputs have received considerably more attention from social science researchers, it is easier to find highly detailed research that is explicitly devoted to these designs, such as the work by Krause (2002) reported above. Consequently, the next three chapters will lack some of this richness and detail.

Saying that qualitative input designs have received more attention from researchers is not, however, the same as saying that they are used more often than the other designs.

Those other designs may appear to be rarer simply because they have not received as much explicit discussion. Hence, it should not surprising that this particular design serves as the point of departure for several of the more complex designs to be considered in Chapter 10.

SUMMARY

Qualitative input designs can use the strengths of qualitative methods to contribute to a core quantitative method in three ways. First, discovery uses the exploratory strengths of qualitative methods when what the subject matter of a survey instrument or a program intervention should be is relatively unclear. Second, development uses the meanings-related strengths of qualitative methods to advance the specification of the content of the quantitative method. Third, definition uses the depth and detail from qualitative methods to identify specific ways of asking questions or implementing programs. Taken together, these three uses for preliminary qualitative inputs make this design the most popular among the four designs that make up the sequential priorities model.

DISCUSSION QUESTIONS

The majority of surveys and program interventions do not need preliminary qualitative input. How would you determine when this kind of additional work could add value? When is it especially useful for meeting the needs of the core quantitative study?

What do you think accounts for the popularity of this design? What factors might make it both widely used and highly visible?

ADDITIONAL READINGS

The examples presented in this chapter serve as the additional readings.

Collier, P. J., & Fellows, C. (with Holland, B.). (2009). *Students first: Improving first-generation student retention and performance in higher education; Final report of program activities 2005–2009.* http://friends.studentsfirst.pdx.edu/files/SFMP final report 2005–2009 final.doc

Krause, N. (2002). A comprehensive strategy for developing closed-ended survey items for use in studies of older adults. *Journals of Gerontology Series B: Psychological Sciences and Social Sciences, 57B,* S263–S274.

O'Brien, K. (1993). Using focus groups to develop health surveys: An example from research on social relationships and AIDS-preventive behavior. *Health Education Quarterly, 20,* 361–372.

CHAPTER 7

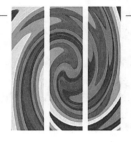

Preliminary Quantitative Inputs to Core Qualitative Research Projects

Overview

The chapter examines the most common uses for preliminary quantitative input designs, which are typically to assist in the selection of data sources for core studies that rely on qualitative methods. It begins with a discussion of the role that small Ns and, especially, the purposive selection of data sources play in qualitative studies. The core of the chapter is organized around four strategies for purposive selection: defining criteria, systematic comparisons, specific information, and theory and application development. Each of these four sections emphasizes the ways in which preliminary quantitative designs can help fulfill these strategies by locating either informants for open-ended interviewing or sites for participant observation. The later sections of the chapter describe other benefits of using preliminary quantitative designs, while the conclusions cover not only this particular design but also the broader issues associated with using either a qualitative or a quantitative method as a supplementary input to a core method.

BASIC USES FOR PRELIMINARY QUANTITATIVE INPUT DESIGNS

Preliminary quantitative inputs occupy the second cell in the broader sequential contributions model (see Table 1.2) because in this design, the researcher begins the overall research project with a supplementary study. In this case, the most basic use for the inputs from the preliminary quantitative study is to locate data sources for a predominantly qualitative project (i.e., either informants for open-ended interviews or sites for participant observation). As in the previous chapter, the strengths of the supplementary method contribute to the effectiveness of the core method. One key difference between these two designs, however, is that the design options described here do not have the high visibility of the designs in the previous chapter. Even though preliminary quantitative inputs are used frequently, they are often taken for granted. One practical result of this difference in explicit attention is the smaller number of examples in this chapter as opposed to the pair of extended case studies in the previous chapter (Collier & Fellows, 2009; Krause, 2002). This reflects the general rarity of detailed, self-conscious descriptions of preliminary quantitative designs (one recent exception to this trend is Barg et al., 2006).

Following the general logic of the sequential priorities model, preliminary quantitative designs begin by addressing the needs of the core method. In this case, qualitative methods often rely on detailed, in-depth data from a relatively small number of carefully chosen sources, which means that the effectiveness of these studies depends on locating high-quality data sources. Quantitative methods offer strengths that can meet this need, as they search large numbers of potential data sources to find the kinds of sites or individuals who match the data collection needs of the core qualitative study. In essence, this amounts to an argument for taking the idea of studying things "in depth" as a serious metaphor: If your strategy for data collection is to dig deeply into a relatively small number of data-rich sources, then it pays to begin with some prospecting that helps you locate sources that are likely to provide the kind of data you need.

In practice, the value of preliminary quantitative inputs stems from two procedural aspects of most qualitative studies: the tendency to rely on small Ns and the emphasis on purposive selection as a procedure for choosing data sources. With regard to relying on small Ns, the intense study of a small number of data-rich sources makes it important to select the "right" sources, and preliminary quantitative methods can help you make appropriate choices. Further, the process of purposive selection in qualitative research means that you are often looking for very specific kinds of research informants or sites to supply the kind of information you need, and quantitative methods can help you locate data sources that will match those purposes.

The next two subsections examine the reliance on small Ns and the emphasis on purposive selection, both as procedural aspects of qualitative methods and as bases for preliminary inputs from quantitative methods. Before doing so, however, it will be helpful to address the concept of sampling as a potential source of confusion about the selection of data sources in qualitative methods.

This chapter consciously avoids the words *sample* and *sampling* because social science research almost inherently links them to implications about the generalizability and representativeness of samples and the larger populations from which they are drawn. Even the common usage of trying a "free sample" of something follows this pattern, since it assumes that trying one example will give you a good sense of what all the other items in the "population" are like. Yet these issues of generalizability and representativeness are seldom a central consideration for selecting data sources in qualitative research. Instead, qualitative methods typically require data sources that allow you to study well-specified phenomena in depth and detail within a well-defined context.

At this point, it is probably too late to modify the idea that any concrete set of data sources is a "sample" of some sort and thus a representation of some larger population. It is still possible, however, to emphasize the difference between the logic for selecting data sources in qualitative research and in quantitative research. Hence, this chapter will avoid the common tendency to refer to "purposive sampling" in qualitative research and will instead speak in terms of the *purposive selection* of data sources.

The Reliance on Small Ns in Qualitative Methods

When you are working with a relatively small number of data sources, you are vulnerable to any problem that leads you to select the "wrong" data sources. Imagine a study based on a dozen open-ended interviews in which your conversations reveal that several of the informants were inappropriate for the study. Equally troubling would be a comparison of two case studies in which you discover that one of the sites has a number of unexpected differences with the other. When small Ns create these kinds of problems, you either need to redesign your study or replace those data sources. One major strength that quantitative methods can contribute to this scenario is the systematic ability to examine a large number of potential data sources, allowing you to screen out the least appropriate cases and concentrate on the most likely candidates for your data collection. The reliance on small Ns thus is not only a major aspect of research designs for qualitative methods but also presents an opportunity for preliminary quantitative input designs to make contributions.

The tendency to rely on small Ns arises from the context-oriented emphasis on depth and detail that is a central characteristic of much qualitative research. The original summary of context-related issues in Chapter 3 (see Table 3.1) pointed out the importance of a "holistic" and "naturalistic" approach to understanding processes as they occur in real settings or in the lives of real people. This typically translates into collecting a great deal of data on a relatively small number of cases. This emphasis on context, depth, and detail is reflected in the classic contrast between qualitative research's tendency to produce "thick data but narrow coverage" from a limited number of carefully selected data sources and quantitative research's reliance on "thin data but broad coverage" from a larger number of randomly selected data sources. Further, this focus on context does not happen in isolation, since the related goals of understanding the meanings of others (subjectivity) and transforming those observations into meaningful theory (induction) are also often best served by working with a limited number of data-rich sources of information. In other words, the essential purposes of qualitative research often lead to the use of research methods that rely on small Ns.

If you are going to collect detailed, in-depth data from a few sources, then it is important that those sources match your goals. For example, qualitative interviewing frequently involves talking intensely with a relatively small number of people—perhaps even taking an intense oral history from just one person (Yow, 1994). Alternatively, studies with group interviews often include fewer than 10 groups. The same considerations apply to participant observation; you are likely to do all your work at a single site, which makes it essential for you select a site that provides sufficient opportunities to learn about the topics that interest you. Thus, the standard approach in both participant observation and open-ended interviewing makes it is crucial to select data sources that will serve your purposes.

Following the general logic of sequential priorities designs, you can use preliminary quantitative data to address the issues raised by relying on small Ns. In particular, inputs from a quantitative study can help you find the "right" cases by searching through relatively large databases. Alternatively, as the beginning of this section noted, you can think of these issues in terms of the costs involved in starting with "wrong" or inappropriate cases. Even relatively thin quantitative data can help you sort out the cases that most likely would be useful for your study. In particular, quantitative databases almost always provide equivalent information for each site or person in the database, and this standardization makes it possible to do systematic comparisons across many potential data sources so you can locate the informants and sites that are most likely to serve your purposes.

Before considering examples of how this works in practice, however, it is necessary to consider a second procedural element of most qualitative research: the purposive selection of data sources. If the use of small Ns puts a premium on finding the "right" data sources, then you need a clear sense of what makes one data source preferable over another. Purposive selection is the main procedure that qualitative researchers use to address this issue, and it also generates opportunities for preliminary quantitative data to contribute to a qualitative score study.

The Reliance on Purposive Selection in Qualitative Methods

Purposive selection, the practice of collecting detailed information from carefully chosen sources, follows directly from the inductive-subjective-contextual nature of qualitative research. If you are going to generate a theory inductively, it has to be a theory about something; if you are going to understand someone's subjective perspective, then you need find people who share that perspective; and if you are going to study something in context, then you need to define the nature of those circumstances. Even if your ideas about whom to interview or what to observe change as the design of your research emerges, you still need to make a decision about where to start.

Deciding on appropriate data sources is only the beginning, however. The next step is finding the right kinds of people to interview or the right kinds of sites to observe, and this is where preliminary quantitative studies can make a valuable contribution. In particular, the strength of quantitative databases for this purpose is their ability not only to give relatively fast access to large number of eligible cases (e.g., people who can tell you about the things that interest you) but also to allow you to search for cases with specific combinations of characteristics. Thus, the process of locating sources of data that will serve your purposes often benefits from a preliminary use of censuses and official statistics, maps and geographical information systems, existing surveys, organizational databases, and so on. Just as the difference between quantitative approaches to "sampling" and purposive selection is a perennial source of confusion in qualitative research, so too is the frequent failure to distinguish between purposive selection and "convenience sampling" (Morgan, 2008). This confusion arises from the fact that two interrelated processes are at work in determining data sources, not just for qualitative methods but also for other most social science methods.

1. You must *define* the eligible criteria that determine who can serve as data sources.

2. You must *locate* a set of data sources who meet those criteria.

In qualitative research, your *procedures* for locating specific data sources may be highly systematic or based on simple convenience, but your *purposes* almost always require you to define the kinds of people and places that can best serve as sources of the information you need. Even though many qualitative studies do rely on "convenience" to locate the people interviewed or the sites observed, it would be highly unusual to find a qualitative study that defined almost anyone or anyplace as eligible to serve as a source of data. This is the essence of purposive selection.

Michael Patton (2002) has provided the best-known summary of what he calls "purposeful sampling" (pp. 230–244). The current account of purposive selection builds on Patton's work but differs from it in two important ways. The first difference is that Patton generated a comprehensive list of 16 specific strategies that qualitative researchers might use to generate "samples," including both random sampling and convenience sampling. In contrast, the system discussed here concentrates solely on "purposive selection" as a general approach.

The second difference between Patton's (2002) original list and the approach discussed here is an emphasis in this chapter on a smaller number of more basic strategies: The present list is limited to four basic strategies for purposive selection. The main issue is not how long the two lists are but rather the number of categories used to describe essentially the same content. While Patton's more detailed summary captures subtle differences among relatively similar approaches, the version presented here favors broader similarities over smaller distinctions. In particular, Table 7.1 consolidates several of Patton's more narrowly focused strategies as "variations" within the four basic strategies discussed here. The next four sections of this chapter show how each of these basic strategies can benefit from preliminary quantitative inputs; hence, the following discussion of Table 7.1 provides only a brief introduction to these four strategies for purposive selection.

The first category in Table 7.1, "defining criteria" for selecting data sources (also known as "criterion sampling"; see Sandelowski, 2000), is essentially a restatement of the underlying logic of purposive selection itself. In particular, any application of purposive selection requires you to state a set of characteristics or eligibility standards for the kinds of sources that can supply the data that will meet your purposes. Preliminary quantitative input designs are most useful for this selection strategy when you need to locate unusual or very specific kinds of people or places. For example, if you want to interview people with a certain set of characteristics, one time-saving strategy would be to search a quantitative database that contains information

Table 7.1	Four Strategies for Purposive Selection of Data Sources

1. **Defining Criteria:** Selects specific types of cases (or people, experiences, etc.) according to carefully stated eligibility criteria.

   Variations: *Typical cases:* Selects sources that typify the subgroup of interest.

   Information intensity: Selects cases based on amount of data.

2. **Systematic Comparisons:** Selects sets of cases according to the similarities and differences between them.

   Variations: *Stratification:* Selects sets of cases across some range of interest.

   Maximum variation: Selects sets of cases to capture diversity.

3. **Special Information:** Selects cases that have unique characteristics or other factors that make them both different and interesting.

   Variations: *Critical cases:* Selects important cases or those with unique experiences.

   Extreme or deviant cases: Selects cases that fall outside the norm.

4. **Developing Theory and Applications:** Selects cases according to their ability to build new theory or challenge existing theory.

   Variations: *Extending:* Selects cases based on emerging insights from earlier work.

   Bounding: Selects "negative cases" to limit range of theory or application.

about people who might match your criteria. Alternatively, if you want to do a case study on some group or organization with specific or unusual characteristics, then quantitative resources for sifting possible sites could be quite useful.

The second strategy in Table 7.1, selecting data sources based on "systematic comparisons," adds one basic feature: the separation of the total data set into two or more subgroups for comparison purposes. In this case, your purposive selection strategy is built around investigating the differences between systematically selected sets of people or places. Adding a comparative dimension requires defining eligibility criteria for at least two categories of data sources, so designs that use systematic comparisons are almost automatically more complex than those that rely on a single set of defining criteria. This also means that comparative studies are especially likely to benefit from the advantages of preliminary quantitative designs that help you assess which cases fall into each of the categories you want to compare. For example, in interview studies, this design would call for people who differ in specific ways, and an appropriate quantitative database would help you locate sets of people who have those contrasting characteristics. Similarly, if your goal is to compare a set of case studies, then you can benefit from information that allows you to classify potential sites according to how well they match different categories.

The third strategy, selecting data sources with "specific information," relies on the insights that you obtain by examining cases that fall outside the typical or "normal" range. In contrast to the first strategy based on defining criteria, searching for cases with specific information often defines potential data sources by characteristics that specify what they are not (i.e., by the things that set them apart and thus make them interesting for your purposes). Sometimes, you are seeking combinations of characteristics that amount to "looking for a needle in a haystack," and preliminary quantitative data can be especially useful for locating the sources of that specific information. For example, if most of the people who pass through a particular organization or program have a typical set of outcomes, but you want to interview those who have unusual outcomes, then organizational records could be an excellent way to locate those people. Alternatively, if you want observe a site that is distinctly different from the mainstream, then quantitative sources can help you identify such an outlier.

The final strategy in Table 7.1, "developing theory and applications," assumes that you are using an emergent research design that encourages a process of evolution in your choices about data sources. The typical goal in this strategy is to use your preliminary analysis from an earlier round of data collection to define a new set of sources that will help you extend what you have learned so far. Once again, preliminary quantitative input designs help you locate cases that are especially well suited for this iterative process of developing theory and applications. For example, if your first set of interviews provided a strong set of insights from one set of data sources and you now want to determine how broadly those insights apply, then you could use a quantitative database to locate participants who differ from those original sources in systematically defined ways. Alternatively, if you began by observing an unusually successful organization and you now want to challenge some of your emerging ideas about the sources of that success, quantitative resources could help you locate sites that either match or differ from the first organization in specific ways.

All four of the data selection strategies shown in Table 7.1 require (1) defining the kinds of data sources that will meet your purposes and (2) specifying a set of procedures for locating the kinds of people you want to interview or the kinds of sites you want to observe. As noted earlier, this process of selecting data sources is especially important when you are working with small Ns, because even a few mistakes in choosing your cases can have a major impact on your research. As with each of the sequential priorities designs, the emphasis here is on using the supplementary method to meet the purposes of the project's core method.

Translating this into the terminology of sequential priorities designs, you should begin by choosing the purposive selection strategy that is best suited to the needs of your core, qualitative study. The next step is to pair that goal with a preliminary quantitative study to locate the desired data sources. The next four sections illustrate applications of designs for each of the purposive selection strategies in Table 7.1, using examples from both open-ended interviewing and participant observation.

USING QUANTITATIVE INPUTS TO SELECT SOURCES BY DEFINING CRITERIA

Qualitative methods require you to select people whose words and stories will help you understand a particular perspective or worldview and to locate cases that will be especially helpful in understanding other related cases (Leech & Onwuegbuzie, 2009). Thus, determining the defining criteria that specify your potential data sources is an essential aspect of purposive selection. By stating the defining criteria for the people or sites that will meet your purposes, you create a set of eligibility standards by which to assess potential data sources for your study. Thus, as pointed out in the earlier summary of defining criteria as a strategy for purposive selection, this is the approach that comes closest to summarizing the general principle of purposive selection itself. All of the various forms of purposive selection inherently rely on specifying appropriate data sources, and the three other strategies in this chapter basically consist of more complex variations on the fundamental principle of using defining criteria.

For qualitative interviews, once you set the defining criteria for selecting the data sources, the obvious question is how you will locate people who meet your purposes. If your criteria are so demanding that they make it difficult to locate enough people, then the strengths of a quantitative input design may make it much easier to find the people you need. Example 7.1 illustrates not only one set of options for using quantitative databases to locate participants for qualitative interviews but also a number of more general points about the advantages of quantitative input designs.

Example 7.1 Finding Cases That Meet Defining Criteria

Pavlovskaya (2002, 2004) examined how privatization as a large-scale economic transformation affected the everyday lives of people in Moscow, Russia. Although there were many studies on the effects of privatization at the "macro" scale, Pavlovskya wanted to learn about "micro" effects on the sources of income people had and how monetary and nonmonetary (in-kind) exchanges flowed through extended families and larger social networks. Hence, her research design focused on qualitative interviews with families in a section of Moscow that had experienced high levels of privatization.

The quantitative phase of her research had two steps, beginning with a systematic search of areas in downtown Moscow that used a computerized geographical information system (GIS). The goal was to map "underprivileged" areas that had undergone rapid transformation following privatization. The GIS database allowed her to link geographical locations with data about both local income levels and building-by-building changes in ownership between the pre- and post-privatization periods. This allowed her to locate a low-income area with a high level of transformation due to privatization.

In the next stage, Pavlovskaya used lists of children in local elementary schools as another quantitative resource to select 30 families for in-depth interviews. She preferred families with children in this age group because "these households experience great pressure to raise income, do domestic work, and take care of the children under very difficult economic circumstances" (2002, p. 283). From these lists, she randomly selected informants who were parents of children in the younger grades.

The large-scale data on Moscow showed major economic growth in the retail and services sectors for the study area, but the qualitative study revealed that many local residents were suffering rather than benefiting from these changes. Residents reported that most of these businesses were "too expensive or irrelevant to their daily lives," forcing them to travel long distances to cheaper outlets or to rely barter and in-kind exchanges within their networks (Pavlovskaya, 2002, p. 286).

The first step in Example 7.1 involved using maps and property records as a resource to narrow down the search for a particular kind of informant, and the same thing can be accomplished through a variety of quantitative sources. This amounts to using sources of "aggregate data" to identify places where you are likely to locate the participants who suit your purposes. Thus, in the current example, it was important to find an area where the residents typified the kinds of experiences that this researcher wanted to study. This kind of aggregate data is not limited to maps or other descriptors of geographical areas. An equivalent approach would be to review the characteristics of organizations or other membership groups to target the ones that are most likely to have the kinds of people you want to interview. In addition, as Table 7.1 notes, there are several common variations on the general strategy of relying on defining criteria, and preliminary quantitative data can also play a useful role in these more specific designs. For example, in the search for "typical cases," examining quantitative databases helps you not only formalize the definition of what it takes to be "typical" but also locate data sources that have this typical set of characteristics.

Of course, the same kinds of resources can assist in locating sites for participant observation. In that case, you would start with a set of defining criteria for the communities or organizations that you wanted to study, and then you would use quantitative databases to help you find sites that met those criteria. Various kinds of official records can be especially useful for this purpose, including directories, maps, and censuses. Examining those records can often give you a sense of the range of sites that are available and how likely it is that there are enough potential locations to meet your criteria. For example, you might discover that there are so many potential sites available that you either tighten your selection criteria or add further criteria. Alternatively, you may learn that your definitions exclude almost every possible site; in that case, having quantitative data available should help you determine the aspects of your defining criteria that are removing the most cases.

Returning to Example 7.1, the goal of locating specific types of people to interview created the need for a more specific database that went beyond the aggregate data available from the original maps. In that study, the researcher used lists of families with children in elementary school to select the specific people she interviewed, and such organizational lists are one of the most common sources of data for quantitative input designs. As this example illustrates, such lists are especially valuable when they are linked to other information about the potential interview sources. Formally, the availability of this additional information is what converts a mere list into a database, and computerized searches become especially helpful when databases contain either many names or a great deal of information about each person. The increasing availability of such computerized databases makes it possible to sift through a large number of potential participants to find the smaller (often much smaller) set of data sources that meet your defining criteria.

Example 7.1 also made use of random sampling for the selection of the people to interview, but it is important to note that this procedure does little to improve the generalizability of such a small sample. (In technical terms, such a small sample would have a very wide margin of error around any estimate that it did produce—see Morgan, 2008.) Instead, this process of randomly drawing from a larger pool comes closer to the experimental procedure of "random assignment" by removing the researcher from the decision about who will or will not be interviewed. Hence, rather than using random sampling for generalizability, a random selection from a pool of people who all meet your defining criteria eliminates any claim that you made a "biased" choice about whom to include as data sources. Once again, the value of this process is connected to the use of small Ns, since "handpicking" even one or two informants could have a substantial influence on your results.

Another noteworthy point from Example 7.1 is that the researcher went to considerable effort to construct the geographical database that served as the first step in locating people to interview. For most quantitative input designs, creating your own database is less common, and you are far more likely to use existing databases (such as the list of elementary school parents in this example). Fortunately, most efforts to create new quantitative databases for a specific study do not have to be as elaborate as the one illustrated in this example.

Survey research provides a useful set of options for collecting your own data in a quantitative input design. Hence, this section concludes with a hypothetical example that creates a data set to pursue another variation on defining criteria, a search for data sources that possess a degree of "information intensity" (see Table 7.1). Rather than assuming that you already have a survey data set that would allow you to locate people who have a high level of familiarity with your topic, Example 7.2 describes a situation in which you could use a survey as screening tool to locate people who have the desired characteristics.

Example 7.2   Creating a Survey to Screen for Eligible Data Sources

Suppose that you want to study the experiences of professors who consistently use technology in their teaching. One way to locate them would be to send out a brief questionnaire that asks about their current use of technology in teaching, years of teaching experience, and how long they have been using the targeted teaching technologies. You also want to include a request for contact information from those who would be willing to participate in a longer, open-ended interview about their experiences.

If you want to do 10 in-depth interviews, you might start by sending out 100 questionnaires. This will provide initial estimates of both the response rate for such a survey and the percentage of the respondents who meet your defining criteria and are willing to be interviewed. On the one hand, if that first wave of surveys produces enough people, then you will not need to waste resources on a larger survey. On the other hand, if there are not enough people, you at least have enough information to estimate how many more surveys you need to send out; meanwhile, you could start interviewing the people you have already found.

As Example 7.2 demonstrates, preliminary quantitative studies can be very brief and purely descriptive, especially when your basic goal to is to screen for people who meet a set of defining criteria. In contrast, a full-scale piece of survey research for hypothesis-testing purposes would typically include not only independent and dependent variables but also additional measures to control for other relevant factors—which would easily add up to a more complex questionnaire. In addition, preliminary surveys in preliminary quantitative designs typically do not require the same technical sampling procedures as full-scale survey research; in particular, they seldom require a true random sample. Remember, your key goal in this design is not to create generalizable estimates of numerical results for the population as whole; instead, you simply need to find a sufficient number of people who meet your defining criteria. As a result, the relatively minimal data set compiled from a basic screening questionnaire may easily be sufficient to locate enough cases with the "depth and detail" that suit your larger purposes. As noted in Chapters 4 and 5, this is another instance in which the sequential priorities model encourages you to use simplified versions of the methods associated with your supplementary study, because you are explicitly designing that study around the goal of contributing to a different core method.

Whether you rely on existing databases, create your own, or use some combination of the two (as in Example 7.1), the essential value of quantitative inputs is to help you locate the data sources that meet your defining criteria. One obvious contribution from the preliminary quantitative portion of the project is the time and effort that it can save you. In many situations, the process of searching potential data sources to find those that meet your criteria will be much easier when you do that search in a data set, rather than by visiting many potential informants to find the right ones or traveling to several potential field sites to find the ones that suit your purposes. Of course, preliminary quantitative screening may only narrow down your search for data sources that match your defining criteria, and you may make further contacts to determine whether those potential data sources are indeed appropriate. Yet, even if preliminary qualitative inputs are only a first step for locating data sources that meet your defining criteria, this design can greatly reduce the time and effort involved in your study.

USING QUANTITATIVE INPUTS TO SELECT SOURCES FOR SYSTEMATIC COMPARISONS

Making systematic comparisons between different subsets of your data sources is the central element in this purposive selection strategy. Whether you are working with two categories of informants or four observation sites, the goal is to learn more about each of them by comparing them to the other(s). In essence, this strategy requires a double application of the basic logic in purposive selection: First, determine the broader domain of data sources that can serve your purposes; then, divide those potential sources into subcategories that will yield interesting comparisons. The value of preliminary qualitative studies follows this same two-step logic, since searches through quantitative databases can help you locate cases that meet both the overall and subcategory membership criteria.

Example 7.3 illustrates the common tactic of using organizational records to sort data sources into separate subgroups for systematic comparison. In this example, a set of medical records created the opportunity to sort interview participants into two related but distinctively different groups for the purpose of data collection. At the analysis stage, this led to a series of comparisons between the two categories of participants, which ultimately revealed different patterns of decision making.

Example 7.3	Differences in Seeking Diagnosis

Morgan (2002) studied how families caring for an older person with cognitive impairment decided when to get a diagnosis for Alzheimer's disease. According to the assessment staff at the clinic, actual symptom severity had little to do with the timing for seeking diagnosis, and medical records confirmed that families were just as likely to bring in patients who had either milder or more severe degrees of cognitive impairment. This led to a refinement of the research question to, Why do some families seek diagnosis for Alzheimer's in the presence of minimal symptoms, while others wait until impairments are considerably worse?

By using data from the medical records on the level of cognitive impairment at diagnosis, it was possible to create two sets of focus groups, separating families who acted in the presence of milder or more severe symptoms. For the participants, this separation into groups that shared similar experiences created a more comfortable conversation by avoiding conflicts over differences (e.g., "I can't believe you brought her in when that was her only problem," or, "Why in the world did you wait so long to bring him in?"). For the researcher, this separation created the basis for comparing the discussions about decisions to seek diagnosis between these two sets of groups.

In this case, comparing the two sets of caregivers showed differences in both when they recognized symptoms and how they responded to them. For example, those who waited until a higher level of cognitive impairment was evidence often had less direct contact with their family member and thus did not recognize how bad things were. Also, even when one family member recognized the existence of a problem, conflict within the family could delay a decision about what to do. Overall, this strategy of purposive selection through systematic comparisons led to both better data quality and clearer insights into the research question.

Research designs that *segment* focus groups into different sets are a common approach with this method (Morgan, 1997). As Example 7.3 shows, segmentation can serve two purposes for focus groups. On the one hand, it typically makes it more comfortable for participants to engage in group discussions by placing them with others who have similar experiences or perspectives. On the other hand, it facilitates analysis of the data by creating clear distinctions between purposively selected subsets of participants. This pair of advantages makes systematic comparisons a popular strategy in focus group research. Of course, it is also possible to use quantitative data to split a set of individual interviews into different segments for systematic comparisons. For example, Bennett, Switzer, Aguirre, Evans, and Barg (2006) administered a brief literacy test as part of their interview recruitment in a population known to have low levels of literacy; although they did not use literacy as a criterion for selecting data sources, their subsequent analyses emphasized systematic comparisons based on the 15% of their informants with low literacy scores.

Although Example 7.3 used organizational records, the study itself was about individual experiences, and those records served as the basis for recruiting participants for the group interviews. Alternatively, preliminary quantitative inputs from official records are often used more directly to select sites for participant observation, as shown in Example 7.4. In that case, a large ongoing study of the effects of classroom size on student performance provided a pool of information for selecting observation sites with larger and smaller classes. One notable feature of this particular study is that the quantitative data allowed the researchers to select observation sites that were roughly equivalent on a number of other criteria, thus increasing the likelihood that size differences were the most important factor being observed. For example, in this case, class size might be connected to urban-rural differences or economic resources. Hence, examining preliminary quantitative data would make it possible not only to identify such associations but also to select sites where the systematic comparisons were not likely to be affected by other factors.

Example 7.4   Comparing Class Sizes in Schools

Although there is a widespread belief that smaller class sizes lead to better student performance, very little research had been done on the classroom behaviors that might lead to such a result. Blatchford, Goldstein, Martin, and Browne (2002) thus undertook a series of studies to compare large and small classes. In addition to systematic quantitative tests of the hypothesis, they also conducted a series of qualitative studies that compared small classes (fewer than 20 students) with large classes (more than 30) to locate differences between these two types of teaching and learning environments.

The project as a whole collected data on more than 10,000 students, concentrating on classes for those ages 4–7 years. Sorting the classrooms by size for the quantitative analyses made it possible to select a set of roughly equivalent larger and smaller classes to compare in the qualitative research project. Thus, the quantitative data served as both the primary basis for one portion of the overall project and as a preliminary input to select the data sources in the qualitative portion of the project.

The research team used case study observations and open-ended comments from teachers to identify nine central themes (Blatchford, Moriarity, Edmonds, & Martin, 2002) related to teaching and learning in smaller versus larger classes, with an emphasis on the amount of attention that teachers could give both students in general and individual students. Additional in-depth observations (Blatchford, 2003) showed differences in teacher-student interaction between smaller and larger classes at the individual, small-group, and whole-class level. Smaller classes consistently produced more teacher-student interaction, while larger classes showed more student-student interaction. In addition, students in larger classes were more likely to engage in off-task activities and disruptive behavior.

Both Examples 7.3 and 7.4 began with an interest in a topic that spanned a full range of a specific selection factor (i.e., degree of cognitive impairment, class size) and then limited their systematic comparisons to the points at the high and low ends on the range (i.e., higher and lower impairment, larger and smaller classes). A variation on this strategy is to select more than one point along the original range to extend the set of comparisons. Table 7.1 refers to this strategy as "stratification," and this is illustrated in Example 7.5 in which a study compared points of view across groups from the lower, middle, and upper ranges of socioeconomic status (SES) within a city. As the example notes, one advantage of using this particular stratified comparison is that it shows one general process seems to be at work across all these levels—a claim that would be difficult to make with data from only the high and low end points. Although there are undoubtedly situations where it would be possible to make stratified comparisons without using quantitative data, it should be obvious that preliminary quantitative inputs are likely to be particularly valuable for this selection strategy.

Example 7.5   Stratified Selection by Social Class

Callaghan (1998, 2005) wanted to understand how social class affected the worldviews of women who were raising preschool-aged children. He investigated these issues through a series of focus groups with women who met regularly in "mother and toddler groups" in local neighborhoods within a larger urban area.

Since all the participants were young mothers, the composition of each focus group was homogeneous with regard to gender and life stage. What differentiated the groups was social class. In particular, Callaghan used a cluster analysis of census data (e.g., type of housing, occupational categories, etc.) to define neighborhoods as more affluent, intermediate, or poor. He then located participants through the member lists of mother-toddler groups in each area. This stratification made it possible to compare similarities and differences in the ways that women across three levels of SES described their gender- and family-related experiences.

In general, Callaghan's comparisons indicated that social class had a powerful impact on these women's lives. In particular, even though women at each SES level recognized and often resented the greater freedom their male partners had, their primary emphasis was on the differences between the values and habits in their class-based neighborhoods. In each social class, the women not only made clear distinctions between

(Continued)

(Continued)

themselves and those who lived in the other two areas but also argued for the superiority of their own way of life. For example, women from the poorer areas claimed they were more open and honest with each other and thus placed a greater value on relationships. In contrast, the women in the higher-status groups emphasized their greater attention to making plans for their own and their family's future.

In this case, the ability to make systematic comparisons across a carefully stratified set of data sources provided strong evidence about processes that operated throughout the larger social setting.

So far, all of these variations on systematic comparisons have operated within a single dimension, whether those comparisons were made between two categories or across several. One extension to this basic approach would be to include more than one dimension, such as using a pair of categorical splits to create a 2-by-2 set of subcategories for systematic comparison (e.g., DeCoster & Cummings, 2004). Once again, the value of using preliminary quantitative inputs to locate sources that match these more complex sets of characteristics should be obvious.

Table 7.1 points to another alternative selection strategy, "maximum variation," which goes beyond using discrete characteristics to define a set of systematic comparisons. When you rely on maximum variation as the basis for selecting your data sources, the goal is to divide the pool of potential sources into subsets that capture distinctively different experiences or perspectives. Example 7.6 demonstrates the logic of maximum variation selection. The researchers collected information about the range of potential data sources and made selections across this range; in addition, this example illustrates a technique for creating your own database rather than relying on existing data sources.

Example 7.6   Mapping for Maximum Variation

Arcury and Quandt (1999) were interested in conducting a yearlong series of ethnographic interviews on health and nutrition with older people in rural North Carolina. This kind of topic can present serious challenges for ethnographic studies, given both the range of people involved and the even wider range of relevant behaviors. Arcury and Quandt addressed these issues by focusing on *sites* as the basis for locating and recruiting participants who reflected the full diversity of the area.

Arcury and Quandt (1999) began by locating a preliminary list of potential sites that might be relevant to the topic they were studying and the people they wished to contact, including community centers, churches, local organizations, health clinics, food markets, etc. They then contacted key informants at each of these sites, both to learn about the specifics of that location and to find out about other potential sites. This approach eventually produced a list of 73 sites across 2 counties. As Arcury and Quandt interviewed the key informants at each site, they built a site-by-site database that included estimates of the number of older people reachable through that site, along with their demographic characteristics on gender, ethnicity, poverty status, and health status. This step also provided a sense of how homogeneous or heterogeneous the potential participants were likely to be at each site.

Next, the staff at each of the sites invited as many potential participants as possible to a meeting, which served as the first step in the recruitment process. In addition, the data on the people who attended each meeting allowed Arcury and Quandt (1999) to update their database about the range of participants at each site. Recruiting from the largest and most diverse sites helped to include a wide range of participants in the study. Further, as the research team examined the demographic characteristics of the participants in early interviews, they were able to detect portions of the local population that they were not reaching (e.g., Native American males). They then searched their database for sites that would help them locate the kinds of participants they needed to meet their goal of maximum diversity.

As Examples 7.3–7.6 demonstrate, systematic comparisons are a powerful strategy for purposive selection, and preliminary quantitative designs can provide a very useful set of inputs to locate the data sources for those comparisons. It is also worth remembering, as noted at the beginning of this section, that systematic comparisons create an additional degree of complexity beyond simply using one set of defining characteristics. In general, the more complex your purposive selection strategy is, the more preliminary quantitative data will offer as a way to locate interview informants and observation sites that meet these more demanding requirements.

USING QUANTITATIVE INPUTS TO SELECT SOURCES WITH SPECIFIC INFORMATION

Selecting sources with special information is a strategy for pursuing sources that have unique attributes—features that make them stand outside the norm. The rarer these combinations of characteristics are, the more likely preliminary quantitative data can help you locate cases that meet your criteria. Note, however, that selecting sources with specific information is not necessarily the same as a looking for sources with unusual characteristics, because almost any purposive selection strategy calls for selecting cases that are unusual in some way or another. Even when you are searching for typical cases, relatively few people or sites may combine all the characteristics you want. More often than not, the key in searching for people or sites with specific information is some characteristic that distinguishes them from other potential sources of data.

In some situations, quantitative data can help you find sources of special information with specific combinations of characteristics that would be difficult to locate in any other way. A good illustration is the ability to locate sites for observations that have changed in specific ways over time by using official records and other databases. For example, you might be seeking organizations that have grown during a general period of decline or urban areas that have experienced substantial amounts of "gentrification." For interview informants, you can follow a similar process by using longitudinal surveys to locate people who have experienced changes that make them sources of special information. Example 7.7 summarizes a study that used ongoing surveys to locate interview informants who had changed in specific ways.

Example 7.7	Special Information About Adaptation to Pollution

By following residents' perceptions of the health threats posed by an oil refinery and asphalt plant, Luginaah, Taylor, Elliott, and Eyles (2002) were able to investigate whether a reduction in emissions at the plant produced a more favorable evaluation of health risks. Although most residents perceived that the level of odors emitted by the plant was down, a subset reported either no change or even an increased level of problems with the smell of the plant's emissions. The researchers thus selected a set of people to interview from both the majority who saw improvement and the smaller group who did not.

Interestingly, the interviews showed little difference in concerns about health risks, regardless of the perceptions about improvements in the smell of emissions. Instead, there was a general concern that the odors where only "secondary" or "superficial" and thus not a good indicator of overall health risks from the plant's emissions—especially for groups such as children who might suffer from long-term exposure.

One important variation on this strategy emphasizes "extreme or deviant cases." This does not imply that these cases are unusual in any absolute sense, however; instead, they stand out in comparison to other data sources, and that is precisely what makes them interesting targets for purposive selection strategy. A good illustration of this general principle is the example of preliminary quantitative inputs in Chapter 1, which described the selection of a set of unusually successful schools (Toch, 1999). In addition, that project involved a preliminary quantitative analysis that was more complex than most of the examples in the current chapter.

Those preliminary analyses used regressions to identify outliers—schools where students performed better on standardized tests than would be expected based on classic predictors like parents' income and education. Thus, if you imagine a scatterplot with schools' average parental income on the horizontal axis and schools' average student test scores on the vertical axis, the typical pattern is a positive correlation in which test scores rise as parental income goes up. In other words, it is typical to find higher test scores in schools from upper-income areas. However, this project used its quantitative analyses to locate the rarer set of schools in lower-income areas whose students performed at an unexpectedly high level. The core qualitative study then examined six of these schools as case studies to gain insights into what it might take to produce high-level performance in what are usually seen as low-resource environments.

In general, this strategy of selecting sources with special information is often identified with locating key informants or observation sites with unique histories. Finding these sources typically involves a considerable amount of personal contact with local "experts." The examples in this section show an alternative approach to searching for sources of special information that can be effective when the likely sources of that information can be targeted through quantitative databases. Once again, those databases may contain information from organizational or governmental sources or information that you collect and organize yourself. Such studies can involve either simple or more complex data collection and analysis techniques. What is more important than this technical variation, however, is the ability to locate the data sources that have the special information you need.

USING QUANTITATIVE INPUTS TO SELECT SOURCES TO DEVELOP THEORY AND APPLICATIONS

The strategy of selecting data sources to develop theories and applications involves choosing cases according to their ability to either build on or challenge existing theories and applications. This version of purposive selection is most commonly associated with the concept of *theoretical sampling* from grounded theory (e.g., Charmaz, 2006; Glaser & Strauss, 1967; Strauss & Corbin, 1998). In that context, the goal is to select new data sources based on what you have already learned so far, which amounts to an explicit and systematic effort to use emerging insights as the basis for decisions about further data collection. For example, if you observed a particular pattern at one site, then you would use that insight in selecting other sites to extend and build on your existing ideas. Likewise, if you reached a set of tentative conclusions from an initial set of interviews, then you might search out categories of people whose experiences could challenge or at least set boundaries around your emerging theory.

Example 7.8 shows an application of this developmental strategy based on grounded theory. In this case, the authors (Dobryzkowski & Noerager Stern, 2003) began by collecting and analyzing a purposively selected set of individual interviews, which produced a set of initial theoretical insights. They then selected two new categories of informants for later rounds of interviews, which helped reinforce some key elements of the earlier interviews while also placing the existing data in a broader perspective. Thus, in classic grounded-theory fashion, the research conclusions emerged from successive waves of data collection and analysis through which the emerging theory pointed to the most useful data sources for the further development of that theory.

Example 7.8	Developing Sources From a Convenience Sample

Dobryzkowski and Noerager Stern (2003) conducted qualitative interviews to learn about the experiences of women who became mothers after the age of 30. For their initial recruitment, the research team contacted a broader range of mothers of varying ages. They made these contacts through a variety of sources, including "word-of-mouth, flyers posted in discount department and grocery stores, in doctor offices and clinics, and an e-mail call for participants placed on a local community college mass mailing system" (p. 244).

They began by conducting 23 interviews with women who had their first child after the age of 30. First, the research team generated an emerging theory from this round of interviews. Then, they choose two additional categories of informants to develop the theory further. Using data on the characteristics of the remaining women who responded to their earlier recruitment, they selected an additional 30 women who either had all their children earlier in life or had at least one child before and another child after age 30. According to Dobryzkowski and Noerager Stern (2003), the interviews with these additional women "were instrumental in helping validate the earlier findings from the original group and in adding depth and range to properties of the variables in the study" (p. 245).

It is important to note, however, that just because the strategy of developing theories and applications can be an important aspect of a grounded-theory approach to qualitative research, these procedures are not in any way *limited* to grounded theory. In particular, this form of purposive selection can be useful whenever you are consciously developing the emergent aspects of a qualitative study. In addition, there is no reason to restrict this strategy to the development of *theory*, since it is just as useful for extending and challenging emerging ideas that are related to practical applications. For example, if you were doing a qualitative program evaluation, you might begin by interviewing a relatively wide range of informants, which would then lead you to pursue specific categories of people whose information would be most useful in developing a deeper and more extensive understanding of that program.

From a procedural point of view, selecting sources for developing theories and applications requires a series of purposively selected data sources in which what you learn in the earlier stages of the study determines the eligibility criteria for the data sources in the later stages. If you had to start over each time you redefined the eligibility criteria for your data sources, this developmental strategy would require a great deal of work. Alternatively, if you maintained a database that included a broad pool of potential informants, as in Example 7.8, it would help you search for data sources that would be especially relevant in developing your theory or application. It can be tricky to create such a database, because it is difficult to predict where your emerging needs might take you. Still, if you have an existing set of resources that is large enough and diverse enough, you may well be able to find the specific kinds of data sources that you need. This is especially likely when your qualitative study is part of a larger research project or program of studies that share the same substantive interests. Example 7.9 illustrates this through the use of a large existing survey, which the core qualitative study mined to locate different categories of interview informants over the course of several waves of developmental selection.

Example 7.9   Developing Sources for a Study of Loneliness and Depression

Barg et al. (2006) conducted a series of studies on the sources of depression in the elderly, starting with a large survey to select participants for several rounds of qualitative interviews. In particular, the researchers used what they learned in earlier interviews to redefine the eligibility criteria for selecting survey respondents in the later interviews.

The qualitative interviewing began with eight older people selected at random from the larger pool of depressed and nondepressed survey respondents. Once again, the point of using random selection was to minimize any biases that might have affected the researchers' starting point, not to generalize from such a small N. The researchers thus began data collection by gaining a general sense of how their target population described and interpreted depression in old age in order to "form ideas for selection criteria for the next subsample" (Barg et al., 2006, p. S331).

One noticeable feature of the first set of interviews was that the informants were more willing to accept what they considered to be problems with anxiety rather than depression. Hence, Barg et al.'s (2006) next set of interviews used the survey data to select respondents who all scored high on anxiety and had either high or low scores on depression. Based on ongoing discussions of the transcripts from the earlier waves of interviews, the research team also pursued rounds of interviews with informants who had a family history of depression, were men in good physical health, had a discrepancy between their depression scores and their doctors' rating of their depression, and were among the oldest participants in the earlier survey study.

Throughout this process, Barg et al. (2006) also purposively maintained a relatively equal number of African Americans and European Americans. The ability to maintain this balance was especially important in this study because several earlier results showed that the two ethnic groups had similar conceptions about depression, and the database made it possible to pursue this issue throughout the development of the theory building.

In both Examples 7.8 and 7.9, the fundamental motivations for using a strategy based on developing theories and applications were to *build on and extend* what was learned from earlier stages of the research. A different goal is to *set boundaries* or limits on your emerging insights. Rather than pushing your ideas too far, it is often wise to examine the range of people or situations to which they apply. From a procedural point of view, setting boundaries once again raises the question of whether the original pool of data sources you generated is wide enough to include people or places that are quite different from the ones you have examined so far. Fortunately, you may not need a large number of alternative data sources for boundary setting, since your main purpose is not to understand these new data sources in depth and detail but rather to understand how and why they set limits on your previous work. One concrete way to implement this search for negative cases is through a variation on what is known as "member checking." Although classic member checking (Guba & Lincoln, 1985) often means going back to the people who provided your original data and getting their reactions to your tentative conclusions, it is also possible to seek out new groups to serve as sounding boards. In particular, a strong database would allow you to search for alternative data sources who are systematically different from the ones who provided the original data. From there, you can explore similarities and differences between their experiences and what you have learned so far.

* * *

Taken together, the four strategies introduced in Table 7.1 capture the most common strategies for implementing purposive selection to define data sources for qualitative studies. Each of the four also provides a clear role for quantitative inputs in helping you locate the kind of data that you need. The value of these preliminary quantitative designs is often to simplify your search for data sources, and this is especially true when you want to find sources with unusual or highly specific characteristics. Another advantage in using quantitative databases is that they allow you to be highly systematic in your selection, since they can tell you a great deal about what is both included and excluded in the group of people you interview or the sites you observe. This ability to make rapid and systematic comparisons across large amounts of data is a key strength of quantitative methods, and the examples in these four sections demonstrate how those strengths can contribute to the process of purposive selection in preliminary quantitative designs.

ADDITIONAL BENEFITS OF PRELIMINARY QUANTITATIVE INPUT DESIGNS

The benefits of preliminary quantitative input designs are not limited to locating data sources. Two additional advantages that researchers have found in the use of preliminary quantitative studies are (1) providing a broader context and (2) generating issues for further data collection and analysis. The second of these additional advantages—which essentially amounts to using quantitative data for exploratory or discovery purposes—is the more controversial of the two. In particular, Chapter 2 singled out the inductive or discovery-oriented purposes of qualitative research as a defining feature that also shaped the specific procedures in qualitative methods. Yet saying that qualitative methods have a particular strength for exploratory work does not eliminate the option of using quantitative methods for that purpose. Similarly, saying that quantitative methods have particular strengths for deductive theory testing is not the same as saying that these methods are limited to that purpose.

Although you typically use the quantitative methods in preliminary quantitative designs in a descriptive fashion to locate specific kinds of data sources, this same work can also lead to unexpected discoveries or insights. Example 7.3 on seeking diagnosis for a family member with Alzheimer's disease provides an illustration. In that case, the medical records revealed a distinct pattern of families being as likely to come to the clinic when symptoms were either milder or more severe, and this confirmed the value of dividing the subsequent focus groups to investigate the potential influence of issues other than symptom severity. The key point here is that important aspects of the research question for this project arose from a preliminary, inductive examination of the available data, even though these data were quantitative. It is thus important to pay attention to the possibility of detecting unexpected patterns and generating potentially interesting research questions during the preliminary quantitative phase for what will ultimately be a predominantly qualitative project.

The second additional advantage—using the data from a preliminary quantitative design as a context for the core qualitative studies—is a more traditional way for this kind of work to provide benefits. This basically amounts to using the same quantitative data that you used to select informants and sites as further background information about both the data sources you select and the broader range of potential data sources. Even when you don't use a quantitative database as a preliminary input for a qualitative study, quantitative information can still help you understand the bigger picture that includes the specific sources you did use.

The typical sources for this kind of background information are the same as those discussed in the earlier sections of this chapter: censuses, government records, maps, organizational records, etc. In terms of purposeful selection, the broader background picture that you can form from quantitative data is especially useful when you are using either typical or deviant cases as your selection strategy. For individual interviews, this information can provide a general context for understanding the circumstances that make the lives and experiences of people who provide the data either typical or unusual. Similarly, in observational case studies, this information can help you place the specific location(s) where you collect your data within the larger range of alternative study sites.

Overall, both discovering patterns in the data and establishing a broader context demonstrate the additional benefits that can result from a more systematic examination of quantitative data as an input to a core qualitative method. Even when those quantitative data are relatively "thin" compared to the depth and detail that you will ultimately emphasize, they can still help you by either revealing important aspects of the topic you are studying or giving you a broader sense of the circumstances that surround the sources of your collected data.

CONCLUSIONS

This chapter completes the examination of preliminary input designs and thus the top half of Table 1.2, which defines the four sequential priorities designs. This thus provides an excellent opportunity to compare the current coverage of preliminary *quantitative* input designs to the previous chapter's discussion of preliminary *qualitative* input designs.

One important difference between preliminary studies that rely on input from qualitative versus quantitative methods is the greater amount of effort that usually goes into preliminary qualitative designs. Even when you are using qualitative methods for supplementary studies, a relatively complex preliminary qualitative study is often needed to develop the content for survey questionnaires and program interventions. In particular, these *qual → QUANT* designs almost always require new qualitative data collection to serve the needs of the core quantitative method. Thus, even though supplementary qualitative studies are typically much smaller and more narrowly focused than full-scale qualitative research, they still require relatively demanding data collection and analysis procedures that are carefully designed to meet specific purposes.

In contrast, preliminary quantitative studies are far more likely to depend on existing databases. Even when you need to create a new quantitative database to locate data sources, the analytic procedures usually require little more than computing percentages and cross-tabulations. Although several of the examples in this chapter go beyond the combination of relying on existing databases and using relatively simple analyses, that pairing is undoubtedly the most common format for preliminary quantitative studies. Thus, the quantitative methods in *quant* → *QUAL* designs are typically less complex than the equivalent qualitative methods in *qual* → *QUANT* designs.

A very different contrast between these two forms of preliminary inputs is the relative amount of attention that each has received. Compared to preliminary qualitative designs, which have received widespread attention, preliminary quantitative methods have played a much less visible role in projects that rely on core qualitative methods. Although the greater effort required for preliminary qualitative studies might explain some of the increased discussion from authors who went to this much trouble, this explanation only begs the question of why those researchers were willing to take on this extra work. One obvious explanation for this willingness to generate a relatively demanding set of inputs is a clear sense of *added valued* from preliminary qualitative designs for certain kinds of quantitative studies. In particular, whenever surveys or intervention programs need to develop new content to be successful, then qualitative methods have obvious strengths to contribute. For these kinds of quantitative projects, widespread acceptance of preliminary qualitative designs reflects a belief that the resulting surveys and programs will be higher in quality because of inputs from qualitative methods.

By comparison, even though preliminary quantitative designs are relatively common, articles from qualitative projects that use this design typically devote little space to the quantitative inputs. Interestingly, while these same write-ups are likely to deal directly with issues central to purposive selection itself, such as the reasons for setting eligibility criteria and the desirability of locating carefully defined data sources, the use of quantitative databases to accomplish these purposes is often mentioned only in passing. This amounts to saying that, although purposive selection is highly valued, there is little perception of the added value of using preliminary quantitative designs in that process. Thus, one interpretation of the relative lack of attention to preliminary quantitative designs is that they are not seen as making a central contribution to projects that rely on core qualitative methods. Instead, it seems that they are mostly treated as a more convenient way to locate the data sources that match a particular set of purposive selection criteria.

Saying that qualitative researchers *do not emphasize* the value added from preliminary quantitative designs is not the same as saying that those inputs *do not contribute* substantial added value. Thus, the examples in this chapter show numerous ways in which preliminary quantitative inputs can enhance the general logic of purposive selection. Returning to the larger comparison between the two preliminary uses of supplementary methods, it is hard to say whether the goal of using preliminary quantitative studies to locate data sources for projects with core qualitative methods is as important as the goal of using preliminary qualitative studies to develop materials for projects that emphasize quantitative methods. Perhaps the supplemental aspects of the designs in Chapter 6 truly do contribute more value than the ones considered here. One thing is certain, however: Preliminary quantitative designs are likely to remain more implicit and less developed unless there is a change in the perceived value of what they can contribute.

SUMMARY

The primary use for supplementary quantitative methods as inputs to a core qualitative study is to assist with the goals related to four types of purposive sampling. First, defining criteria uses supplementary quantitative inputs to locate cases that meet specific criteria for inclusion in the qualitative study. Second, systematic comparisons generate sets of cases that have some desired contrast or difference between the data sources. Third, specific information uses quantitative inputs to find sources that are particularly interesting or important. Fourth, theory and application development locates data sources that are particularly useful for theoretical purposes, such as extending existing work by finding new data sources that can build on earlier ideas. Overall, although these quantitative input designs are relatively widely used, they have received less attention than other designs within the sequential priorities model.

DISCUSSION QUESTIONS

The kinds of systematic inputs that quantitative methods can make to purposive sampling primarily take the place of more informal procedures, such as convenience sampling. When is this kind of systematic sampling most likely to be an advantage for qualitative research? When is it worth the additional time and effort?

Quantitative input designs are relatively common but don't receive much attention in the literature. What do you think are some of the reasons for this lack of visibility?

ADDITIONAL READINGS

The examples presented in this chapter serve as the additional readings.

Arcury, T. A., & Quandt, S. A. (1999). Participant recruitment for qualitative research: A site-based approach to community research in complex societies. *Human Organization, 58,* 128–133.

Barg, F. K., Huss-Ashmore, R., Wittink, M. N., Murray, G. F., Bogner, H. R., & Gallo, J. J. (2006). A mixed-methods approach to understanding loneliness and depression in older adults. *Journal of Gerontology: Social Sciences, 61B,* S329–S339.

Bennett, I., Switzer, I., Aguirre, A., Evans, K., & Barg, F. (2006). "Breaking it down": Patient-clinician communication and prenatal care among African American women of lower and higher literacy. *Annals of Family Medicine, 4,* 334–340.

Blatchford, P. (2003). A systematic observational study of teachers' and pupils' behaviour in large and small classes. *Learning and Instruction, 13,* 569–595.

Blatchford, P., Goldstein, H., Martin, C., & Browne, W. (2002). A study of class size effects in English school reception year classes. *British Educational Research Journal, 28,* 169–185.

Blatchford, P., Moriarity, V., Edmonds, S., & Martin, C. (2002). Relationships between class size and teaching: A multimethod analysis of English infant schools. *American Educational Research Journal, 39,* 101–132.

Callaghan, G. (1998). The interaction of gender, class and place in women's experience: A discussion based in focus group research. *Sociological Research Online, 3.* Retrieved from http://www.socresonline.org.uk/3/3/8.html

Callaghan, G. (2005). Accessing habitus: Relating structure and agency through focus group research. *Sociological Research Online, 10.* Retrieved from http://www.socresonline.org.uk/10/3/callaghan.html

Dobryzkowski, T. M., & Noerager Stern, P. (2003). Out of synch: A generation of first-time mothers over 30. *Health Care for Women International, 24,* 242–253.

Luginaah, I. N., Taylor, S. M., Elliott, S. J., & Eyles, J. D. (2002). Community responses and coping strategies in the vicinity of a petroleum refinery in Oakville, Ontario. *Health and Place, 8,* 177–190.

Morgan, D. L. (2002). Seeking diagnosis for a cognitively impaired family member: Evidence from focus groups. In G. D. Rowles & N. E. Schoenberg (Eds.), *Qualitative Gerontology: A contemporary perspective* (2nd ed., pp. 213–233). New York, NY: Springer.

Pavlovskaya, M. E. (2002). Mapping urban change and changing GIS: Other views of economic restructuring. *Gender, Place, and Culture, 9,* 281–289.

Pavlovskaya, M. E. (2004). Other transitions: Multiple economies in Moscow households in the 1990s. *Annals of the American Association of American Geographers, 94,* 329–351.

CHAPTER 8

Follow-up Qualitative Extensions to Core Quantitative Research Projects

Overview

This chapter examines designs in which a supplementary, qualitative follow-up study moves a project beyond the results from a core quantitative study that has already been completed. It is thus the first of the designs that is based on making further contributions to what was learned in a core study—in this case, extending the results obtained through either a survey or an experimental intervention. The chapter is organized around three basic motivations for using a qualitative follow-up design after a survey or a program intervention is used as a core quantitative method. First, *exploration* seeks explanations for how and why a particular set of results occurred; this motivation often arises when one seeks the sources of the original results. Second, *investigation* pursues a further examination of the results from the quantitative data; it often involves interpreting specific patterns in the data. Finally, *illustration* describes the basis of the quantitative results; it typically concentrates on demonstrating relatively well-understood aspects of the quantitative data. Taken together, these uses for qualitative extension designs demonstrate how the strengths of supplementary qualitative methods can extend what was already learned in a prior quantitative study.

This chapter marks a notable transition from the two previous chapters, which presented designs in which a supplementary method contributed preliminary inputs to a core method. In contrast, this chapter and the next one cover designs in which the supplementary method serves as a follow-up extension to the core method. These designs begin with the assumption that you have completed the core study and now want to use a supplementary study to follow up on and extend what you have already learned. This leads to a pair of possible sequential priorities designs: *QUANT → qual* and *QUAL → quant*.

The shift of designs that use the supplementary method from a preliminary to a follow-up position involves more than just the sequencing of the methods. In addition, the use of the labels *input* and *extension* signals a difference in the role that the supplementary study plays within the overall project. The concept of extension emphasizes going beyond existing results. In this chapter, the results from the core, quantitative portion of a project serve as a starting point, and the purpose of the additional qualitative study is to add to or extend those results. As always, the needs of the core method determine the goals and procedures that you use in the supplementary method, but now you are beginning with a set of quantitative results in hand, and following that study with an additional qualitative study will take you beyond what you already have learned with your core method.

Given the conceptual shift associated with follow-up extension designs in general, it will help to consider the specific strengths that a follow-up qualitative study can contribute to an earlier core quantitative study. First, because the core quantitative methods place a heavy reliance on the *deductive* testing of hypotheses derived from prior theory, the data generated may provide only limited resources for investigating unexpected or poorly understood results. The value of using a follow-up qualitative method is that you can use an *inductive* approach to explore the sources of those results and generate hypotheses that go beyond what you measured in the original study. Second, the emphasis on an *objective* approach in quantitative methods may make it difficult to illuminate your procedures and results with an understanding of the research participants' perspectives, but a qualitative follow-up can examine aspects of the participants' *subjective* interpretations. Finally, there may be additional value in supplementing the *generality* of quantitative results with the kind of *context-specific* depth and detail that qualitative methods can provide.

In general, the most common reason for using supplementary qualitative studies is to provide more information about the processes that produced the original quantitative results. In many ways, the message is that if you want to know more about why program participants acted the way they did or why survey respondents said what they did, then why don't you ask them?

BASIC USES FOR FOLLOW-UP QUALITATIVE DESIGNS

There are three common reasons for using $QUANT \rightarrow qual$ designs: exploration, investigation, and illustration. The key distinction here comes from how well defined the needs of the core quantitative study are. With exploration, the purpose is to produce broad insights into how and why a particular set of results occurred. For example, your goal might be to understand either an unsuccessful intervention or an unexpected survey result. With investigation, the goal is to explain specific patterns in the quantitative data. For example, your goal might be to determine why one set of intervention participants performed better than another set or why a group of survey respondents had scores that were either above or below expected levels. Finally, follow-up studies that concentrate on illustration provide descriptions of the sources for the quantitative portion of the project. For example, you might present a case study that highlights the success of an intervention, or you might describe specific survey respondents to "put a human face on the data."

Each of these designs begins with set of quantitative results that define the desired contribution from a supplementary qualitative study. In particular, they demonstrate how the strengths of qualitative methods can extend the results from a core quantitative study. This goal of using the follow-up study as an extension of the core method will be a common theme in both this chapter and the next.

QUALITATIVE FOLLOW-UP DESIGNS FOR EXPLORATION

When a qualitative follow-up study is based on exploration, the goal is to engage in a discovery process that sheds new light on the quantitative portion of the project. In many cases, this corresponds to understanding the how and why behind the quantitative results. Intervention research is especially likely to pursue this path when the results from a project are hard to understand. In other cases, this motivation is a useful match to the relatively exploratory goals in the quantitative study. Survey research is especially likely to rely on this discovery-oriented design when the original goal is to describe an unfamiliar population or poorly understood phenomenon; in that case, the qualitative portion of the study can expand on what you learned in the core study. In either case, the key distinguishing feature of exploration as a motivation in qualitative follow-up studies is the need to go beyond the topics covered in the original research and collect new data that will help explain the results from the core study.

Using Qualitative Follow-up Designs to Explore Results From Interventions

The original example of qualitative follow-up designs, Example 1.5 in Chapter 1, described a study in which a highly promising mental health intervention failed for poorly understood reasons (Chinman et al., 2001; Davidson et al., 1997). Specifically, the readmission rate was unexpectedly high for patients who had been coached in skills that should have increased their capacity for independent living. By using follow-up focus groups, Davidson et al. determined that the supportive nature of the program environment served as an attractive lifestyle for the patients, one that was preferable to life outside the treatment facility. By exploring the source of the original result, the qualitative study offered an explanation for the program's failure to increase independent living.

This example illustrates one common reason why interventions fail: They produce unintended consequences that counteract the original program goals. An entirely different source of problems is programs in which the intervention is implemented at only a low level—the intervention fails because it was never actually put in place. Example 8.1 describes a qualitative follow-up study that revealed this kind of implementation problem.

Example 8.1	Discovering Increased Problems Due to Low Implementation Rates

Under President George W. Bush, the US Department of Education restricted the funds it provided for interventions in programs that had a strong evidence base for their success, which almost always meant that the program had been proven in a random, controlled trial. This federal policy also insisted that any such program be implemented exactly as it was originally developed to maintain that proven effectiveness.

This policy has been quite controversial. My own contact with it came through a graduate student in one of my seminars who was involved in assessing the effectiveness of a school-based drug and alcohol treatment program. The goal was to institute a unified program across grades in a system in which all the students from a single middle school moved up to a single high school. Because only two officially approved programs matched this goal, the local school system was restricted in using its federal funding to using one of those two programs. The seminar student sought my help because the local school system's evaluation of what was supposedly the more successful of these two approved interventions showed that drug and alcohol use actually increased after the school put that program in place.

As part of a qualitative follow-up investigation, the student conducted a series of interviews with teachers who were supposed to deliver the program content. What she found was a radical misfit between this program and the local schools. In particular, the pair of local schools served middle- and upper-income suburban areas where over 80% of the high school students went on to college, while the original program had been developed in a low-income neighborhood in New York City that had a very high drop-out rate. As a result of this mismatch, many of the teachers in her interviews indicated that they had made little or no use of the program. These teachers consistently reported a fear that using such obviously inappropriate materials would severely reduce their credibility regarding drug and alcohol issues. These were the only approved teaching materials on the topic, however, so substance abuse issues often received less attention than in previous years. Thus, the failure to implement this intervention resulted in an overall decrease in the efforts that were targeted at the intended outcome.

One interesting difference between the studies of Chinman et al. (2001) and Davidson et al. (1997) and Example 8.1 is the extent to which the researchers followed up on the results from the supplementary qualitative study. In Example 8.1, the research ended with the qualitative supplement, which discovered a highly believable explanation for an unexpected outcome. In contrast, the first two studies went a step further by using the findings from the qualitative study to revise the original program. In other words, the researchers generated a hypothesis about the poor performance of the initial intervention, and they tested this hypothesis by systematically modifying the program. The success of the revised program provided strong empirical evidence for the value of the hypotheses that were generated through the supplementary qualitative study. This project thus extended the original qualitative follow-up design with a further quantitative study, which suggests the more complex designs that will be covered in Chapter 10.

Using Qualitative Follow-up Designs to Explore Results From Surveys

The classic use of supplementary follow-up interviews with surveys is to develop explanations that are not available within the survey data. In particular, the goal is often to learn about the sources of the results from the participants themselves, as opposed to speculating without data. Example 8.2 demonstrates several explanations that came from listening to the survey respondents.

Example 8.2 Interpreting Exploratory Quantitative Data

Blackhall, Frank, Murphy, and Michel (2001) used qualitative interviewing to follow up on the results from an earlier quantitative study on differences among four ethnic groups in their preferences with regard to end-of-life care. The original survey focused on a comparison of European, African, Korean, and Mexican Americans (Blackhall et al., 1999), and it found substantial differences across the four ethnic groups with regard to beliefs and preferences about terminal care.

The researchers' in-depth interviews of survey respondents in the four ethnic groups included an item about whether patients should be told the truth about a diagnosis of fatal cancer. In the survey, nearly 90% of both European Americans and African Americans agreed that the patients should be told, while only 65% of Mexican Americans and 47% of Korean Americans said that the patient should be told this information. Blackhall et al. (2001) noted: "Although large differences among the attitudes of our groups. . . . are apparent from the survey data, the reasons for those differences cannot be determined from the survey responses alone" (p. 61).

The follow-up qualitative interviews used the equivalent of a *neutral probe technique,* repeating the original survey question—once again asking whether terminally ill cancer patients should be told the truth—and then probing *why* people choose their responses. One of the largest differences that emerged from the interviews was agreement among European Americans and African Americans that knowing is an important part of "patient autonomy," a prevalent theme in these two groups. In contrast, Korean Americans and Mexican Americans were more likely to say things related to a theme that "it is cruel to tell" because this knowledge can cause psychological as well as physical suffering. In addition, Korean Americans expressed culturally specific beliefs about family responsibilities (*hyodo,* in Korean) that emphasized taking care of both the physical and emotional needs of relatives during illness. *Hyodo* would be violated by the cruelty of telling a family member distressing news.

The full set of themes that Blackhall et al. (2001) discovered also provided insights into more subtle differences that were not detectable in the survey data. In particular, although both European Americans and African Americans emphasized the general theme of patient autonomy, European Americans were more likely to link this to the further theme of "getting your things in order"—planning for the consequences of a terminal illness—while African Americans were more likely to link their statements about autonomy to the opportunity to "get right with God" and deal with spiritual needs (2001, pp. 63–64). Thus, even though the European and African Americans gave similar responses to the original survey item, there were potentially important differences in their reasons for those answers.

In Example 8.2, using probes to hear more from study participants about the original survey question raises an interesting issue: What if this qualitative data had been collected through an open-ended question within the initial survey? In all likelihood, this would still have produced a *QUANT → qual* design, because the important distinction is *not when you collect the data but how you use it*. In particular, the analysis would almost certainly follow the same pattern as above, starting with the results from the quantitative data and then using the qualitative data for further exploration. Thus, open-ended questions in surveys can provide the basis for qualitative extensions, even though the data are collected simultaneously.

Another notable feature of the previous example was that the qualitative follow-up study used participants from the original survey. In many cases, it will not be possible to reinterview the survey respondents, so the alternative is to conduct the qualitative interviews with a new set of participants. When possible, one desirable strategy is to use the same sampling procedures used to identify survey respondents to locate participants for the follow-up interviews. This may, however, not be necessary for exploratory work, as demonstrated in Example 8.3.

Example 8.3   Using Secondary Data for Exploratory Analysis

Rowlingson and McKay (2005) were interested in how socioeconomic origins affected the experiences of women who are known as either "lone mothers" (in Britain) or "single mothers" (in the United States). Because relatively little research had been devoted to this topic, they conducted secondary analyses on a series of large-scale surveys from Britain to find out whether women whose fathers were either working-class or largely absent had different experiences as lone mothers than those from from middle-class backgrounds. In addition, they examined a series of open-ended interviews with lone mothers from an archive of recent qualitative studies, as well as data from other qualitative studies on choices about motherhood.

(Continued)

(Continued)

Their analysis of the survey data showed that women who came from a family where the father was either working-class, unemployed, or absent were far more likely to become lone mothers than women who came from more middle-class families. This led Rowlingson and McKay (2005) to a new question: "Why is there such a strong link between socio-economic disadvantage and single lone motherhood?" (p. 35). Their qualitative follow-up work pointed out two relevant factors that accounted for the experiences of women from lower versus high socioeconomic backgrounds. First, women made different choices about motherhood itself, especially about terminating the pregnancy versus becoming a lone mother. For the more middle-class women, becoming a lone mother was often considered a serious disruption to their ongoing educational and career plans; in contrast, women from lower-class backgrounds often had undesirable options with regard to employment, which made the potential rewards of motherhood more attractive. Second, women from disadvantaged backgrounds who became mothers were more likely to decide against marriage because their potential husbands had worse economic prospects than they did. Thus, as Rowlingson and McKay noted, "far from rejecting the 'traditional' notion of a two-parent family, these women had very high, traditional standards for prospective partners" (p. 37). More specifically, several of the participants in the qualitative study used their own parents' troubles as a justification for preferring lone motherhood over a bad marriage.

This last explanation—that women become lone mothers because they reject unsuitable partners—is a good example of how using a qualitative follow-up study for exploratory purposes can add value to the research. By learning from the accounts of lone mothers themselves, Rowlingson and McKay (2005) were able to generate an explanation for the survey results that was not merely plausible but interesting in its own right.

Both Example 8.2 and 8.3 show the value of using a qualitative follow-up design to explore the sources of results from core survey data. Of course, there is no guarantee that results from a qualitative study will provide conclusive explanations of survey results. The strengths of qualitative methods are in generating hypotheses rather than testing them. Thus, if you want to *test* the hypotheses that a qualitative study generates, you need to return to the same strengths that drove the original quantitative study.

QUALITATIVE FOLLOW-UP DESIGNS FOR INVESTIGATION

When the motivation for the supplementary study is investigation, the goal is to conduct systematic, purpose-driven work to understand a pattern of results from the core quantitative study. More often than not, the goal is to understand why the quantitative research produced nonsignificant results. In principle, if you conduct a well-designed and well-executed study, then negative results should lead you to reject the null hypothesis and conclude that there was no effect. But if a great deal of effort went into an intervention, wouldn't you want to understand why the program failed to produce the expected impacts? And if the hypothesis your survey was testing had important theoretical support, wouldn't you want to understand as much as you could about why the hypothesis was not supported? In either of these cases, a qualitative follow-up study based on investigation allows you to pursue the specific pattern of results from the quantitative findings.

Using Qualitative Follow-up Designs to Investigate Results From Interventions

The designs in this section deal with interventions that are implemented at both the individual level and in organizations such as schools and clinics; that is, either individuals or organizational sites are the *unit of analysis* for testing the extent to which the program produced a desired set of outcomes. From the point of view of the supplementary qualitative study, individuals and groups both represent potential bases for further investigation of poorly understood results from a larger intervention program.

For many interventions, the classic quantitative test is a comparison of pretest and posttest scores to examine the average amount of change associated with participation in the program. Figure 8.1 shows a hypothetical version of such an assessment of a program delivered in organizational units. Each of the sites in this project is scored in terms of how much it changed between a pretest given before the intervention and a posttest given afterward. Following the scores from left to right shows that two of the sites experienced very little change, most of the sites showed some improvement, and the two sites on the far right had higher levels of improvement. In this example, the numerical results show the all-too-common result of a nonsignificant "trend in the right direction": The overall average score on the outcome measure rose somewhat but not by enough to be statistically significant.

Figure 8.1 draws attention to an important aspect of this nonsignificant result, because the overall average change reflects a mix of different amounts

| Figure 8.1 | Varying Outcomes for Cases in a Program Intervention |

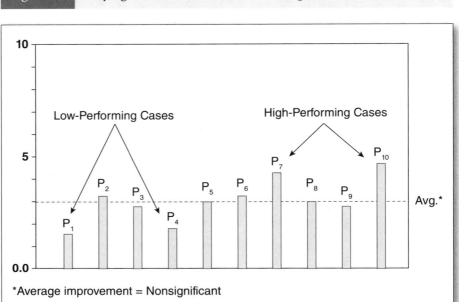

*Average improvement = Nonsignificant

of change across the full set of sites. Averaging these outcomes produces a small positive effect. Program evaluators who experience results such as those in Figure 8.1 are often left with the frustrating feeling that the program might indeed have worked—after all, the overall effect was in the predicted direction—but they are unable to explain why the effect was not as strong as they expected. In this situation, a follow-up qualitative study can make a major contribution by investigating the possible sources of poorly understood results.

When you have a pattern of results that is similar to that in Figure 8.1, focusing solely on the average effect misses most of the story. Looking at the difference between the sites in the diagram indicates that an effective strategy for a follow-up qualitative investigation would be to compare the more successful and less successful cases within the overall project. Hypothetically, if you could transfer elements of the high-performing cases' success to the rest of the sample, this would lift the overall average. For example, specific factors may have facilitated the high performers' success—perhaps "champions" took the lead in implementing the intervention. Similarly, focusing on the less successful subset could identify ways to improve the outcomes in such cases. For example, perhaps internal dissension about "ownership" of the intervention created a systematic set of barriers. Finding ways to encourage facilitating factors while minimizing barriers could produce a revised version of the intervention, which in turn might have a statistically significant result.

One of the central features of this design is an approach to purposive sampling that uses what Chapter 7 called *systematic comparisons*. It emphasizes a pairwise investigation of more and less successful cases. One reason for using the idealized summary in Figure 8.1 is to show that variations on a systematic comparisons sampling strategy make the most sense when there is substantial variation in the outcome variable. In this example, the overall set of cases indicates strong differences between more and less successful outcomes, which creates the basis for purposive sampling. The alternative that you need to avoid is a project in which all the outcomes are clustered around a result of "no effect"; this would eliminate the basis for using a systematic comparisons strategy for selecting cases. Another way to think about this caveat is that this design is only appropriate when you find a clearly noticeable spread between higher and lower scores.

Even when such a spread exists, however, it is not guaranteed to be meaningful. In particular, if the variation in the outcomes is nothing more than random scattering, then comparing the best and worst performers would be meaningless. Unfortunately, there is no a priori way to tell the difference between systematic and random variance in your outcome variables. This is especially problematic because it turns out that humans have a hard time detecting and accepting randomness. This issue is well known in social psychology (see Nisbett & Ross, 1980), where there are numerous demonstrations that humans have difficulty investigating an apparent pattern and concluding that it is nothing but random. To understand how this might work, imagine that Figure 8.1 represented schools and the results truly were random—a budget shortfall in one school, unusually high teacher turnover in another school, a serious dispute between the parents and the principal in another, and so on. Yet if you sorted those random outcomes into pools of best and worst outcomes on the intervention, then there would seem to be a very strong reason to investigate and explain those differences by *systematically looking for factors that were related to the intervention*. Further, as Box 8.1 discusses, examining random rather than systematic variation creates logical as well as practical problems.

> **BOX 8.1**   Sampling on the Dependent Variable
>
> Discussing the *QUANT → qual* design in terms of a need to explain some nontrivial amount of variance in the quantitative study's outcomes highlights another aspect of this design: It is based on what quantitative researchers call "sampling on the dependent variable." This idea of investigating aspects of your original theory according to the results from testing that theory follows the inductive goal of generating hypotheses in qualitative research, but it violates the deductive nature of quantitative research. In particular, if the variation in the outcomes is nothing more than random scattering, then comparing the best and worst performers can be highly misleading.
>
> Sampling on the dependent variable can be a serious problem for this kind of qualitative follow-up study, but only if the variation in outcomes truly is largely random. If you unthinkingly followed the quantitative dictum that you should never sample on the dependent variable, then you would miss all those situations in which systematic but poorly understood differences are seen between more and less successful cases. This is a serious error because it means wasting all the resources that went into the original intervention by concluding that it had no effect and giving up on it, even though potentially fixable problems might have been detected by a qualitative follow-up study. In the classic language of hypothesis testing, this amounts to a "false negative," because you concluded that the intervention had no effect when its effects were actually present but obscured by other factors.

It is thus important to remember that, from the point of view of the core quantitative method, you are conducting further analyses that occur "after the fact" (i.e., they depend on the outcomes from your original hypotheses). To avoid a self-fulfilling prophecy, such that you are almost certain to find meaning in the results because this is what you are looking for, you need to think about this problem at every step when you are using a qualitative follow-up design to investigate quantitative results. Ask yourself: Do your qualitative observations reveal logical linkages that create a coherent sense of the processes that distinguish more and successful sites? Or do your results sound more like a set of separate explanations for the different sites that you are comparing? One way to keep these questions in mind is to remember that your goal in this kind of investigation is to *generate hypotheses,* and one of the key virtues of a good hypothesis is using the simplest explanation to account for the widest range of outcomes.

As we've seen, using qualitative follow-up designs allows one to learn lessons that go beyond the results from the original quantitative study. One of the most useful applications of this principle with intervention programs is to develop new approaches that can enhance the effectiveness of a revised version of the intervention.

Targeting and Tailoring

Two of the most important mechanisms for revising interventions are targeting and tailoring. On the one hand, *targeting* means limiting the types of people the intervention is designed to serve so that you enhance effectiveness by concentrating on the groups that are most likely to benefit. Thus, in targeting, you make changes in the target population that the intervention is designed to serve rather than modifying the intervention itself. On the other hand, *tailoring* means modifying the program to match different needs of different groups of people so that you enhance effectiveness by moving away from a one-size-fits-all approach. Thus, in tailoring, you maintain the overall target population while producing different versions of the intervention that are optimized to different groups of people.

Example 8.4   Targeting and Tailoring

Schumacher et al. (2005) used a variety of qualitative follow-up studies to examine a large intervention trial that sought to increase the role of drugs in reducing and managing chronic pain in cancer patients. These drugs had the potential to be addictive, so the intervention relied on specially trained nurses, who carefully monitored and assisted patients with using the drugs. Examining the quantitative results identified a subgroup of participants who failed to show positive results because they almost never used the intervention drugs. Interviews with these patients uncovered the fact that they were basically opposed to using drugs to control their pain, especially if there was any chance that the drugs might become addictive. Schumacher et al. concluded that such patients were poor candidates for the intervention in question.

This is a case in which targeting would be an appropriate response. Because the qualitative follow-up study made it possible to identify the kinds of patients who would not use this particular intervention, future interventions could identify such patients in advance and assign them to a different pain control strategy.

(Continued)

(Continued)

In a different segment of the same study, Schumacher et al. (2005) reported on opportunities for tailoring future versions of the intervention. Through interviews with the nurses from the original intervention, the team identified three key difficulties to overcome: finding the optimal combination of medications, finding the optimal doses, and finding the optimal timing for administering the medications. Because different patients had different problems, the nurses in the original study spent a considerable amount of time "tailoring prescribed regimens to meet individual needs" (p. 273). Thus, future versions of the intervention could develop separate protocols according to the type of difficulties that patients were having.

Example 8.4 shows applications of targeting and tailoring at the individual level, and this same logic can be demonstrated with Figure 8.1. Here, the most obvious form of targeting is to drop sites that are likely to perform poorly from future versions of the interventions. To accomplish that, however, you need to be able to identify sites where the intervention is likely to perform poorly. Thus, if the supplemental qualitative study identified a set of barriers that would predictably block the effectiveness of the intervention, then future versions of the intervention could be targeted to avoid those sites. As the idealized example in Figure 8.1 demonstrates, targeting sites where the intervention is more effective is far more likely to produce a significant effect.

Figure 8.1 also makes it possible to demonstrate tailoring by suggesting that future versions of the intervention should operate differently in sites identified as poor, average, or high performers. In particular, the qualitative study might identify strategies for reducing barriers and emphasizing facilitators, which would lead to specific variations on the overall program that are tailored to address either barriers or facilitators or both. Future versions of the program could thus be more effective by offering alternatives that would meet the specific needs of specific groups of people.

This discussion of tailoring and targeting demonstrates the value that qualitative follow-up designs can add when used to investigate the findings from program interventions. In particular, when a quantitative study produces nonsignificant results, you might be led to give up on a well-thought-out and well-conducted program. Instead of walking away, however, you can use a supplementary qualitative study to help explain the pattern of results in the core quantitative study.

Using Qualitative Follow-up Designs to
Investigate Results From Survey Research

Examining *outliers* is one of the clearest situations in which further qualitative investigation can help you clarify the findings from analyses that rely on correlation regression. In this case, the bulk of the data support the original predictions, but the results are not significant because a subset of cases deviate from the overall pattern of results. Scatterplots are the classic tool for locating outliers. In particular, a scatterplot provides a direct visual representation of the relationship between two variables, and such relationships are the heart of hypothesis testing. In addition, because scatterplots draw your attention to how the full set of cases is distributed across the pair of variables, they also point to outlying cases that deviate from the pattern in the majority of data.

In Figure 8.2, a scatterplot shows clearly the simple case in which one extreme outlier disrupts the hypothesized relationship. This figure also indicates two possible benefits from this kind of outlier analysis. First, in purely statistical terms, removing a set of outliers can reveal a significant relationship within the larger data set. Second, a substantive examination of the outlying cases can provide insights into what makes them different from the majority. Qualitative follow-up designs are especially useful with survey data when you can bring these two aspects of outlier analysis together, using a qualitative investigation of a set of outliers to explain why those cases fail to fit an expected statistical prediction. In other words, searching for outliers shows what differs between the statistically expected and actually observed patterns in the data, and a qualitative follow-up study seeks to understand why those differences occurred.

Figure 8.2 illustrates how outliers can distort the results in qualitative data; in addition, it shows the value of not just detecting these outliers but also investigating why they differ from the rest of the cases. In this study, the hypothesis being tested is that increased healthcare spending will lead to increases in life expectancy. Analyzing the full data set of 20 industrialized nations produces a nonsignificant result; both the slope of the regression and the explained variance are very close to zero. The strongest source of this unexpected result is a single outlying case—the United States, which has by far the largest expenditure on healthcare but one of the lowest scores for life expectancy. Repeating the analysis without that one outlier raises the explained variance from zero to 16% (correlation = .40).

Examining substantive reasons behind outlier status for the United States would almost certainly emphasize that it is the only country in this data set that does not have a centralized, national healthcare system. On the one hand, this

Figure 8.2   The Impact of Outliers in Quantitative Analysis

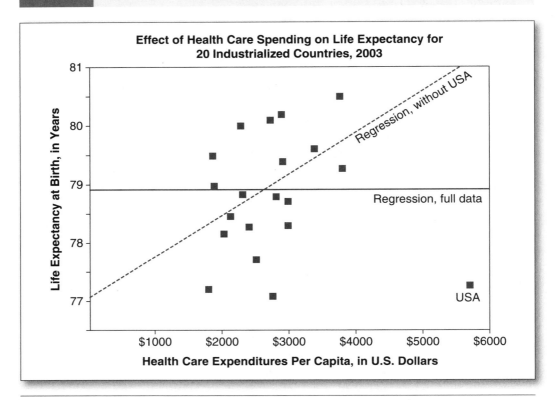

Source: Organization for Economic Cooperation and Development (2003).

drives the level of expenditures in the United States upward due to the for-profit nature of much of its healthcare system. On the other hand, the lack of government-subsidized healthcare creates underserved populations whose limited access to healthcare has negative effects on life expectancies. Examining this outlying case thus yields an explanation for *why* the original data failed to show a relationship between healthcare expenditures and life expectancy.

Once again, it is important to remember that, from the point of view of the core quantitative method, this kind of qualitative follow-up design amounts to a post hoc explanation that is most useful for *generating hypotheses*. Consider the proposed explanations for why the United States is an extreme outlier with regard to healthcare expenditures and life expectancy in Figure 8.2, namely, the lack of a centralized healthcare system and existence of underserved segments of the population. While those explanations use what we know about healthcare in the United States to build an argument about why its position is so different from that of other industrialized countries, those explanations were only generated after the fact, once we knew that the U.S. situation needed special attention. Further, the United States could be different in a great many other ways with regard to both health expenditures and life expectancy, so the explanations offered here are only a few of the many potential hypotheses that might explain this outlier.

While an example with a small data set that is disrupted by a single outlier is useful for demonstration purposes, most qualitative follow-up studies on survey research involve more complex data sets and more complicated issues related to outliers. Example 8.5 presents such a study in which a well-designed survey failed to find any evidence for a strong theoretical prediction. This is a good illustration of using a qualitative follow-up design to investigate the kinds of negative findings that would typically prevent the publication of results. By going a step further, however, this project was able to locate a number of factors that might not only account for the lack of significant results in this particular survey but also play an important role in any future research on this topic.

Example 8.5   Following Up on Nonsignificant Results in a Survey

Thoits (1995) explored the impact of stressful life events that were either central or more peripheral to survey respondents' personal identities. Although she predicted that "identity-relevant" events would be more distressing than events that were not related to central identities, she in fact found no difference. Before rejecting her hypothesis, Thoits carefully examined several alternative measures of each of her key variables, as well as a number of other statistical techniques for estimating the predicted effects, with no improvement in the results.

Although it would have been possible to "reject the data rather than the theory," that was not an easy option to justify for this study. In particular, this study used a high-quality data set gathered from two waves of longitudinal surveys. These surveys began by determining the importance of identities and followed up by assessing the occurrence of life events and changes in psychological distress 2 years later. Combining the strong

(Continued)

(Continued)

design with the range of alternate measures available implied that even if the hypothesized relationship was relatively weak, there should have been some evidence for its effects.

Thoits investigated the unexpected results by using the richness of her overall data set to create a set of case studies. Each case used the two waves of data and the multiple measures of the key variables to characterize changes in respondents' lives, and it combined that data with responses to several open-ended items and the brief narratives that interviews provided to summarize each interview. She selected her cases through a purposive definition that located respondents who had experienced at least one life event in three of the most common and important identity areas: work, parenting, and love and marriage. A random sample of 50 such cases showed that approximately 30% fit the hypothesized pattern, so Thoits concentrated on understanding the experiences of the 70% who did not match her theoretical predictions.

Examining these "disconfirming cases" revealed five patterns that each occurred in at least 20% of those cases. One key element in all these patterns was the importance of *context* for understanding how the intersection of life events and identities affected well-being. For example, one set of respondents who were experiencing troubles associated with a key role did not show the predicted distress at the loss of that role because they experienced this change as a "relief."

These patterns led to more detailed hypotheses that went beyond what could be tested in the original research design. Thus, the results of this qualitative follow-up generated a set of related hypotheses, which brought to light a series of additional factors that affected how the life events in valued identities were related to levels of psychological distress.

The article by Thoits (1995) in Example 8.5 is one of the best examples of a thorough qualitative follow-up study dedicated to the investigation of poorly understood results from a survey. Even so, one aspect of the design for the qualitative portion of the project needs further attention: the use of a random sample to select the cases that received a detailed follow-up. Chapter 7 presented a strong argument in favor of the use of purposive sampling techniques in qualitative studies, and Example 8.5 nicely demonstrates the inefficiency of a random sample for this kind of work. In particular, a substantial proportion of the cases in the random sample were rejected and not analyzed because they did not meet the target criteria. Since this approach produces a nonrandom subsample, it would have made much more sense to begin with the kind of purposive sample that was based on the same defining criteria that were ultimately used to weed cases out of the random sample.

This points to a general strategy for selecting the subset of cases that you should examine from a survey or other large data set when you are using a qualitative follow-up design to investigate poorly understood results: *Concentrate on the cases that are most important in creating the difference between the predicted and the observed outcomes.* This approach was obviously applicable in the previous discussion about outliers, but how can you implement the same kind of logic when you are working with a large data set that isn't affected by a small number of extreme outliers? Figure 8.3 lays out a general set of procedures for dealing with this issue.

The top half of Figure 8.3 uses simulated data to present an idealized scatterplot for a high correlation. Thus, if you predicted a strong relationship between two variables, then the scatter of points in Figure 8.3a would be similar to your expected results. Alternatively, if your results showed no correlation between the two variables, your observed results would be similar to those plotted in Figure 8.3b. Comparing the patterns for a strong relationship and a correlation of zero points to two elements of the data, as indicated by the arrows. First, the high correlation indicates that low scores on the independent variable (on the x-axis) would be matched by low scores on the dependent variable; second, there should be an equivalent match between high scores on the independent variable and high scores on the dependent variable. Instead, the random data show that cases with low scores on the independent variable are matched by "higher than expected" scores, while high scores on the independent variable correspond to "lower than expected" scores. From this perspective, the random data contain a relatively large set of what would be considered outliers in terms of the results expected from a strong correlation.

You can apply this pattern to the study by Thoits (1995) in Example 8.5. She predicted that life events that affected more central identities would lead to higher levels of distress. Instead, she actually observed a zero correlation, which involved both (1) differences at the lower end of the independent variable, because people who experienced changes in less central identities also experienced unexpectedly high levels of distress, and (2) differences at the upper end of the independent variable, because people who experienced changes in more central identities did not experience high levels of distress. Thus, when Thoits concentrated her qualitative follow-up study on disconfirming cases, she was

Figure 8.3 Distribution of Observations With No Correlation Versus High Correlation

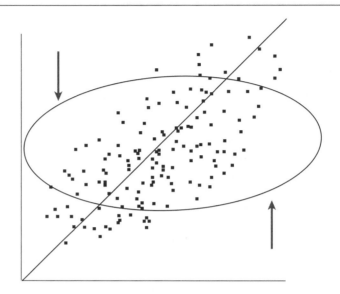

a) Scatter Plot With High Correlation and Outline of Plot for No Correlation

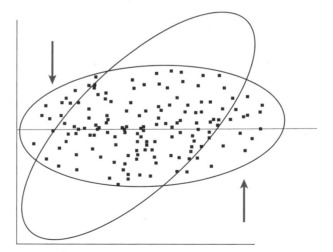

b) Scatter Plot With No Correlation and Outline of Plot for High Correlation

targeting two sets of outliers where the observed values did not match her statistical predications. Stated in more general terms, anytime you predict but fail to observe a strong relationship between an independent variable and some outcome, you should pay particular attention to cases at the low and high ends of the independent variable.

In general, a study that fails to support your original predictions does not mean your study doesn't have any implications for future research. In particular, if a well-designed study fails to support a widely believed hypothesis, that could be exactly the kind of result that requires additional investigation. Searching for the sources of nonsignificant results displays the more general logic behind qualitative follow-up designs. Rather than simply abandoning disappointing results, you can use the designs in this section to dig deeper into the specific aspects of your data. Without this kind of further investigation, your quantitative analyses produce "mute facts" with many possible interpretations.

USING QUALITATIVE FOLLOW-UP DESIGNS FOR ILLUSTRATION

Beyond the exploration and investigation of results from quantitative studies, one of the most powerful uses for qualitative follow-up studies is to illustrate the sources of the quantitative results. This motivation for adding to the core quantitative data takes advantage of the strengths that qualitative methods have for providing context. In this case, the qualitative data can provide depth and detail to convey more information about the quantitative data. Thus, when you use supplementary qualitative results for illustration, your goal is to create a sense of how real people are connected to the findings from quantitative methods. This can be thought of as "putting a human face on the data."

Using Qualitative Follow-up Designs to Illustrate Results From Interventions

One general approach to using illustrative data from qualitative data is the *success case method* (Brinkerhoff, 2003, 2005). Originating in program evaluation, this technique seeks out the sources of more successful outcomes within a program. It operates by carefully screening for cases with especially positive results and then generating rich case studies that demonstrate the reasons behind these success stories. From the current perspective, the success case method systematically uses supplementary qualitative data to illustrate the reasons why successful programs are producing positive outcomes.

| Example 8.6 | Illustrating Success in a Program Intervention |

One project that made especially good use of the success case method was the Well-Integrated Screening and Evaluation for Women Across the Nation (WISEWOMAN) intervention, a nationwide effort to reduce health problems and chronic disease among low-income women (Lewis, Johnson, Farris, & Will, 2004). In particular, the program generated success stories that called attention to specific sites within the larger program, and it used these examples to illustrates paths to success for other units. As the authors noted,

> Within every successful health promotion program are people who have compelling stories to tell. Writing their stories and sharing them with others is an effective way of conveying how a program works, why it is successful, and how others can launch similar programs. (p. 616)

Lewis et al. (2004) presented a 10-step process for generating success stories, which they illustrated through a detailed discussion of a successful program that promoted physical fitness by using the cultural values of women living in a Native American village in rural Alaska. They then used the report on this program as a further example of how they wrote up the success cases in their program. This example thus serves a dual function. On the one hand, it illustrates the sources for the positive outcomes at this particular site. On the other hand, it illustrates how to make effective use of a case study to communicate how and why the overall program is succeeding.

Without the kind of illustration done in Example 8.6, there is always a question of whether programs actually function in the ways they were intended. In particular, if the program succeeds, is that due to the predicted effects of the intervention? Providing illustrative data that connect the results to the program supports the argument that the reasoning behind the intervention indeed operated as expected.

Using Qualitative Follow-up Designs to Illustrate Results From Surveys

The key distinction between using $QUANT \rightarrow qual$ designs for illustration as opposed to exploration or investigation depends on how well the results from the quantitative study matched the original predictions. When your findings do indeed support your hypotheses, then an illustration of the human experiences and processes that produced those results is one way that a qualitative follow-up study can contribute additional strengths to the research project as a whole. Example 8.7 makes a strong case for using illustrative qualitative data. The researchers in this example collected qualitative data in parallel with the core quantitative study and then selected the appropriate qualitative data afterward.

Example 8.7   Telling the Stories Behind the Results

Underserved populations are systematic segments of patients who cannot get access to or afford decent healthcare. In their book *Just Don't Get Sick,* Seccombe and Hoffman (2007) described the experiences of former welfare recipients and their families who lost healthcare coverage under the agreement to end "welfare as we know it" during the 1990s.

The core method in Seccombe and Hoffman's (2007) study was a longitudinal survey that first interviewed former welfare recipients while they were still eligible for healthcare benefits and then reinterviewed the same sample a year later, when 40% had become uninsured due to the new, much stricter rules. In addition, approximately 1 in 7 of the respondents participated in relatively unstructured qualitative interviews following each survey.

As you might expect, the book contains numerous tables and figures that document the changes during the year when many of these low-income families lost their guaranteed benefits. And as you might also expect, those tables and figures show increasing health problems, which produced financial problems, which in turn combined to create substantial disruptions in lives of many of these families—especially when the healthcare problems affected either the primary wage earner or a young child who then needed additional care. If Seccombe and Hoffman (2007) had relied solely on this quantitative summary, the reader would be left to imagine the complexities that families faced in dealing with these problems when they lost their healthcare.

To put a human face on their data, Seccombe and Hoffman (2007) used their qualitative data to begin each chapter with an extended account of one person's experiences. The first chapter opens with the struggles of Molly, who attempted to deal with the bureaucracy that had improperly cut her off her young daughter's benefits. She herself experienced a life-threatening complication in pregnancy after losing her birth control prescription, which hit her with a bill of $14,000 for the surgery and a single night's hospital stay. Perhaps Molly had it worse than most, but then we read about Bob, a diabetic who did find healthcare insurance but couldn't afford doctor visits due to his policy's $3,000 deductible; and Sarah, who lived in her patents' basement while caring for a young son

(Continued)

(Continued)

with cerebral palsy; and Kelly, who was unable to manage a $12 monthly copay on her insurance while simultaneously coping with a combination of her own Parkinson's disease and bipolar disorder plus her son's severe learning disabilities.

These stories confront the reader with the very real consequences behind a simple statistic such as the 40% of welfare recipients who lost their healthcare coverage. Moreover, by beginning each chapter with an illustration from the qualitative follow-up study, Seccombe and Hoffman (2007) went beyond putting a human face on the data to create a deeper human context for understanding the statistics that followed.

In studies where the qualitative findings mostly consist of examples that demonstrate the mechanisms described in the original theory, it may appear that the main contribution from illustration is simply "good storytelling" that makes the results more convincing. There is, however, a more important point involving the fundamental logic of testing theories by rejecting the null hypothesis that the results could have been due to chance alone. When you report that a result is "statistically significant," you are stating that it is unlikely that the data are random—and that is all that you are saying. Hence, rejecting the null hypothesis allows you to conclude that there is a pattern in the data, but it does not provide any evidence that your original theory was the source of that pattern. Although in rare circumstances the theory in question is the only possible explanation for the pattern of findings in your study, it is far more likely that a number of alternative explanations could have produced the nonrandom pattern you observed.

Illustration thus contributes additional strengths to the project as a whole by addressing the issue of alternative explanations for the results. On the one hand, it shows that the processes that produced the results match the predictions of your original theory. On the other hand, it shows how the predictions from alternative explanations fail to fit what you observed in your qualitative follow-up study.

CONCLUSIONS

For each of the designs in this chapter, the core quantitative methods provide a starting point that determines the goals of the supplementary qualitative follow-up study. The qualitative data *extend* the original quantitative results, a possibility that seldom exists in the preliminary input studies described in the two previous chapters. There, the central thrust of supplying predefined kinds of data was unlikely to have an impact on the basic goals of the core study. In contrast, studies that follow up on the results from an earlier core study may well move the original research in new directions.

Thus, the point is noted throughout that qualitative follow-up studies have a strong potential for generating new hypotheses. This fits well with the important goal of reaching conclusions when the results have implications for further research. While those who lack experience sometimes make sarcastic remarks about how the conclusions sections in research articles always call for further research, those who actually study the topic in question often find this to be the most interesting portion of the entire article. Therefore, the additional hypotheses that you generate may be especially important.

Finally, with regard to the status of qualitative follow-up designs within the general framework of the sequential priorities model, these studies are gaining recognition. One obvious advantage of these studies is the clear value that the supplementary qualitative methods contribute. Another advantage is the relatively straightforward integration of the two sets of results because of the direct connection between the follow-up data and the original study. Thus, within the four sequential priorities designs, qualitative follow-up studies are in the process of becoming well justified and widely recognized.

SUMMARY

Qualitative follow-up designs can extend the results from a core quantitative study in three basic ways. When the goals are exploratory, the supplementary qualitative method extends the quantitative results by searching for explanations associated with unexpected or poorly understood outcomes from the quantitative data. When the goals are investigative, the qualitative follow-up study furthers the basic purposes of the quantitative study by pursuing a deeper understanding of patterns in the original data. When the goals are illustrative, the purpose is to demonstrate the bases for quantitative results—how and why the research came out the way it did. Taken together, these three uses for qualitative follow-up designs promote their increasing use and visibility.

DISCUSSION QUESTIONS

Studies that use qualitative follow-up designs for exploratory purposes are especially useful when the core quantitative method produces unexpected results, but these designs are often created "after the fact." Can you plan in advance to study things that don't work out as expected? If you were writing a grant proposal, how would you justify a plan to use a qualitative follow-up design for exploratory purposes?

When are qualitative follow-up designs used for illustrative purposes likely to be most valuable? How would you defend this kind of study against the charge that it is merely anecdotal storytelling?

ADDITIONAL READINGS

The examples presented in this chapter serve as the additional readings.

Blackhall, L. J., Frank, G., Murphy, S. T., Michel, V. (2001). Bioethics in a different tongue: The case of truth-telling. *Journal of Urban Health, 78,* 59–71.

Blackhall, L. J., Frank, G., Murphy, S. T., Michel, V., Palmer, J. M., & Azen, S. P. (1999). Ethnicity and attitudes towards life sustaining technology. *Social Science and Medicine, 48,* 1779–1789.

Lewis, S. D., Johnson, V. R., Farris, R. P., & Will, J. C. (2004). Using success stories to share knowledge and lessons learned in health promotion. *Journal of Women's Health, 13,* 616–625.

Rowlingson, K., & McKay, S. (2005). Lone motherhood and socio-economic disadvantage: Insights from quantitative and qualitative evidence. *The Sociological Review, 53,* 30–49.

Schumacher, K. L., Koresawa, S., West, C., Dodd, M., Paul, S. M., Tripathy, D. . . . Miaskowski, C. (2005). Qualitative research contribution to a randomized clinical trial. *Research in Nursing and Health, 28,* 268–280.

Seccombe, K., & Hoffman K. A. (2007). *Just don't get sick: Access to health care in the aftermath of welfare reform.* New Brunswick, NJ: Rutgers University Press.

Thoits, P. A. (1995). Identity relevant events and psychological symptoms: A cautionary tale. *Journal of Health and Social Behavior, 36,* 72–82.

CHAPTER 9

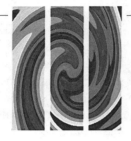

Follow-up Quantitative Extensions to Qualitative Research Projects

Overview

This chapter presents two basic uses for supplementary quantitative methods that follow up on core qualitative studies. The first is to use the deductive strengths of quantitative methods to test hypotheses that were generated by the results of the qualitative study. In this case, the emphasis is on operationalizing the results from the qualitative study to supply the variables that are necessary for quantitative methods. In addition, the same logic that applies to generating and testing hypotheses applies to assessing the more complex theories that can be built from qualitative studies. The second major motivation for quantitative follow-up studies is to show that the results of the qualitative study have implications that extend beyond the specific context of those results. Here, the goal is to use the strengths of quantitative methods to demonstrate the greater generality of the original qualitative findings. Taken together, these two motivations for following up on a core qualitative study show how the strengths of supplementary quantitative methods can extend qualitative results.

BASIC USES FOR QUANTITATIVE FOLLOW-UP DESIGNS

Quantitative follow-up designs fall into the fourth and final cell in the sequential priorities model (Table 1.2). Like the $QUANT \rightarrow qual$ designs discussed in the last chapter, these extend a core method. In this case, however, a supplementary quantitative study provides additional strengths that contribute to a core qualitative study, or *QUAL* → *quant*. Qualitative research studies typically result in inductively generated theories that arise from subjective interpretations and from data that are developed within a specific context. The question, then, is how you can extend these results with the additional strengths of quantitative methods.

Using a quantitative method to add value to qualitative study is not as simple as it might appear. The issue here is the "politically charged" relationship between the larger fields of qualitative and quantitative research. Quantitative research and quantitative methods have often held a dominant position in this relationship; hence, a central issue for *QUAL* → *quant* designs is what it means for a quantitative follow-up study to "enhance" the findings from a core qualitative study. To illustrate this problem, consider the implications of saying that your quantitative follow-up study will "validate" or "verify" the qualitative findings. This implies that the results of qualitative methods should not be fully accepted until they have been "proven" by quantitative research. It is important to understand that this is not merely a question of vocabulary. Instead, it reflects political, historical, and cultural issues that continue to resonate with members of the qualitative community (e.g., Denzin, 2010, 2012).

The current position is that the supplementary quantitative methods in *QUAL* → *quant* designs provide additional evidence to support the results from the qualitative study. It is certainly not the case that qualitative results *require* further support before they can be taken seriously. Instead, using a quantitative follow-up design means that you have additional goals that go beyond the typical stopping point for stand-alone qualitative studies. This chapter examines two such motivations. First, it looks at deductive processes that pair generating hypotheses with testing them. Here, the point is to increase the *credibility* of the qualitative results by showing they can be converted into meaningful measures that perform in predictable ways.

The second well-developed motivation for quantitative follow-up designs is to demonstrate greater *generality*. Here, your goal is to build on the context-specific results of the qualitative core study to show that they apply more broadly. In other words, the interpretations of a set of carefully selected interviews are not limited to just that set of participants; instead, they are likely to apply to other similar participants. Equivalently, if your insights come from a carefully designed case study, then the goal is to show that those findings are also likely to appear in other, similar settings. As noted in Chapter 3, the goal here is not to produce a formal statement of statistical generalizability. Instead, the purpose of pursuing evidence for greater generality is to indicate how results are applicable beyond the context of the original set of observations.

Once again, it is important to emphasize that there is no inherent need either to test qualitative theory building or to demonstrate the generality of qualitative findings unless you have specific goals that would benefit from these additional strengths. Thus, the fundamental logic of follow-up designs is to enhance the results of one study by extending them in ways that would not be possible using the methods from the original study. Whether you are testing the results of your theorizing or moving beyond the context in which you constructed those results, you need to have purposes that call for this particular design, and these two basic purposes serve as the basis for this chapter.

TESTING HYPOTHESES WITH FOLLOW-UP QUANTITATIVE METHODS

Chapter 3 noted that one of the most frequent goals of qualitative research is to develop results inductively by moving from observations to the creation of theory. Theories can vary greatly in their complexity, however. At the simplest level, qualitative analysis produces statements about the relationship between two concepts, such as "This kind of person is more likely to engage in this kind of behavior." At a more complex level, the results take the form of models that systematically relate a number of concepts. From the point of view of the qualitative core method, this amounts to a distinction between generating hypotheses and building theories. In either case, the point of the quantitative follow-up model is to support the results from your qualitative interviews or participant observation, an objective that differs from the traditional quantitative goal of determining the "truth" of preexisting theory.

The current definition of a hypothesis begins with the classic idea of predicting a relationship between two theoretical concepts. Of course, in practical terms, you cannot test a hypothesis (or assess a theory) until you *operationalize* it in terms of measurable variables. This description of hypothesis testing in a quantitative mode implies a corresponding procedure for hypothesis generation on the qualitative side. On the one hand, you need to be clear about the qualitative concepts that go into the hypothesis—from a quantitative perspective, this corresponds to defining measurable variables. On the other hand, you need to be explicit about the relationship between the theoretical concepts in question—from a quantitative perspective, this corresponds to specifying testable relationships.

Within qualitative research, a major resource for both defining measurable variables and specifying testable relationships is the common practice of stating the results as a set of themes. Often, the results section of a qualitative article will begin with an announcement that is literally equivalent to "There were three (or four or five) key themes in the data." These themes typically provide well-defined links between sets of actors and types of behavior. When a theme is cast in this format, it is relatively easy to translate it into an empirical claim such as "If a set of research participants has a given set of characteristics, then they will be more likely to . . ." Rewriting a theme in an "If . . . then . . ." formulation is almost certain to give you a testable hypothesis. In particular, this formulation often leads to the specification of independent and dependent variables (i.e., if a research participant, or setting, has a given set of characteristics, then this has a predictable implication for the dependent variable). This leads to a first set of exemplary studies, in which the core qualitative study generates hypotheses about the linkage between an independent and a dependent variable (prior to a second set of examples that examine the role of quantitative follow-up studies in assessing more complex theories).

Testing Basic Hypotheses

Once you have translated a theme into a statement about a testable relationship, you still need to operationalize the variables that go into the test. Within the literature on quantitative follow-up quantitative designs are three basic ways to accomplish this conversion of qualitative concepts into the measurable variables:

1. *Categorize* research participants or settings according to groups that match key elements in the qualitative themes.

2. *Score* the participants or settings according to the extent that they exhibit the relevant aspects of a theme.

3. *Transform* the variable in question by creating a quantitative measure that matches the equivalent qualitative concept.

Operationalizing variables by categorizing cases according to themes begins by developing a system of thematic criteria that can distinguish different types of participants. The next step is to place each participant in a specific subgroup within this system. In essence, you are creating a single, nominal variable and assigning each participant to one of the categories within that variable. In a hypothesis-testing mode, this kind of categorical variable often plays the role of an independent variable with an interval-level dependent variable, as in Example 9.1.

Example 9.1	Categorizing Thematic Material to Create an Independent Variable

Using qualitative research for exploratory purposes is quite common, but following up on it by analyzing quantitative data is much less so. Drach-Zahavy and Pud (2010) began their project with exploratory interviews about when and why hospital-based nurses made errors in administering medication. Given the lack of theory in this area, they relied on the discovery-oriented strengths of qualitative methods as their core method. They were particularly interested in the effectiveness of various learning mechanisms.

Using open-ended interviews with individual nurses, Drach-Zahavy and Pud (2010) studied the sources of learning that guided practice at different steps in the process of administering medication. The result was a set of themes that uncovered four patterns of learning mechanisms. The authors thus developed the hypothesis that the rate of errors would be affected by learning mechanisms. They tested this hypothesis through a set of regressions that first examined the effects of control variables and then assessed the additional effects of the four learning mechanisms. In this case, the qualitatively derived variables generated a highly significant increase in the explained variance, from 23% to 40%.

For a variation on testing relationships that relies on a categorical specification of the independent variable, consider Example 9.2. Here, the authors (Hult, Wrubel, Bränström, Acree, & Moskowitz, 2012) utilized both demographic variables and existing quantitative measures as dependent variables. This choice is particularly interesting because they did not prespecify the relationships that they were testing. Instead, they examined the characteristics of their qualitatively derived independent variable in terms of its effects across a range of quantitative variables. This is certainly problematic from a purely statistical point of view, because it tests a large number of hypotheses with a small number of cases. More generally, it violates the widespread advice against conducting a "fishing expedition" with quantitative data. This is, however, a good example of the difference between the standards involved in doing quantitative analysis as a supplementary study than as a stand-alone study. In a quantitative follow-up study, the goal is to learn more about the nature of the themes discovered in a core qualitative study, which makes it appropriate to do "exploratory" quantitative analysis.

| Example 9.2 | Interpreting the Characteristics of a Categorical Independent Variable |

To understand the dynamics of disclosure and nondisclosure of HIV status, Hult et al. (2012) followed a set of 50 newly diagnosed patients over 9 months. In addition to in-depth, individual interviews, they also conducted a survey that included demographic data as well as a series of widely used scales and indices. Their qualitative data allowed them to identify four styles of disclosure, ranging from nearly complete nondisclosure through almost universal disclosure.

As a next step, Hult and colleagues (2012) used the content of the participants' individual interviews to assign each person to one of the four styles of disclosure. They then examined how the dependent variables from the survey varied across these categories. In a first series of tests, they found very few differences across the measures related to demographic characteristics and physical health. In contrast, there were a number of differences on self-reported measures related to stigma and social support. Overall, examining the survey data as a follow-up to the qualitative study made it possible to cover a broader range of measures in a more systematic fashion than would have been possible with the qualitative data alone.

The second approach to converting qualitative concepts into quantitative variables, scoring, changes themes to numeric scores and requires an explicit judgment process. By far the most common approach is for the qualitative team to produce a rating for each participant according to the content of what the participant said about a given theme. In essence, you are putting together an ordinal- (or arguably interval-) level variable on which each participant is ranked from low to high. Within mixed methods research, this kind of scoring process is one way of "quantizing" qualitative data (Sandelowski, Volis, & Knafl, 2009). In the present case, this means that the original data are collected qualitatively and then translated into quantitative variables. Example 9.3 summarizes two studies that used scoring approaches.

| Example 9.3 | Scoring Thematic Information to Create Variables |

Seal, Eldrige, Kacanek, Binson, and MacGowan (2007) were interested in the factors that make those who are released from prison either more or less likely to be incarcerated again. Their qualitative interviews with recently released prisoners revealed four themes related to social support and to reintegration into the larger society. They then scored each of their participants as low, intermediate, or high on each theme to create ordinal independent variables, including a fifth, global rating of "reintegration." They then showed that their thematic variables produced significant differences in hard drug usage, risky sexual behavior, and actual recidivism.

Cunningham et al. (2000) investigated the extent to which psychological factors predicted the survival of patients with advanced cancer. Through an analysis of detailed qualitative data, they produced a set of psychosocial themes, which they then translated into 5-point Likert scores. In addition, they collected several standard questionnaire measures of well-being. Compared to the survey-based measures of well-being, the qualitatively based measures consistently showed a stronger relationship with survival times.

The third approach to converting themes for quantitative testing is to transform the content of the theme into an equivalent variable, and the most common ways to transform themes are to use an existing scale or create a new scale. When one creates a new scale, the process is the same as in typical quantitative measurement, beginning with a series of separate variables or *items* that are combined into the ultimate scale. Interestingly, this is often the goal in preliminary qualitative input studies, in which the *qual* → *QUANT* design helps generate the items that go into the scale. This opens up the option of using the core qualitative data as a basis for creating the content of a scale in a follow-up quantitative study, as shown in Example 9.4.

| Example 9.4 | Using Thematic Information as the Basis for Creating Scales |

When teenagers visit doctors accompanied by their parents, the parents frequently do almost all the talking. Beginning with qualitative interviews with teens, van Staa (2011) discovered that adolescents wished to be involved in these conversations, even though they readily acknowledged their frequent silence. Based on these interviews, she created a questionnaire instrument that measured aspects of self-efficacy related to hospital visits. This 11-item scale was administered through an online survey. Then she used multivariate regressions to predict which teens had gone to the doctor alone as well as which ones were likely to ask questions when they visited the doctor. The results showed that the qualitatively based predictor remained significant after controls for a variety of demographic variables, such as age, gender, and education, as well as a series of health-related variables, such as number of recent doctor visits.

What categorizing, scoring, and transforming have in common is the transformation of themes from qualitative results into variables that work within the limits of quantitative methods. Stated as a hypothesis, the results from qualitative research present themes that need to be stated as pairs of independent variables. The next step is to go beyond these two-variable relationships to examine qualitative studies that produce more complex results.

Assessing More Complex Theories

Moving beyond the testing of basic hypotheses means following up on the classic qualitative goal of building theories. If theories consist of relationships among a set of concepts, then the simplest version of a theory is a statement about the systematic connections among three variables. One of the most interesting forms of three-variable relationships is an interaction effect, in which the relationship between two variables depends on the value of a third variable. These models are also known as *moderator effects* because the effect of the independent variable on the dependent variable differs across the levels of a third, moderator, variable. For example, in the United States, higher rates of education are associated with higher levels of income, but this effect is stronger for men than for women; thus, the strength of the relationship between income and education depends on gender as a third variable.

Qualitative studies that describe interaction effects are especially likely to specify relationships that are *context dependent,* meaning that the relationship is notably stronger in one set of circumstances than another (e.g., "This kind of behavior is more likely to produce a given outcome for this particular subgroup of participants"). From a quantitative point of view, these statements are directly translatable into hypotheses that can be tested via either analysis of variance or regression, as shown in Example 9.5.

Example 9.5   Generating and Testing Model-Based Interaction Effects

Hospital-based trauma resuscitation teams provide emergency care to patients such as gunshot victims. Yun, Faraj, and Sims (2005) reported on their tests of a series of hypotheses that they derived from a year of ethnographic observations and interviews. In particular, they believed that the effects of different styles of leadership would depend on the specific circumstances in which that leadership occurred.

In this case, senior physicians provided the leadership for each incoming patient, and they exhibited two broad forms of leadership. On the one hand, physicians who acted as directive leaders told the other members of the team what to do throughout the treatment process; on the other hand, empowering leaders were more likely to encourage the other members of the team to initiate their own actions. A classic two-variable model would test whether one or the other of these leadership styles produced better quality of care; however, Yun and colleagues (2005) argued that the situation was more complex. Based on their observations, they concluded that the effectiveness of one form of leadership or the other depended on the nature of the case. In particular, they hypothesized that the effectiveness of leadership style would depend on both the severity of the case being treated and the level of experience among the team members.

To test these hypotheses, Yun and colleagues (2005) used a transformation approach that created a series of realistic scenarios, each of which portrayed a different combination of leadership style, severity of injury, and level of team experience. They then had members of trauma teams use an 8-item scale to rate the quality of the healthcare delivered in each case. As predicted, the effect of leadership style on healthcare quality depended on the severity of the case: In the more severe cases, leadership style was felt to make little difference, but in less severe cases, an empowering style was associated with better outcomes. With regard to team experience, the quantitative data also matched their prediction: Leadership style did not matter as much for less experienced teams, but more experienced teams were seen as benefiting from empowering rather than directive leaders. The effects of leadership style were thus contingent on the specific circumstances surrounding the case.

Of course, qualitative research often produces theories that have more complexity than that associated with interaction effects. It is rare, however, to see quantitative tests of such full-fledged theories. At a minimum, this kind of theory testing requires a model that systematically interrelates the themes from the qualitative results. Rather than working with two or three variables, it is necessary to measure several variables and make a formal specification of their full set of connections. Most of the models that appear in the qualitative literature are too abstract to meet these criteria, but Example 9.6 illustrates one way to accomplish this goal.

| Example 9.6 | Testing a More Complex Theoretical Model |

Wuest and Hodgins (2011) created a statistical model to test a theory that Wuest had built from a series of studies on women who served as caregivers for family members. Using a grounded theory approach, Wuest described a set of salient concepts, including the quality of the past relationship with the care receiver and the caregiver's sense of obligation to the care receiver. To test the model, the researchers transformed these theoretical constructs into quantitative scales, some of which were newly created for this study and others of which were drawn from existing quantitative measures. All of these variables were systematically related to each other through structural equation modeling (i.e., by constructing a *path model*).

The beginning stages of this model controlled for a series of background variables, such as hours spent in caregiving, while the main section of the model specified a series of relationships among the caregiver's sense of obligation, health outcome, and health promotion. The analyses supported the theory's predications, including a two-step, "indirect" path by which the negative aspects of past relationships promoted a sense of obligation, which in turn had a negative impact on health outcomes.

The theory-testing logic in Example 9.5 translates a system of relationships into a hypothesized set of paths in a structural equations model, which is a promising approach to operationalizing more complex qualitative theories. In particular, this process requires specifying whether each variable in the model either does or does not have direct connections to every other variable. When these variables correspond to a relatively small set of key concepts, this procedure produces a compact and testable statement of a qualitatively based theory.

DEMONSTRATING THE GREATER GENERALITY OF QUALITATIVE RESULTS

The primary goal in using *QUAL → quant* designs to demonstrate generality is to establish that the original results were not context specific. The most common way to accomplish this extension of the core method is through surveys. By using a survey, you are making the case that the original results are not limited to either the people you talked to in qualitative interviews or the sites where you worked with participant observation. Even a small, well-targeted survey can help establish a claim about greater generality. In contrast to surveys, experimental designs are a rarer technique for demonstrating generality due to the greater effort that they typically involve—but this also means that there are untapped opportunities in using experiments as evidence for generality.

Like theory testing, generality requires the operationalization of key qualitative concepts, and it requires the original results to be statistically assessable relationships. In this case, you want to go a step further by showing that the patterns in the qualitative data can be not only substantiated but also applied more broadly. Generality is thus an additional strength of quantitative methods that can be used in quantitative follow-up designs. Once again, however, it is important to distinguish establishing generality from the goals of standalone qualitative studies. Adding generality as a strength is only relevant when you have clear reasons for extending your results beyond their original context. When you want to move beyond the context in which original results occurred, the goal of demonstrating greater generality calls for the strengths of a quantitative follow-up design.

Using Surveys to Demonstrate That Qualitative Results Are More General

Surveys are especially useful for answering questions about whether qualitative results are more widespread, which is basically an issue of *prevalence*. Finding an equivalent pattern of results in a survey with a new set of participants indicates that the original results are not limited to the specific context where they were observed. Instead, they can be predictably located in other reasonably equivalent circumstances.

Surveys in quantitative follow-up designs typically differ from full-scale survey research in two ways. First, they often rely on relatively small sample sizes (e.g., 20 to 100 participants). Second, they typically use purposive rather than random sampling (see Chapter 7). In essence, you are proposing that your original results point to an appropriate place where a limited but carefully chosen sample will produce a similar set of results. Thus, relatively small, nonrandom samples can be sufficient to support the greater generality of the qualitative results, as shown in Example 9.7. Still, there is no reason to limit the quantitative portion of a *QUAL → quant* project to a small-scale survey, as shown in Example 9.7. (See Box 9.1 for a further discussion of this issue.)

Example 9.7	Using a Survey to Establish the Prevalence of Qualitative Results

In Chapter 1 (Example 1.6), I described a project in which I used a survey to follow up on the results of a series of focus groups with recent widows (Morgan, 1989). This was the first study I did that indicated the importance of the negative as well as the supportive aspects of relationships, and this was an unusual finding at the time. As noted in Chapter 1, I found the same results when I followed up on that stand-alone qualitative study with survey data from a convenience sample of fewer than 50 older people. This supplementary study accomplished several things. First, it showed that the results I observed in the qualitative study could be operationalized and tested via survey data. Second, it showed that the results were not limited to recently widowed women but could also be found more broadly. Based on this demonstration of the generality of the original results, I received a substantial grant to investigate a more elaborate statistical model with a much bigger survey.

Example 9.8	Using a Survey to Establish the Prevalence of Qualitative Results

Cross-cultural research presents a situation in which qualitative data can reveal patterns in beliefs and behaviors that researchers would not expect, based on Western assumptions. Houston, Harada, and Makinodan (2002) thought that something like this might help explain the extremely high incidence of tuberculosis among Vietnamese immigrants.

Beginning with extensive qualitative interviewing, Houston and colleagues (2002) discovered that their participants distinguished between two types of tuberculosis—a psychological form and a physical form. For the psychological form, the primary cause was seen to be exhaustion, so the preferred treatment was reducing stress rather than seeking medical care. In contrast, physical tuberculosis corresponded to the Western conception of the disease, which led to the same responses as patients seeking treatment from standard Western medicine.

To demonstrate that these results applied within the larger community, the research team conducted a survey with Vietnamese respondents to investigate their understanding of and responses to tuberculosis. Through a set of tables with percentages, Houston and colleagues (2002) showed that members of this culture did indeed believe in two forms of tuberculosis, which corresponded to two separate sets of health beliefs about symptoms, causes, and treatments. The researchers concluded with a series of recommendations about the importance of developing educational programs to help recent Vietnamese immigrants recognize that both forms of tuberculosis were infectious diseases that would be spread through close contact.

BOX 9.1   Size of Study Versus Priority of Study Revisited

When introducing the notation for mixed methods research designs, Chapter 4 noted that the *size* of a study is not the same as the *priority* that the study receives within the sequential priorities model, and the Houston et al. (2002) study in Example 9.8 is a case in point.

Despite the fact that claims of generality can often be made with relatively small, nonrandom samples, Houston and colleagues (2002) conducted a survey of over 500 people with a random sample of potential respondents who had Vietnamese last names. This was clearly a large and expensive study, yet it was treated as supplementary within their design. The reason is that almost every aspect of the survey was driven by the needs of the earlier qualitative study. This approach produced an article that paid a good deal more attention to the design of the qualitative portion of the research than to the design of the quantitative study. In addition, the presentation of quantitative results was limited to simple tables that matched the findings from the qualitative study. In other words, the results of the core qualitative study were the dominant feature in the project as a whole.

One obvious question is why Houston et al. (2002) conducted a major quantitative study to substantiate a straightforward set of qualitative results. Although the authors did not address this issue directly, they did explicitly state that they wanted to use their results in the next phase of their research program, in which their goal was to do a large-size intervention. A full-scale survey was thus useful to justify the expense of such a program, even if it was more than the authors needed to show the generality of their original qualitative findings.

A Further Possibility: Using Experiments to Demonstrate Greater Generality

The most common strategy for establishing greater generality relies on the specific strengths of surveys as a method for quantitative research. There is, however, no reason why you cannot use an experimental approach to go beyond the conclusions that you reached through a core qualitative study. This approach requires a central relationship to be investigated, in which the intervention itself serves as the independent variable that affects a specific outcome variable. The operationalization of the hypothesis thus involves creating an intervention that captures the key principles from the qualitative data. By showing that an experimental program does have the predicted effect, you are presenting evidence that the effects you observed in your qualitative study were not limited to what you learned in that particular context.

It is easy to understand why experimental interventions are a relatively rare tool for generating evidence of the greater generality of qualitative results. Compared to surveys, experiments are typically both more expensive and more complex to conduct. This does not necessarily have to be the case, however, if the intervention takes the form of a relatively small demonstration program. In this case, the goal is not to prove the efficacy of the intervention, just as the goal of using a small, targeted survey is not the same as that of using a full-fledged survey with a representative sample. Instead, the point of a demonstration program is more likely to be proof of a concept so that it is reasonable to believe that the steps you took in creating this small version of the intervention would reasonably apply to a larger version.

One of the key possibilities for converting qualitative results into demonstration programs is to provide evidence for the transferability (Lincoln & Guba, 1985) of the results. The quantitative extension expands on the original context of the results by specifying additional settings where you would observe the same outcomes. Hence, the lessons you learned from the original results have broader application. In this case, operationalization consists of translating your qualitative conclusions into an intervention that embodies your insights from the original study. In addition, you need to specify the kinds of sites where transferability is likely to occur.

Imagine that you conducted an in-depth observation in a school that you specifically selected because it was unusually successful in some way. Based on those observations, you might obtain not only a sense of the sources of this success but not also become convinced that implementing similar programs in other appropriate schools would be feasible. You could address this claim about transferability by putting a demonstration program into practice at another site. Reproducing your qualitative results as an intervention would be strong evidence for the soundness of your original conclusions.

Overall, transferability amounts to a specific form of generality by which you show that the results from one context can apply in a broader range of settings. In essence, the researcher needs to answer these questions: To what settings are these results transferable? Under which circumstances? These specifications are especially important for making claims about the generality of potential interventions to avoid overextending the relevance of the original qualitative results.

CONCLUSIONS

Considering the place of quantitative follow-up designs within the larger sequential priorities model, it is perhaps fitting that this final design is also the least common of the four. In part, this current low level of usage is due to a long-standing and understandable concern with the supposed need to validate or verify qualitative results with further quantitative research. In addition, limitations arise from the effort involved in operationalizing variables. More recently, however, these barriers have been receding in recognition of the value that quantitative supplements can add to core qualitative studies. Thus, quantitative follow-up designs are increasing in popularity.

One source of this wider acceptance is the pairing between generating and testing hypotheses. The idea of generating hypotheses has long been recognized as one of the strengths of qualitative research; yet this strength is of little use if those hypotheses do not produce further research. The answer proposed here is to take the themes that result from qualitative research and restate them as "If . . . then . . ." relationships between measurable variables. When this kind of reformatting makes sense, it is a strong argument for using *QUAL → quant* designs.

The popularity of quantitative follow-up designs is also enhanced by the goal of showing that results of qualitative studies apply more generally. Qualitative researchers rarely expect their findings to be restricted to just the set of participants they interviewed or just the settings they observed. Instead, they want to convey a broader message. When it is important to give a concrete demonstration of this wider applicability, the strengths of a supplementary quantitative method can make a meaningful contribution to the results from a core qualitative study.

Taken together, these two trends suggest that use of quantitative follow-up designs will continue to grow. Of course, this does not mean that all four of the designs in the sequential priorities model will reach a kind of parity such that each is equally common. The level of use that each of these designs receives will be a function of the purposes it serves and the extent to which those purposes serve the needs of social science researchers. The point is not to promote one option in comparison to the others; instead, the goal is to put forth a set of powerful and practical research designs that extend the range of purposes we can serve.

SUMMARY

There are two primary uses for supplementary quantitative methods as a follow-up to a core qualitative study. One is to test hypotheses and theories that were generated as results in the qualitative portion of the project. The other is to extend the generality of a set of qualitative results beyond the specific context in which they originally occurred. Both of these approaches require the operationalization of the qualitative results into measurable variables and testable relationships.

DISCUSSION QUESTIONS

How relevant do you think the history of qualitative and quantitative research is to the *QUAL → quant* design? In particular, what do you think of the idea that quantitative methods can "validate" the results of qualitative studies?

How do you feel about operationalizing qualitative concepts as variables and then specifying statistically testable relationships between these variables? When is this a useful set of procedures, and when does it go too far beyond the original goals of qualitative research?

ADDITIONAL READINGS

The examples presented in this chapter serve as the additional readings.

Cunningham, A. J., Edmonds, C. V., Phillips, C., Scoots, K. I., Hedley, D., & Lockwood, G. A. (2000). A prospective, longitudinal study of the relationship of psychosocial work to duration of survival in patients with metastatic cancer. *Psycho-Oncology, 9,* 323–339.

Drach-Zahavy, A., & Pud, D. (2010). Learning mechanisms to limit medication administration errors. *Journal of Advanced Nursing, 66,* 794–805.

Houston, H. R., Harada, N., & Makinodan, T. (2002). Development of a culturally sensitive educational intervention program to reduce the high incidence of tuberculosis among foreign-born Vietnamese. *Ethnicity & Health, 7,* 255–265.

Hult, J. R., Wrubel, J., Bränström, R., Acree, M., & Moskowitz, J. T. (2012). Disclosure and nondisclosure among people newly diagnosed with HIV: An analysis from a stress and coping perspective. *AIDS Patient Care and STDs, 26,* 181–190.

Morgan, D. L. (1989). Adjusting to widowhood: Do social networks really make it easier? *The Gerontologist, 29,* 101–107.

Seal, D. W., Eldrige, G. D., Kacanek, D., Binson, D., & MacGowan, R. J. (2007). A longitudinal, qualitative analysis of the context of substance use and sexual behavior among 18- to 29-year-old men after their release from prison. *Social Science and Medicine, 65,* 2394–2406.

van Staa, A. (2011). Unraveling triadic communication in hospital consultations with adolescents with chronic conditions: The added value of mixed methods research. *Patient Education and Counseling, 82,* 455–464.

Wuest, J., & Hodgins, M. J. (2011). Reflections on methodological approaches and conceptual contributions in a program of research on caregiving: Development and testing of Wuest's theory of family caregiving. *Qualitative Health Research, 21,* 151–161.

Yun, S., Faraj, S., & Sims, H. (2005). Contingent leadership and effectiveness of trauma resuscitation teams. *Journal of Applied Psychology, 90,* 1288–1296.

Part 3

Additional Issues

CHAPTER 10

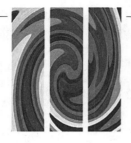

Multipart Sequential Designs

Overview

The simplest way to extend the basic designs discussed in the previous chapters is to increase the number of sequential methods from two to three. Even this minimal change creates a number of possibilities, only a few of which are truly interesting. Among the large number of possible three-part designs, this chapter focuses on projects that alternate between supplementary and core methods. The first of these designs relies on a core quantitative method with supplementary qualitative methods in both the preliminary and follow-up positions: *qual* → *QUANT* → *qual*. The key strength of this format is that it allows both of the supplementary methods to make their own contributions to the core method. The same is true of alternating designs that use a qualitative core: *quant* → *QUAL* → *quant*.

Moving beyond three-part designs to even more complex combinations of qualitative and quantitative methods raises both practical concerns with regard to logistics and broader issues with regard to integrating multiple sets of results. Again, alternating supplementary and core methods leverages a useful set of strengths in a manageable format by creating a "chain" of studies that revolve around a consistent core that can be either qualitative or quantitative. Overall, the strengths of these designs arise from their close connection to sequential priorities model; they use its four basic designs as building blocks to create more complex combinations of qualitative and quantitative methods.

E ach of the four designs in Chapters 6 through 9 paired a sequence of one qualitative and one quantitative method. Going beyond these two-part designs to multipart designs is not as simple as it might seem. In particular, if there are 4 basic two-part designs, then there are at least 16 possible three-step designs. Studies that create sequences of four or more methods within a single project are, understandably, even more complex. In discussing this complex set of options, there is thus a trade-off between being relatively exhaustive and emphasizing a small but powerful set of designs. The approach here is to concentrate on practicality and therefore to be selective within the larger, more complex set of multipart sequential designs.

The most straightforward way to emphasize practicality in the development of multipart designs is to build on the existing designs in the sequential priorities model. Chapter 5 argued that what made the four basic designs so practical was that they were both *accessible* and *dependable*. In terms of accessibility, using the existing designs as a foundation means that the lessons from Chapters 6 to 9 provide a strong starting point for understanding what it means to expand a two-part design into three parts. Further, relying on the proven process of combining supplementary and core methods increases the dependability of three-part sequences. Hence, assembling more complex projects from the original set of four basic designs enhances both the accessibility and dependability—and thus the practicality—of these multipart projects.

FORMATS FOR THREE-PART DESIGNS

It makes sense to begin by considering the possible ways that you might add to one of the basic sequential priorities designs. In the case of a preliminary qualitative input design, one obvious option is to include another supplementary qualitative study as a follow-up. To understand the potential uses for this three-step design, it helps to break it into an underlying sequence of basic designs:

$$qual \rightarrow QUANT$$

$$QUANT \rightarrow qual$$

$$qual \rightarrow QUANT \rightarrow qual$$

This reformatting shows how the core quantitative method stands at the center of this design, with an alternating set of qualitative supplementary studies coming before and after it. The first step in this three-part design uses a preliminary qualitative input design to maximize the effectiveness of the core, quantitative study. The next step is a follow-up qualitative extension to pursue the results from the same core study. Thus, the two supplementary qualitative studies each serve distinct purposes: the first as input and the second as follow-up. Note also that, from the point of view of the project as a whole, the designs of both supplementary qualitative studies are driven by the needs of the single core quantitative method.

This design is clearly powerful because the core quantitative method draws on the strengths of both supplementary qualitative methods. In particular, the first step in the process improves the effectiveness of the quantitative study before it enters the field, and the second step investigates issues that go beyond the results from the core study. Overall, the alternation between the two qualitative supplements and the quantitative core means that a *qual* → *QUANT* → *qual* design builds on the effectiveness of both the *qual* → *QUANT* and *QUANT* → *qual* designs.

Now consider a three-step design in which you again begin with a qualitative input design and then add a supplementary quantitative follow-up study:

$$qual \rightarrow QUANT \rightarrow quant$$

This example is less interesting than the previous one because it does not meet the essential goal of combining methods that have different strengths. Instead, following a core quantitative study with another smaller quantitative study would be a straightforward practice within existing versions of quantitative research. Hence, this three-part design adds little to the original *qual* → *QUANT* design.

Next, consider the pair of designs that you get when the third method adds another core study to a project that begins with a preliminary qualitative input design:

$$qual \rightarrow QUANT \rightarrow QUANT$$

$$qual \rightarrow QUANT \rightarrow QUAL$$

The first of these designs is also less interesting, because you are using the traditional practice of following one quantitative study with another. With regard to the second design, following up on a quantitative core study with a qualitative core study signals a major change in direction, because the third stage of the research will be dominated by the goals and needs of this new qualitative study. As noted in Chapter 5, such an attempt to pursue different core methods within the same project is problematic because it creates competing priorities, in which the needs of each core study are set up to drive the design of the other. By comparison, the use of a single core method, such as in a *qual* → *QUANT* → *qual* sequence, is notably more straightforward.

This set of possible additions to a *qual* → *QUANT* study leads to three principles:

1. By *alternating* the supplementary studies in the *qual* → *QUANT* → *qual* design, the research benefits from the contribution of different strengths to the same core study. In contrast, the other designs illustrate potential problems that apply to a number of other three-part designs.

2. Sequences that include two adjacent qualitative or quantitative methods are less interesting, because this pairing is unlikely to bring additional strengths to the overall project.

3. Three-part designs that include two different core methods require a major shift in direction that is difficult to perform within one research project.

To see how these principles apply more broadly, consider designs that begin with a quantitative input design. Combining the original preliminary input with a quantitative follow-up yields the following sequential logic.

$$\text{quant} \rightarrow \text{QUAL}$$

$$\text{QUAL} \rightarrow \text{quant}$$

$$\text{quant} \rightarrow \text{QUAL} \rightarrow \text{quant}$$

The result is an alternating pair of quantitative supplementary studies conducted before and after a core qualitative study. In this case, the first step is an input design to maximize the effectiveness of the core, while the second follows up on the results from the same core study. As with the first design considered above, these two supplementary quantitative studies serve separate purposes, while the design for the overall project is driven by the core qualitative method.

Once again, this pattern of alternation around a single core study produces a powerful design by combining the strengths of the two underlying designs. On the one hand, the *quant* → *QUAL* component can help you locate the most useful sources of data before the core qualitative study enters the field. On the other hand, the *QUAL* → *quant* component allows you to either test hypotheses from the core qualitative results or extend the results' generality.

Next, compare this alternating design to the three others that also build on a quantitative input design:

quant → QUAL → qual

quant → QUAL → QUAL

quant → QUAL → QUANT

As before, the first two designs are less interesting due to pairing adjacent qualitative methods and thus extending a core qualitative study with yet more qualitative data. The third of these designs illustrates the other potentially problematic aspect of three-part designs since it contains two kinds of core studies, thereby requiring a change of direction within a project.

Taken together, these comparisons demonstrate the general value of the two types of alternating designs: *qual → QUANT → qual* and *quant → QUAL → quant*. Another argument in favor of these designs is the relative ease of addressing issues related to integration. Because each of these designs has a single core study, you can use needs of that core method to determine the content of the two supplementary studies. Interestingly, this logical argument also corresponds with practice, because variations on these two designs are the most common examples in the literature. Hence, this chapter will concentrate on three-part designs that alternate a pair of supplementary methods of the same type around a single core method of the contrasting type.

ALTERNATING DESIGNS WITH A QUANTITATIVE CORE

Alternating a quantitative core study with supplementary qualitative input and follow-up is undoubtedly the most common format for three-part sequences. This makes sense because of the popularity of both the underlying *qual → QUANT* and *QUANT → qual* designs. In particular, the benefits from preliminary and follow-up qualitative studies apply to both surveys and program interventions used as quantitative core methods.

For survey research, the value of qualitative methods as a preliminary input is well known. As noted in Chapter 6, the strengths that qualitative methods contribute as inputs can serve purposes related to the discovery, development, and definition of survey measures. Additionally, a qualitative follow-up design can either illustrate results that conform to the predictions of the survey or investigate results that diverge from original expectations. Example 10.1 uses both of these strengths in the process of creating a new survey instrument.

Example 10.1	Combining Qualitative Input and Follow-up With Survey Research

Luyt (2012) began his project on measuring masculinity with the familiar strategy of using a qualitative input design to generate a survey instrument. In this first step, he conducted individual interviews and focus groups with members of several different ethnic groups in South Africa. This led to the identification of a series of major themes, which Luyt converted to a series of survey questions. A factor analysis of these items led to three subscales: Toughness, Control, and Sexuality.

On the one hand, the results of the quantitative investigation were encouraging; on the other hand, they also pointed to additional work that needed to be done. The instrument was successful with regard to its ability to measure the core concepts of perceptions of masculinity; however, it also needed substantial work to achieve a more complete degree of equivalence across multiple ethnic groups. Luyt (2012) examined this issue through a set of focus groups in which participants were separated by ethnicity. Overall, the examination of both the qualitative and quantitative data pointed to a set of detailed revisions of the questionnaire.

For intervention programs, the strengths of an alternating *qual* → *QUANT* → *qual* design provide benefits that are similar to those in which survey research is the core quantitative component. In particular, the qualitative input in the first stage can assist in creating a program that is well suited to the participants. In the second stage, a qualitative follow-up gives the opportunity to learn more about why the program performed in the ways that it did. Example 10.2 makes this point, describing an alternating design in which the core quantitative study was a program intervention.

Example 10.2	Combining Qualitative Input and Follow-up With a Program Intervention

Farquhar, Ewing, and Booth (2011) used qualitative methods to both develop and assess an intervention that they developed to relieve breathlessness in patients with advanced lung disease. In the first step, their preliminary qualitative research developed and refined the features of the potential program. At the core of this project was a demonstration study on the feasibility of the intervention. The final step in the overall design used a series of qualitative interviews to learn more about the practical performance of the program. These results led to important revisions in the protocol for a planned larger intervention.

Interestingly, Farquhar and colleagues (2011) concluded their presentation by discussing this three-part design as the basis for a full-sized intervention that would include mixed methods interviews at regular points throughout. In that case, this set of studies might collectively be considered preliminary aspects of that larger core study.

In general, it seems likely that *qual* → *QUANT* → *qual* designs will continue to be the most popular type of three-part designs. For one thing, they can build on the relatively large experience base that goes with both *qual* → *QUANT* and *QUANT* → *qual* designs. Because the purposes behind each of these underlying designs are well understood, it is easier to see the value of combining those strengths into a three-part study.

ALTERNATING DESIGNS WITH A QUALITATIVE CORE

Alternating supplementary quantitative methods around a core qualitative method also benefits from the relatively clear understanding that exists for the two underlying studies. Remember from Chapter 7, however, that while *quant* → *QUAL* studies are common, they are relatively unrecognized within the literature. In addition, *QUAL* → *quant* designs are becoming better known but are still not highly visible. This means that both of the components in this design are not as well developed as the equivalent segments within a *qual* → *QUANT* → *qual* design.

As with alternating designs in general, the quantitative input and quantitative follow-up studies contribute different strengths to the project as a whole. Beginning with a supplementary quantitative study is especially useful for locating participants who meet the criteria for purposive sampling. The strengths that you gain from this kind of quantitative input are, however, quite different from the strengths of testing hypotheses and demonstrating generality. Example 10.3 makes this point with a project that used a series of case studies as its core method.

Example 10.3	Combining Quantitative Input and Follow-up With a Program Intervention

"Positive deviance," a technique illustrated by Bradley et al. (2009), starts by identifying programs or individuals that perform well above the typical level in their field. This phase of research seeks to understand the sources of this success through case studies. The first part of Bradley and colleagues' design thus began by using quantitative databases to locate a purposive sample of cases for in-depth qualitative analysis. The goal was to generate systematic hypotheses about the source of the success among these cases. Then the second phase of this research design tested the hypotheses from the first phase.

Bradley and colleagues (2009) examined aspects of cardiac care in which there was considerable variation in performance across hospitals. By searching a large national database, they were able to identify a set of hospitals that were notably faster in delivering crucial elements of care to heart attack victims. In particular, they identified 11 hospitals that had substantially improved the timing of care delivery within the past 4 years and thus were in an especially good position to describe specific actions that had upgraded performance. These cases thus exhibited "positive deviance" because they functioned at a higher level than their peers. Bradley et al. then visited each of these sites and collected over 100 qualitative interviews from a diverse range of staff. Based on their analysis of this data, they identified a set of strategies that were likely to be associated with faster delivery of high-quality cardiac care.

As a final step, Bradley and colleagues (2009) conducted a large, Web-based survey of randomly selected hospitals in which the factors that had emerged in the case studies became variables in the survey. They conducted statistical analyses on the hypotheses from the qualitative study and isolated six strategies that were clearly related to better practices. The ultimate result was a series of sources of success that could apply to a wide range of care settings.

Overall, both *qual* → *QUANT* → *qual* and *quant* → *QUAL* → *quant* formats for alternating designs point to the value of alternating the strengths of preliminary input and follow-up extension designs with those of a core study. From the standpoint of logistics, the overall design process is simplified when the needs of a single core study are used as the basis of both the preliminary input and follow-up extension studies. From the standpoint of integration, it is possible to rely on the well-known contributions of preliminary inputs and follow-up extensions. Taken together, these two advantages make a strong case for alternating designs with a single core study.

MANAGING THE COMPLEXITY IN LONGER SEQUENTIAL DESIGNS

There is, of course, no reason why multipart designs need to be limited to three steps, but the complexity of adding more studies to a sequence creates a pair of difficulties. The first set of problems is mechanical or logistical. Bringing more components into a design requires you to develop effective and efficient strategies for collecting and analyzing multiple sets of data. Consider a sequence of two core quantitative studies that also includes a full set of supplementary inputs and follow-ups. This leads to a five-part sequence:

$$qual \rightarrow QUANT \rightarrow qual \rightarrow QUANT \rightarrow qual$$

Even this simple expansion can require considerably more resources, including the need for a project to remain in the field for an extended period of time.

This design also points to a second set of difficulties, which arise from the need to integrate the increasing range of results from the larger number of studies. Thus, although the logistical problems in longer sequences may be mostly a matter of project management, the issues involved in integration are likely to be more troublesome. In particular, the more core studies that you include within a project, the more demands there will be on the supplementary studies. While a five-part sequence like the one shown here can probably be dealt with by extending the previous recommendation for three-part designs, it may well represent the upper limit for such alternating sequences.

The fundamental problem with research designs at this level is managing the complexity of longer, multipart sequential designs. Two reasonably well-known approaches to these difficulties come from the literature on program interventions. The first strategy involves using *process evaluation,* which creates a series of interconnections between the qualitative and quantitative components within an intervention. The second strategy is to link separate projects in a larger *research program,* which consists of an ongoing sequence of projects.

Process Evaluation and Dual-Track Sequential Designs

Process evaluation studies (Patton, 2002) are an alternative to *traditional summative evaluations,* which only assess outcomes at the end of an intervention.

In contrast, process evaluations rely on continual monitoring of the intervention throughout the project. At their best, process evaluations provide you with systematic links across the multiple sets of data that you collect throughout an ongoing intervention program. These linkages can be formalized as a *dual-track sequence,* as illustrated in Figure 10.1.

Figure 10.1   A Dual-Track Sequence Design With Quantitative Core Studies

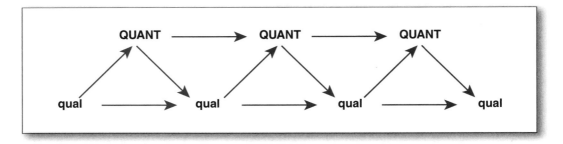

The dual tracks in this system consist of alternating sequences of core and supplementary methods. The purpose of the alternating interconnections in a dual-track sequence is to increase integration between the two ongoing series of qualitative and quantitative methods. Compare this to the simple alternating chain that includes three core studies:

$$qual \rightarrow QUANT \rightarrow qual \rightarrow QUANT \rightarrow qual \rightarrow QUANT \rightarrow qual$$

As an illustration of how this kind of dual-track sequence can work, consider Example 10.4, which describes a study that used three waves of qualitative and quantitative interviews as well as a set of qualitative cases studies that continued throughout the project as a whole.

Example 10.4   An Alternating Chain of Core Quantitative and Supplementary Qualitative Studies

The 2012 study by Youngs and Piggot-Irvine, in which they evaluated a large-scale training program for advanced teachers who wanted to become principals, provides two examples of a dual-track sequence of qualitative studies with core quantitative steps. In the first example, they examined the role of support from the principals in the teachers' own schools. This topic was not originally included in the set of topics that the authors had antici-pated studying; instead, it was located through their preliminary analysis of the qualitative data. Based on that insight from a first qualitative step, their initial round of quantitative data showed that principals who recruited one of their own teachers into the program were more likely to apply the pro-gram goals. These findings, in turn, led the authors to increase their atten-tion to both the qualitative and quantitative data with regard to the support provided by principals. In particular, the qualitative data provided more detailed information about how this support operated in the experiences of individual teachers, while the quantitative data pointed to the importance of this support for teachers from smaller schools.

A second illustration concerns lessons about the relevancy of the over-all curriculum. In this case, early results from two continuing case studies pointed out that nearly all of the material was devoted to the principal's role with regard to teaching and learning in the school, but this ignored the equally important work involved in management functions related to budgets, school property, and personnel issues. These early qualitative findings were not sufficient to require changes throughout the program, but when subsequent questionnaires also showed that participants felt there were gaps in the curriculum, this information was enough to focus more attention on training for management functions. After this change on the qualitative side, there were clear indications of greater program satis-faction, while on the quantitative side, there were major increases in par-ticipants' rating of their ability to apply the knowledge they were acquiring.

Process evaluations are not a panacea, however. In particular, placing a study under the broad umbrella of "process evaluation" is no substitute for careful attention to integrating the qualitative and qualitative components in the project. As Example 10.5 illustrates, it is still essential to consider how the core and sup-plementary methods will be integrated to meet the overall needs of the project.

Example 10.5	A Less Successful Case of Process Evaluation as an Alternating Chain Design

Munro and Bloor (2010) used a process evaluation approach to assess a school-based drug prevention program, which unfortunately was not suc-cessful. In principle, the process evaluation should have shed light on this

(Continued)

(Continued)

failure by allowing the evaluators to track each stage of the process as it unfolded. In Munro and Bloor's judgment, however, the process evaluation itself was also unsuccessful, because the various pieces of the evaluation came to an end along with the program itself. So, by the time the ultimate outcome became known, there was no further data collection to explain the program's major finding.

In terms of the basic designs covered here, the source of the problem in Example 10.5 was the lack of a genuine supplementary qualitative follow-up study, which would have provided the ability to pursue poorly understood results. This led to an inability to *integrate* the sequence of studies, because the needs of the core methods were not met. From the point of view of a dual-track sequence design, this example points to the importance of surrounding the core studies with a carefully designed series of supplementary studies.

The value that dual-chain sequences offer for process evaluations in program evaluation raises the question of whether similar advantages exist for survey research as an alternative source of core quantitative methods. The obvious equivalent is a series of surveys within a longitudinal series. The key difference here is the inability to modify the content of surveys in such a sequence. Thus, when you conduct a process evaluation, you are tracking an evolving process, but when you do a longitudinal survey, you need to preserve your measures from one wave of data collection to the next. At most, the supplementary studies can point to the advantage of adding new measures, but this contribution is unlikely to require the full apparatus of a dual-track chain.

What about multipart designs with a sequence of qualitative core studies? It is easy to diagram a dual-track design with core qualitative studies and an alternating series of supplementary quantitative studies, as shown in Figure 10.2, but this kind of design is likely to be rarer than its core quantitative equivalent. The reason is that the dual-track format is best suited to projects that have distinct waves of data collection within a longitudinal study, and that is an unusual model for qualitative research. Still, it is quite possible to imagine a series of qualitative studies that rely on supplementary quantitative studies to aid in either the selection of participants or the testing of results. Specifically, this kind of design would match a long-run interest in theoretical sampling. As described in Chapter 7, theoretical sampling uses the emerging theory from

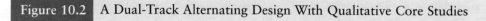

Figure 10.2   A Dual-Track Alternating Design With Qualitative Core Studies

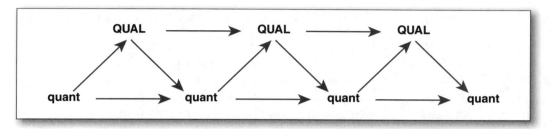

earlier portions of a project to determine the next set of research participants. The goal is to enhance the effectiveness of each wave in the qualitative core by choosing participants who will make the maximum contribution to what you have learned so far.

Overall, these dual-track designs demonstrate the larger strategy of managing the complexity of multipart sequences by using the underlying logic of the original sequential priorities model. In particular, the design process is simplified by thinking in terms of how the strengths of the supplementary methods can contribute to the needs of the core methods. The same can be said of the process of integrating the results of the different methods, because the roles of both the supplementary and core methods are well understood.

Research Programs as a Strategy for Extending Sequential Designs

The essential defining criterion of a research program is that it links a set of separate projects. As opposed to the methods within a single project, each project within a sequence produces a set of results that can stand on its own. This means that there are two sequential processes: one that links the studies within each project and another that links those projects into a larger research program. To illustrate this distinction, recall from Example 10.2 that Farquhar et al. (2011) reported a *qual* → *QUANT* → *qual* project in which the core study was a demonstration program. In addition, they stated their intention to continue this work with a full-scale intervention that would involve both qualitative and quantitative interviews. Reformulating these two projects as a research program suggests one possible design:

$$[qual \rightarrow QUANT \rightarrow qual] \rightarrow QUANT$$

Or, depending on the complexity of the second project in the research program, the overall design might look like this:

$$[qual \rightarrow QUANT \rightarrow qual] \rightarrow [qual \rightarrow QUANT \rightarrow qual]$$

In this extension of the basic notation, each set of studies within a pair of brackets is a separate project that can serve as part of the longer sequence in a research program. Example 10.6 demonstrates this process: The authors (Nastasi et al., 2007; Nastasi, Jayasena, Summerville, & Borja, 2011) created a series of interventions, each of which began with a preliminary qualitative input study to maximize its effectiveness. In addition, they used the first of their interventions as the basis for the second project in their program, and so on. Here is a representation of the overall research program:

$$[qual \rightarrow QUANT] \rightarrow [qual \rightarrow QUANT] \rightarrow [qual \rightarrow QUANT] \ldots$$

Example 10.6   Creating a Chain of Qualitative Input Designs

Nastasi et al. (2007) described an intermediate stage in their research program in which they concentrated on a project whose aim was to provide mental health services to Sri Lankan youth. An important goal was to ensure that the intervention would be culturally appropriate for this set of participants. This led the researchers to undertake a detailed preliminary qualitative study, which also made use of their findings from an earlier project on sexual risk prevention for Sri Lankan youth.

As a next step in their research program, Nastasi, Jayasena, Summerville, and Borja (2011) adapted the previous program on mental health services to respond to the crisis produced by the tsunami of 2004. In this case, the need for mental health services was provoked by the disastrous flooding that occurred in Sri Lanka, but the general findings from the earlier work also remained relevant. Even though this was their third project with youth in this culture, the authors wanted to be sure that their programming was appropriate in this post-disaster setting. Hence, this project also began with a preliminary qualitative input study, which helped them adapt their previous work on mental health services.

Example 10.6 illustrates how research programs manage logistical complexity while at the same time leading to a clean process of integration. On the one hand, when you work within each separate project, you can use a sequential design to maximize the practicality of that project. On the other hand, when you connect the results from each project to the next, you can create a sequential design that operates across the full set of projects. The Nastasi et al. (2007) example also demonstrates another of the major advantages of research programs: a straightforward path to integration. The strategy is to achieve integration within each component and then treat the next study as a follow-up that extends the results of the prior work. Once again, the central logic of the sequential priorities model serves as a basis for creating more complex research designs.

CONCLUSIONS

The basic lesson from this chapter is that the underlying logic in the sequential priorities model can be extended to the creation of multipart designs. In particular, relying on the four designs in the sequential priorities model provides a solid basis for developing more complicated multipart designs. As noted at the beginning of the chapter, these more complex designs can be practical because of their close relationship to the four well-established designs in the original sequential priorities model. Thus, those four designs can act as basic building blocks for the construction of designs that become increasingly complex while maintaining their practicality.

SUMMARY

This chapter has emphasized multipart designs that alternate supplementary studies around a single core method. On the one hand, a *qual → QUANT → qual* design can be used both to create the content for the core method and to follow up on the results from that method. On the other hand, a *quant → QUAL → quant* sequence can contribute to both selecting the original research participants and extending the results of the core qualitative method.

Even more complex versions of alternating designs, with more than three parts, hold promise for developing longer sequences of methods that are both practical to use and well integrated. Underlying each of these designs are the basic building blocks supplied by the original sequential priorities model.

DISCUSSION QUESTIONS

The designs in this chapter rely on the alternation in either *qual → QUANT → qual* or *quant → QUAL → quant* designs. Can you think of other equally useful designs, and, if so, what are their specific advantages?

The most complex designs considered here require several repetitions of qualitative and quantitative methods. How realistic is it to include so many components within a single research project? What other options can you propose?

ADDITIONAL READINGS

The examples presented in this chapter serve as the additional readings.

Bradley, E. H., Curry, L. A., Ramanadhan, S., Rowe L., Nembhard, I. M., & Krumholz, H. M. (2009). Research in action: Using positive deviance to improve quality of health care. *Implementation Science, 4,* 1–11.

Farquhar, M. C., Ewing, G., & Booth, S. (2011). Using mixed methods to develop and evaluate complex interventions in palliative care research. *Palliative Care, 25,* 748–757.

Luyt, R. (2012). A framework for mixing methods in quantitative measurement development, validation, and revision: A case study. *Journal of Mixed Methods Research, 6,* 294–316.

Munro, A., & Bloor, M. (2010). Process evaluation: The new miracle ingredient in public health research? *Qualitative Research, 10,* 699–713.

Nastasi, B. K., Hitchock, J., Sarkar, S., Burkholder, G., Varjas, K., & Jayasena, A. (2007). Mixed methods in intervention research: Theory to adaptation. *Journal of Mixed Methods Research, 1,* 164–182.

Nastasi, B. K., Jayasena, A., Summerville, M., & Borja, A. P. (2011). Facilitating long-term recovery from natural disasters: Psychosocial programming for tsunami-affected schools of Sri Lanka. *School Psychology International, 32,* 512–532.

Youngs, H., & Piggot-Irvine, E. (2012). The application of a multiphase triangulation approach to mixed methods: The research of an aspiring school principal development program. *Journal of Mixed Methods Research, 6,* 184–198.

CHAPTER 11

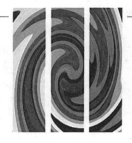

Finding the Expertise to Combine Multiple Methods

Overview

Projects that combine qualitative and quantitative methods obviously require a range of skills, and this chapter considers three ways to build the level of expertise that it takes to do this kind of research. First, you could develop an acceptable level of proficiency in both of the methods that you will be using. Second, you could create a research team whose members supply different kinds of research skills. Third, you or someone else on the research team could develop a different kind of expertise based on a *boundary-spanning role*. A person in this role works back and forth between the needs of different methods. Each of these approaches has advantages and disadvantages; these are the primary topics of this chapter.

Where are you going to find the expertise that it takes to do a project that combines both qualitative and quantitative methods: Are you going to master both kinds of methods yourself? Are you going to put together a team that combines the various skills you need? Or are you going to rely on some other option? Of course, the answers to these questions will vary depending on whether you are doing a smaller project, for which it might indeed be possible to do everything yourself, or a larger project, for which some kind of teamwork might be inevitable. Fortunately, the fundamental advantages and disadvantages of these basic options remain similar, despite the importance of size. Table 11.1 provides a general overview of the trade-offs involved.

Starting with the left-hand column, individually mastering both qualitative and quantitative methods requires a high degree of preparation, especially if you expect to develop a true degree of mastery in both areas. One obvious advantage of this approach is that it nearly eliminates the need for communication across different research specialties, which were described in Chapter 5. In addition, having a known level of mastery in each area should greatly reduce the likelihood that you will inadvertently design a project that exceeds your skill level. Of course, these advantages come at the cost of questions about the level of expertise that any one person can provide. In particular, trying to do everything yourself can require either persistent efforts to maintain a high level of expertise or a willingness to settle for doing projects that make fewer demands on your skills.

In contrast, the division of labor in team-based projects means that each member of a well-chosen team can rely on prior specialized training to provide a given set of skills. This typically means the people in charge of each method will have a higher level of expertise than a single researcher who tries to cover everything. In this case, however, there is an obvious trade-off in terms of communication and coordination of problems. As Chapter 5 noted, these problems

Table 11.1	Three Sources of Expertise in Integrating Methods		
	Individual Mastery	Teamwork	Boundary Spanning
Preparation	High and ongoing level of preparation is needed to master separate skills in each area.	Minimal level of additional preparation is needed due to use of existing skills within the team.	Usually requires prior preparation in one method plus close familiarity with another.
Strengths	Ensures a known level of mastery for each skill; requires minimal coordination.	Can provide very high-level skills for each method.	The role specializes in skills and coordination necessary for a specific set of methods.
Weaknesses	One person is unlikely to have high-level skills for each method.	Team may lack experience in integrating methods; coordination requires extra effort.	This is not currently a research specialty; skills are limited to specific combinations.

are particularly likely when team members who specialize in either qualitative or quantitative methods lack experience with the tasks involved in integrating the two. Overall, working as a team, through it brings together additional skills, also may create a whole new set of problems.

The third column in Table 11.1 emphasizes integration as a specific, important skill, one that is essential for spanning the boundary between the qualitative and quantitative studies that make up a mixed methods research project. If you develop skills in boundary spanning, you go beyond an emphasis on one method to understand how to connect with a different method. Thus, if you are a quantitative researcher with a background in surveys or intervention programs, you would acquire the skills necessary to interface with the qualitative methods that are the most valuable additions to your existing skill set, and the same would be true if you were a qualitative researcher who selectively learned aspects of quantitative methods that would contribute to your own core methods. The practical advantage of this approach is that researchers who already have skills in one area do not have to acquire a full set of skills in another area; instead, they merely learn enough to interface with others who do have those skills. One potential disadvantage of this approach, however, is that boundary spanning between multiple methods is not recognized as a form of expertise, especially in comparison to in-depth specialization in either qualitative or quantitative methods.

Table 11.1 highlights technical issues in training and the trade-offs between different approaches to doing integrated research, but other concerns need to be addressed as well. In particular, political issues can arise in any of the priority sequence designs if the researchers associated with the lower-priority method confuse the *supplemental status of that method in this particular project* with an assertion of *lower status for that method within the overall hierarchy of techniques* for collecting social science data. Hence, each of the following sections will consider both practical and political issues, along with the training, skills, and resources that are necessary to integrate qualitative and quantitative methods.

INDIVIDUAL MASTERY AS A BASIS FOR INTEGRATING METHODS

Following the logic of Table 11.1, the first question is how you would acquire the skills necessary to conduct both qualitative and quantitative research. Among more senior researchers, this has traditionally meant switching from one type of research to another. Historically speaking, nearly all of these transitions have been from quantitative to qualitative research, and given the contentious history between the two, these researchers were often undertaking profound career changes. In the past, such shifts took the form of rejecting one kind of research and its procedures and swearing allegiance to an entirely different way of doing things. Now, however, the increasing acceptance of mixed methods research offers an additional option.

Rather than switching fields completely, someone with extensive training in either qualitative or quantitative methods also has the option of extending their training from one area to the other. This is obviously a challenging and highly demanding task, but given the historical precedent of researchers making wholesale changes from one type of research to the other, adding an area of expertise is hardly out of the question. The obvious issue for more experienced researchers who want to make such a transition is how to find the time and resources to acquire a very different skill set.

The question of how to acquire a dual mastery of both qualitative and quantitative methods is rather different for graduate students and other beginning researchers. Not only do they have more time available for this training, but many fields have experienced a considerable shift in methods teaching, such that introductory courses are now likely to give comparable coverage to both qualitative and quantitative methods. Textbooks' move away from their strictly quantitative nature of earlier eras means that the most recent generations of students have been routinely introduced to the kind of work that goes into, and the kinds of results that come out of, both kinds of research. If you were exposed to this more evenhanded approach to research options right from the beginning, then you are more likely to understand at least the basic issues involved in mastering both qualitative and quantitative methods. Further, textbooks on research methods are increasingly likely to give attention to mixed methods along with qualitative and quantitative methods.

Along with acquiring an initial mastery of multiple methods, there is also the issue of how to maintain adequate proficiency in both areas. Here, there is a notable distinction between skills used in data collection and those used in data analysis. For both qualitative and quantitative methods, the skill sets involved in data collection are considerably more stable than those needed for data analysis, for which you need to engage in ongoing *professional development*. This book has, of course, emphasized data collection as a step in which the combination of qualitative and quantitative methods occurs, and it may be that your projects will place greater importance on integrating data collection with correspondingly less emphasis on integration during analysis. Even so, it is worth noting that data analysis is the area that is most likely to demand your consistent attention to keep your skills from becoming outdated.

So far, this presentation has made it seem as if you need to acquire equally high-level skills in both qualitative and quantitative methods, but the underlying logic of the sequential priorities model offers a different option. In particular, when you are using a sequential priorities design that relies on a core qualitative method, then your mastery of the supplementary quantitative method only has to be sufficient for the specific purposes that it serves. This typically requires less skill than using that same quantitative method to produce results that can stand on their own. Of course, the same logic applies when you use a core quantitative method: Your mastery of the supplementary qualitative methods needs to be sufficient for that limited purpose but not for producing a full-scale qualitative study.

Finally, another issue that needs to be addressed is the size of the project. Projects for which the lead researcher supplies the expertise in both kinds of methods tend to be smaller than team-based projects—if only because the ability of teams to put together skill sets that would be very rare in a single individual allows them to tackle greater complexity. For smaller projects, you may be able to undertake nearly all of the tasks yourself. For larger projects based on individual leadership, the most likely difference is that you will supervise a number of assistants. It is important to note, however, that these assistants typically take on narrowly defined tasks, which makes this way of organizing research different from the division of labor among experts that defines team-based approaches to integrating methods.

This additional supervisory responsibility often means more than just looking over the work of several people, because larger projects often require a more complex organizational structure to support the project as whole. Even so, these organizational constraints do not require any additional skills in research methods. Instead, you need to recognize that doing something that falls within your own range of research skills is not necessarily the same as supervising a number of potentially less skilled people doing the same work. Hence, if you need to train and supervise people in work that is near the limits of your own skills, then you definitely run the risk of being overwhelmed by a larger project.

TEAMWORK AS A BASIS FOR INTEGRATING METHODS

Chapter 5 has already described many of the challenges involved in teamwork for sequential priorities designs, and nearly all of these same issues apply to mixed methods research in general. At a minimum, both halves of the research team need to have some understanding of what the other can and cannot do. Chapter 5 also emphasized the difference between relatively passive sharing of information and more active collaboration at every stage of the research process. Teamwork in integrating qualitative and quantitative methods thus requires skills that go beyond expertise in research methods.

One of the most basic characteristics of a team is its size. Because two-person teams are the simplest, they serve as a useful point of introduction. The assumption is that two-person teams represent a division of labor such that one of you has more expertise in qualitative methods and the other in quantitative methods. The most obvious question here is the extent to which you and your partner are familiar with one another's methods. On one extreme is mutual familiarity; on the other extreme is separate specialization with little overlap. In between, there is a situation commonly described by analogy as sharing a common language, or being "bilingual," between the qualitative and quantitative members of the team (e.g., Curry et al., 2012; O'Cathain, Murphy, and Nicholl, 2008). Note, however, that mere "bilingualism" falls short of the "biculturalism" that may be necessary for integrating different methods. At that level, both researchers have a deeper understanding of both the practices and belief systems associated with the "foreign" form of research.

Just as important as sharing a common language is for research partners to master a third language, that of mixed methods research. This important aspect of preparation goes into any kind of teamwork in this area. As Chapter 5 pointed out, this kind of research involves a series of steps that require an ongoing process of coordination. This means that being half of a two-person team requires more than just communicating with your partner while carrying out your own responsibilities. A far better plan is to work together throughout the length of the project.

So far, the discussion of a division of labor has been limited to separate skills in the qualitative and quantitative arenas, but the mixed methods designs considered here also point to a division between core and supplementary methods. The key concern here is a political one, namely, that assigning the supplementary methods to a secondary role is not the same as turning the person in charge of those methods into a "junior partner." Instead, both halves of the team must recognize that the needs of the core method will not be met without the appropriate results from the supplementary method. Once again, Chapter 5 points to the importance of explicitly working out how the integration of the core and supplementary methods will occur.

Finally, it is important to move beyond the exclusive domain of research methods to consider a number of other factors that can either separate or unite the partners in a two-person research team. Are they from the same discipline? Are they equally senior or junior? And do they share the same stakes in the outcome of the research project? These concerns are not limited to mixed methods research; they are important concerns for any kind of teamwork. Given the complexity of teamwork for mixed methods research, however, these additional concerns can easily come into play. For example, what is the potential for conflict when a more senior person has responsibility for the supplementary contribution to a project while a junior person is in charge of the core method?

Even this brief introduction to teamwork makes it clear why one of the potential limitations of mixed methods research is the additional time and effort that goes into it. In many ways, a two-person team is an excellent solution to this issue, because you will almost certainly need to work together on a routine basis, not just because you are doing mixed methods research.

Multiple-Person Teams

There is some truth to the idea that larger teams just raise more complex versions of the same issues that occur in two-person teams. What is worth noting, however, is how fast this complexity grows. Georg Simmel's (1950) well-known comparison of dyads and triads demonstrated the multiple forms of interaction that were possible in three-person but not two-person groups, and the potential issues with group dynamics continue to multiply as group size grows. As a result, it is wise to create a well-defined organization for teams with four or more members, and Table 11.2 indicates several factors that go into this process.

Each of the major categories in Table 11.2 shows a set of options that move from lower to higher *levels of integration within the team* as a whole. Thus, the category of team culture moves from the relatively low level of integration implied by shared vocabulary, to a tighter integration among the team members at the level of mutual respect, and the highest level of integration with mutual understanding. As noted in the discussion of bilingualism above, the ability to translate each other's concepts and jargon takes you only so far. Mutual respect goes further to include an appreciation for the ways that each member contributes to the team as a whole. At the highest level of integration in team culture, mutual understanding means knowing why your partners think and act in the ways they do. To extend the analogy of bilingualism, mutual understanding implies a form of biculturalism, such that team members have a richer appreciation of each other's beliefs and practices.

Table 11.2	Characteristics of Teamwork in Mixed Methods Research
Team Culture	
Shared Vocabulary	Team members are "bilingual" with regard to each other's typical procedures and specific jargon.
Mutual Respect	Team members understand the value of each other's contributions and value what the others can offer.
Mutual Understanding	Team members understand the "why" behind each other's methods and research designs.
Division of Labor	
Multidisciplinary	Qualitative and quantitative researchers each possess separate strengths that operate in parallel.
Interdisciplinary	Qualitative and quantitative researchers work together to make use of each other's strengths.
Transdisciplinary	Qualitative and quantitative researchers share their strengths in ways that that affect how both methods operate.
Leadership	
Communication	Leader(s) encourage exchanges that allow both qualitative and quantitative researchers to follow each other's activities.
Coordination	Leader(s) bring together qualitative and quantitative researchers to discuss each other's decisions.
Collaboration	Leader(s) actively unite qualitative and quantitative researchers for shared decision making.

Next, the division of labor dimension captures how closely the qualitative and quantitative members of the team work together throughout the research process. The three-part distinction among multidisciplinary, interdisciplinary, and transdisciplinary teams draws on related distinctions from Shulha and Wilson (2003) as well as O'Cathain et al. (2008). One common metaphor used to describe this dimension involves Venn diagrams, which show with only slightly overlapping circles that multidisciplinary team members operate in a largely separate fashion. This low level of integration is unlikely to be adequate for the degree of integration required by the research designs covered here. Instead, teams need to function with the kind of overlap that is captured in the concept of interdisciplinary research. At the highest level of integration—a transdisciplinary approach—the qualitative and quantitative members of the team engage in a united partnership such that each consistently facilitates the participation of the other.

Finally, leadership is crucial to larger teams. As Chapter 5 argued, simply exchanging communication is typically insufficient in mixed methods research. In particular, if there are multiple members on each team, then working together effectively is almost certain to require explicit coordination of your activities. At the highest level of integration, mutual collaboration emphasizes a shared sense of participation and accomplishment that goes beyond merely managing the efficiency and effectiveness of the team.

There is an obvious attraction to attaining the highest level of team integration through a culture of mutual understanding, a transdisciplinary division of labor, and a collaborative leadership style. Even so, it is important to think about the time and effort that this kind of teamwork requires, especially in complex research projects with large teams. In many situations, a moderate level of integration may be all that you need. A different solution, however, involves a variation on two-person teams in which one person takes responsibility for the qualitative portion of the team while another person takes responsibility for the quantitative portion. Example 11.1 demonstrates a number of specific techniques that can increase the chances for success with this form of integration.

Example 11.1 Coordinating a Mixed Methods Study

Corden and Hirst (2008) described their partnership as the leaders of the qualitative and quantitative portions of a research project as follows: One author was in charge of collecting and analyzing semistructured interviews, while the other did secondary analysis of longitudinal survey data. To coordinate their ongoing work, they held a series of team meetings on a biweekly basis, at which the members of the entire project team shared their various data collection and analysis protocols. At a minimum, this allowed each half of the overall team to think of their own work in terms of what the other half was planning; beyond that, it allowed both the qualitative and quantitative sides to make adjustments in their designs and activities to maximize their mutual relevance. This same process of sharing at regular meetings continued as the two portions of the project began to

(Continued)

(Continued)

produce preliminary reports, which were circulated to the team as a whole. In addition to emphasizing team building across the project as a whole, the two authors also shared a single, high-level research assistant who routinely worked with both of them. Moreover, they created detailed documentation throughout as a way not just to keep a record of their process but also to use the process of creating the documentation as a way of monitoring their success in communicating with each other.

BOUNDARY SPANNING AS A BASIS FOR INTEGRATING METHODS

Table 11.1 positions boundary spanning as a midpoint between individual mastery of separate skills and a team-based approach to those same skills. As the name implies, operating in this role means being a bridge between the qualitative and quantitative researchers on a project. Researchers who play a boundary-spanning role are occupying a special position in the division of labor that connects what would otherwise be separate specializations. Boundary spanning requires you to move back and forth between the two teams. From the team's point of view, creating such roles is a strong strategy for improving coordination between the two methods.

There are two likely points of origin for this kind of boundary spanning. In one, you already have a background in the core method, so you can provide the specific skills necessary to interface with the supplementary portion of a project. The other alternative is to make the connection through an identification with the supplementary method. In this case, you would have not only the skills necessary to carry out a stand-alone study with the methods in your area of expertise but also a further expertise in working with core projects that use the alternative methods.

At present, the most realistic example of this kind of work would be a qualitative researcher providing inputs to quantitative projects and, more specifically, focus group researchers doing preliminary work for survey researchers (Morgan, 1997). Given the relatively well-developed nature of projects that use qualitative inputs, it is not surprising that this is also the area where the most work has been done on developing boundary-spanning roles. Indeed, it is not unusual to find large-scale survey operations that include a specialized unit devoted to focus groups and qualitative researchers who work full-time to create inputs to surveys. The head of this unit then provides the boundary-spanning contacts with the survey side. In line with the design cycle from Chapter 5, half of the project would consist of agreeing on a research design for the focus groups that would meet the needs of a given survey. After that, you would be in charge of conducting the groups and ensuring that the results meet the desired goals.

As noted above, there are actually two options for generating a boundary-spanning role: The other alternative in this example would be someone from a survey organization making the connections with the source of the qualitative inputs. This division of labor is more common when the survey organization does not have any employees who are in charge of doing qualitative research. In that case, one member of the survey team can routinely be in charge of hiring the focus group moderators, ensuring they understand the precise needs of a specific survey, and working with the focus group researchers on a continuing basis to make sure they are producing relevant material.

Of course, this one rather specialized example does not exhaust the possibilities for boundary spanning; instead, it is simply the best developed. In particular, there is nothing to stop researchers in a core qualitative project from hiring quantitative researchers to generate contributions from a supplementary method. Thus, survey researchers could either supply preliminary inputs to locate specific categories of research participants or conduct a follow-up study to demonstrate the broader generality of a set of qualitative results. Regardless of whether your own expertise is in qualitative or qualitative methods, your goal in boundary spanning should be to maximize the contributions from one method to the other.

The example of using focus groups as qualitative inputs to quantitative methods is also notable in terms of the limitation shown in Table 11.1, namely, that boundary spanning is not widely recognized as a kind of expertise in mixed methods research. The fact that it does exist in one specific set of circumstances provides at least a provisional model for extending this approach to other kinds of research designs. Still, the likely expansion of large-scale mixed methods projects in the future points to the need for this research specialty as a resource for such projects.

As a final word on boundary spanning, it is also worth considering the kind of preparation required for this kind of work. One clear advantage of this approach is illustrated by considering the knowledge required for mastery of both qualitative and quantitative methods. Instead of gaining full-scale proficiency in both types of research, you would be pursuing your own division of labor between acquiring both a core and a supplementary set of skills. Add in a familiarity with the general principles of mixed methods research, and you are ready to perform a boundary-spanning role.

SUMMARY

Doing mixed methods research requires expertise in both qualitative and quantitative methods. One obvious but difficult way to provide this expertise is for a single researcher to achieve a relatively high level of mastery in both kinds of research. As an alternative, an increasingly common approach is to use teams of researchers and divide the work between those who execute the qualitative and quantitative components. A third option is to occupy a boundary-spanning role that uses skills in making connections between methods.

DISCUSSION QUESTIONS

Do you have an equal interest in both qualitative and quantitative methods? How do you plan to balance your interests in these two sets of skills when you do mixed methods research?

Is a boundary-spanning role a realistic option for you? Does your field recognize the potential for this approach to provide expertise in mixed methods research?

ADDITIONAL READINGS

On the issues involved in using teams to do mixed methods research, see the following:

Curry, L. A., O'Cathain, A., Plano Clark, V. L., Aroni, R., Fetters, M., & Berg, D. (2012). The role of group dynamics in mixed methods health sciences research teams. *Journal of Mixed Methods Research, 6,* 5–20.
O'Cathain, A., Murphy, E., & Nicholl, J. (2008). Multidisciplinary, interdisciplinary, or dysfunctional: Team working in mixed-methods research. *Qualitative Health Research, 18,* 574–585.

CHAPTER 12

Conclusions: Further Thoughts About Research Design

Overview

Too often, accounts of the research process give an oversimplified version of how research decisions are made. Hence, this chapter questions and problematizes the classic advice that "your theory should determine your research method." Rather than a top-down approach, in which theory drives methods, the approach here advocates a cyclical version of the linkage among research questions, research methods, and available data. In addition, even if "how-to" decisions about research methods are ideally driven by "why-to" decisions, in a very real sense, choices about research methods influence choices about research questions. In particular, the lifelong investment that researchers make in achieving research skills means that they rarely take on questions that require major changes in methods. Finally, it is impossible to ignore a series of outside factors that affect real-world decisions about research—including the researcher's personal interests, the influence of audiences, and the availability of resources to do the research. A consideration of the need to balance personal interests, desired audiences, and available resources provides a more realistic view of the research process.

The emphasis in Part 2 was almost exclusively technical. After that lengthy coverage of how to do research, decisions about why to do research one way rather than another are the topic of this final chapter. The need to make decisions has been a major theme throughout this book. Thus, one of the key goals has been to describe a wide range of practical ways of doing mixed methods research. This technical approach has many advantages, but it can have the disadvantage of giving an overly mechanical sense of how research operates. Too much emphasis on the methodological aspects of research ignores many real-world issues. This last chapter addresses these concerns by returning to the three big principles that served as the basis for the conclusions in each of the chapters in Part 1:

1. Every successful research project requires two things: a meaningful research question and an appropriate way to answer that question.

2. Deciding how to do your research depends on a clear understanding of why you are doing the research.

3. Choosing research methods that can accomplish your research goals requires knowing both what your options are and how to evaluate those options.

There is, however, one major difference in how this chapter addresses these issues. This time, the order of the three principles is reversed. This reordering reflects a shift in direction. The book as a whole has moved from more abstract material in Part 1 (i.e., choosing meaningful research questions and appropriate research methods) to more explicit consideration of research design in Part 2 (i.e., interrelating how-to and why-to concerns) and finishing with the last several chapters on detailed applications of research methods. In contrast, this final chapter's ordering of the three principles moves from data-related concerns to research design and ends with more abstract concerns.

* * *

3. *Choosing research methods that can accomplish your research goals requires knowing both what your options are and how to evaluate those options.*

This principle addresses choices about methods by stressing the knowledge you need to make good decisions. Mixed methods research provides an unusually broad range of ways to apply methods, and selecting effective combinations can be challenging. From the earliest chapters, this book has stressed understanding the different strengths of different methods as a basis for making these decisions. In addition, the division of labor between core and supplementary methods provides a strategy for combining the separate strengths of qualitative and quantitative methods. The sequential priorities model is thus devoted to responding to the issues involved in making choices about research methods.

Even so, the knowledge that you need to make good choices about methods almost always goes beyond abstract "rules" about methodology because your choices must respond to the specific goals that guide your overall research project. At the most basic level, the range of options you can consider is limited to those that are capable of answering your research question, and your standards for evaluating those options will be determined by how well they fit your ultimate goals.

These same points also occur in discussions about how to link theory and methods. In this case, *theory* refers to the substantive topics that a research field is investigating, and *methods* refers to the techniques for collecting and analyzing data to address those topics. Figure 12.1 presents a simplified summary of the most common set of assumptions about how to connect theory and methods. In this version, you begin with a goal drawn from theory, which determines your research, which in turn determines the methods you will use to collect and analyze data.

You will frequently hear the logic of Figure 12.1 summarized in statements such as "Your theory should determine your research method." This is sound advice. Your research has to be about something, and selecting a question that

Figure 12.1 The Classic Advice on Making Decisions About Research Methods

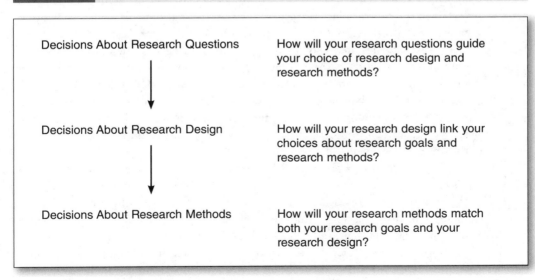

your field considers worth pursuing ensures that your project is about something important. This need to link purposes and procedures has also been a central theme throughout this book. In actual research projects, your research methods (*procedures*) are driven by your research questions (*purposes*). What is missing from this formulation, however, is the need to recognize that the actual pairing of purposes and procedures always occurs in context. The same is true of Figure 12.1, which provides a very general statement that ignores the specific concerns involved in any given research project. In other words, this advice is too general to be of much use in making on-the-ground decisions about real-world research. The next section thus presents a more realistic description of the research process.

   2. *Deciding how to do your research depends on a clear understanding of why you are doing the research.*

   This second principle emphasizes the importance of research design as the point at which the choice of research methods meets the needs of the research question. As such, it definitely deals with the intersection between research purposes and research procedures. This intersection is represented by the need to treat choosing research designs as decision making. This book has addressed these issues through not only the sequential priorities model as the source of four basic designs but also through the more specific designs that were covered within each of the central chapters. In addition, the numerous empirical examples have consistently demonstrated how designs work in practice.

   Given the central place of research design throughout this book, it is important to avoid an overly abstract understanding of this process. Research questions, research designs, and research methods all need to be combined into a common framework. Although Figure 12.1 has obvious value as a strategy for making these connections, it also has limitations. In particular, more experienced researchers will readily acknowledge that this summary is an oversimplification. In particular, it is too linear. In actual practice, each of these decisions may both influence and be influenced by the others. Figure 12.2 summarizes this more interdependent version.

   One new feature that Figure 12.2 introduces is the active role that the availability of data can play in the research process. Rather than simply serving as the end point for research activities, access to data can either stimulate your theoretical thinking about the uses for that data or provide you with insights into the methods that apply to that data. Rather than operating as the lowest and most mundane element in research, the availability of data is often a crucial influence on other research decisions, and this summary includes it as an equal partner.

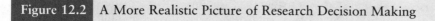

Figure 12.2   A More Realistic Picture of Research Decision Making

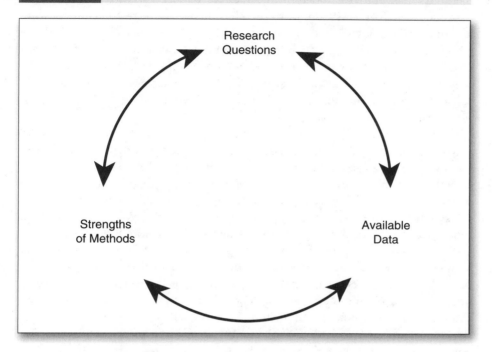

The biggest change that Figure 12.2 makes in the components of the research process is to move beyond theory as the determinant for the other elements. Rather than starting with theorizing as an isolated stage in the process, you need to consider it within a more dynamic setting. Comparing Figures 12.1 and 12.2 indicates that the claim that "your research question should determine your research method" is an overly straightforward account of both *how* decisions about research are made and *why* they are made the way they are. Rather than a top-down, linear process that moves from theory to method, actual research design decisions allow you to change the research questions themselves in response to the opportunities and limitations that are created by either methods or data. Linking these components in a cycle calls attention to the contingency of these decisions: Each shift of your thinking regarding one element also influences the issues that are most important for the other two.

Within this cycle, it is important to recognize the path that leads from choices about methods to choices about research questions. Allowing for this influence directly violates the standard advice that the research question should determine the research method. Yet, in practice, your existing research skills impose the most obvious constraint on your selection of research questions.

Once you have invested a considerable amount of time in mastering a set of methods, it is hard to find the time it takes to learn wholly new methods. Consider the effort it would take to switch from doing open-ended interviewing and qualitative analysis to doing survey research and statistical analysis. While a few researchers do make such large-scale transitions, most people settle into a pattern in which they match their research questions with the technical skills they already have or can easily acquire. Indeed, strong prior commitments to research methods probably do more to influence your choice of research questions than vice versa.

A different question is whether your research interests actually are driven by theory or whether you wish to pursue a more practical and applied set of interests. Many of the uses for qualitative, quantitative, and mixed methods come directly from efforts to solve problems related to health, education, or social welfare. While academic research—and thus the teaching of research in academic settings—is often "theory driven," applied research typically uses a much more flexible approach to joining the elements in the research design cycle.

If the standard portrait of the research process is so artificial, why does it get so much emphasis? The answer to this question lies in the way that we teach beginning researchers. Helping novice researchers get started often involves a great deal of oversimplification, and a statement like "Your research question should determine your research method" is just such an oversimplification. On the one hand, this straightforward picture of research is useful for teaching basic principles to beginners; on the other hand, it ignores many of the practices that actually guide experienced researchers. The kinds of things that help you get started with research methods are not the same things that will help you master the complexities of social science research. The next section goes a step further in providing a more realistic understanding of the research process.

1. *Every successful research project requires two things: a meaningful research question and an appropriate way to answer that question.*

As useful as this principle is, it too is an oversimplification. This simplification is accomplished by failing to consider the tacit meanings behind the words *meaningful* and *appropriate*. Research questions are not inherently either meaningful or meaningless, and research methods are not intrinsically either appropriate or inappropriate. Instead, these are human value judgments that occur in every discipline and research area.

The established researchers in your field have "community standards" about which research questions are most meaningful and which methods are most appropriate for pursuing those questions. When you explain your research questions, you must do so in terms that address the current assumptions and debates within your field. Then, when you try to convince your colleagues about the appropriateness of your methods, you need to take into account the range of techniques that researchers in your field typically use. Any attempt to create a successful research project occurs in a social world, and any realistic view of the research process has to take a variety of social influences into account. Figure 12.3 moves in that direction.

Although Figure 12.2 provides a more realistic view of how research questions and methods are chosen, it still suffers from a very serious limitation: It portrays the decision making involved in research as a purely intellectual process that is disconnected from outside influences. Figure 12.3 addresses this issue by locating the connections among research questions, methods, and data within a broader array of forces. From this perspective, a match among theory, methods, and data is a necessary element of the research process, but that information is not sufficient to say why a given piece of research was done in a given way.

In particular, Figure 12.3 gives a major role to your own personal interests, pointing to the larger factors that make a research question meaningful or a

Figure 12.3   Putting Research Decisions in Context

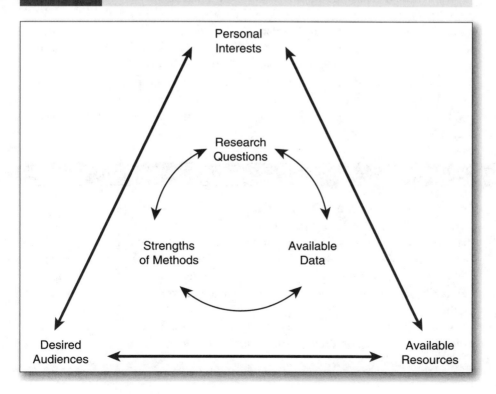

method appropriate *for you* as a researcher. The biggest influence on your choices about research questions and methods is almost always your personal interests—the experiences, values, and goals that motivate you. You do not make your choices in a vacuum, however; the potential audiences for your work often shape the choices you make. And it is obvious how resources can limit your choices, since you may not be able to afford to do either what you would prefer to do or what others want you to do. Ultimately, your choices about research questions and methods involve a complex balance among your own interests, the audiences you want to address, and the resources you have available.

Among the "outside" factors that influence the research process, the role played by your desired audiences is especially important because it often introduces political concerns and power dynamics. Who will decide whether your questions are meaningful and your methods appropriate—the members of a thesis committee? a journal editor? a grant review panel? This need to *justify* your choices is at the center of the research design process. A proposed research design amounts to a claim that a given set of methods will be appropriate for answering a corresponding set of questions, and this claim has to convince some audience.

Even though decisions about how to do a particular research project are unquestionably influenced by the community standards in a field, it is vital to recognize the potential for innovation. You are not forced to accept your field's current assumptions about either "meaningful" questions or "appropriate" methods. Instead, there is what Thomas Kuhn (1977) called an "essential tension" that every field experiences between the competing priorities of building on well-established standards and encouraging innovative new directions. As a result, standards are constantly evolving, and your choices can in a very real way influence the standards in your field.

CONCLUSIONS

Innovations in methods can have influences that reach beyond technical, how-to issues, and mixed methods research is an excellent example of how the standards for research continue to evolve. Only a decade ago, it would have been much more difficult to justify combining qualitative and quantitative methods. Now, the perception that mixed methods research offers new options has transformed the classic choice between either qualitative or quantitative methods.

When a new approach to research, such as combining qualitative and quantitative methods, becomes available, the first thing that is likely to change is a field's approach to answering existing questions. Options that used to be outside the realm of possibility are now practical. The ability to do a better job of answering existing questions is a major accomplishment, but the most important advances in research methods go beyond this. Creating the ability to ask new questions is what makes a new approach to research truly powerful. Things that people never even thought of grow into major research topics.

Thus, the largest changes in what researchers believe their methods can accomplish also create change in the research questions researchers ask. The development of mixed methods research is a demonstration of the mutual influence of research questions on research methods and vice versa. In many ways, your sense of what your options are and how to evaluate them has expanded dramatically. Your ideas about how to do research will now operate within a new understanding of what it means to do research one way rather than another. And your beliefs about appropriate methods will never be the same.

SUMMARY

The classic advice that beginning researchers receive is that "your research question should determine your research method." This amounts to an assertion that theory should come first in the research process, but this perspective is in many ways unrealistic. Instead, research is best thought of as a cyclical process in which choices about research methods influence choices about research questions and in which the researcher's personal interests play a major role in all decision making.

DISCUSSION QUESTIONS

If the process of becoming a researcher is different from the version that is taught in introductory methods classes, what is a more realistic view of how researchers obtain their skills across a career? How could the teaching of research methods take this process into account?

What are the sources of your preferences with regard to research methods? In your own case, does it make sense to say that your choices about research questions have determined your choices about research methods?

How much influence do your "desired audiences" have on your choices with regard to research methods? How easy will it be for you to justify your preferred approach to research?

ADDITIONAL READINGS

On the progression from being a novice in a field to obtaining greater mastery, see the following:

Benner, P. E. (1984). *From novice to expert: Excellence and power in clinical nursing practice.* Reading, MA: Addison-Wesley.
Dreyfus, S. E. (2004). The five-stage model of adult skill acquisition. *Bulletin of Science, Technology, and Society, 24,* 177–181.

On the influence that research communities have on their members, see the following:

Kuhn, T. S. (1996). *The structure of scientific revolutions* (3rd ed.). Chicago, IL: University of Chicago Press.

References

Arcury, T. A., & Quandt, S. A. (1999). Participant recruitment for qualitative research: A site-based approach to community research in complex societies. *Human Organization, 58,* 128–133.

Barg, F. K., Huss-Ashmore, R., Wittink, M. N., Murray, G. F., Bogner, H. R., & Gallo, J. J. (2006). A mixed-methods approach to understanding loneliness and depression in older adults. *Journal of Gerontology: Social Sciences, 61B,* S329–S339.

Bazeley, P. (2012). Integrative analysis strategies for mixed data sources. *American Behavioral Sciences, 56,* 814–828.

Bazeley, P., & Kemp, L. (2012). Mosaics, triangles, and DNA: Metaphors for integrated analysis in mixed methods research. *Journal of Mixed Methods Research, 6,* 55–72.

Beista, G. (2010). Pragmatism and the philosophical foundations of mixed methods research. In A. Tashakkori & C. Teddlie (Eds.), *SAGE Handbook of mixed methods in social & behavioral research* (2nd ed., pp. 95–118). Thousand Oaks, CA: Sage.

Bennett, I., Switzer, I., Aguirre, A., Evans, K., & Barg, F. (2006). "Breaking it down": Patient-clinician communication and prenatal care among African American women of lower and higher literacy. *Annals of Family Medicine, 4,* 334–340.

Berry, W. D., & Feldman, S. (1985). *Multiple regression in practice.* Thousand Oaks, CA: Sage.

Blackhall, L. J., Frank, G., Murphy, S. T., Michel, V. (2001). Bioethics in a different tongue: The case of truth-telling. *Journal of Urban Health, 78,* 59–71.

Blackhall, L. J., Frank, G., Murphy, S. T., Michel, V., Palmer, J. M., & Azen, S. P. (1999). Ethnicity and attitudes towards life sustaining technology. *Social Science and Medicine, 48,* 1779–1789.

Blaikie, N. W. H. (1991). A critique of the use of triangulation in social research. *Quality and Quantity, 25,* 115–136.

Blatchford, P. (2003). A systematic observational study of teachers' and pupils' behaviour in large and small classes. *Learning and Instruction, 13,* 569–595.

Blatchford, P., Goldstein, H., Martin, C., & Browne, W. (2002). A study of class size effects in English school reception year classes. *British Educational Research Journal, 28,* 169–185.

Blatchford, P., Moriarity, V., Edmonds, S., & Martin, C. (2002). Relationships between class size and teaching: A multimethod analysis of English infant schools. *American Educational Research Journal, 39,* 101–132.

Blumer, H. (1969). *Symbolic interactionism: Perspective and method.* Englewood Cliffs, NJ: Prentice-Hall.

Bradley, E. H., Curry, L. A., Ramanadhan, S., Rowe L., Nembhard, I. M., & Krumholz, H. M. (2009). Research in action: Using positive deviance to improve quality of health care. *Implementation Science, 4,* 1–11.

Brannen, J. (1992). *Mixing methods: Qualitative and quantitative research.* Aldershot, UK: Avebury.

Brinkerhoff, R. O. (2003). *The success case method: Find out quickly what's working and what's not.* San Francisco, CA: Berrett-Koehler.

Brinkerhoff, R. O. (2005). The success case method: A strategic evaluation approach to increasing the value and effect of training. *Advances in Developing Human Resources, 7,* 86–101.

Bryman, A. (1988). *Quantity and quality in social research.* London, UK: Unwin Hyman.

Bryman, A. (2006). Integrating quantitative and qualitative research: How is it done? *Qualitative Research, 6,* 97–113.

Callaghan, G. (1998). The interaction of gender, class and place in women's experience: A discussion based in focus group research. *Sociological Research Online, 3.* Retrieved from http://www.socresonline.org.uk/3/3/8.html

Callaghan, G. (2005). Accessing habitus: Relating structure and agency through focus group research. *Sociological Research Online, 10.* Retrieved from http://www.socres online.org.uk/10/3/callaghan.html

Campbell, D. T. (1956). *Leadership and its effects upon the group* (Ohio Studies in Personnel, Bureau of Business Research Monograph No. 83). Columbus: Ohio State University.

Campbell, D. T., & Fiske, D. W. (1959). Convergent and discriminant validation by the multitrait-multimethod matrix. *Psychological Bulletin, 56,* 81–105.

Charmaz, K. (2006). *Constructing grounded theory: A practical guide through qualitative analysis.* Thousand Oaks, CA: Sage.

Chinman, M. J., Weingarten, R., Stayner, D., & Davidson, L. (2001). Chronicity reconsidered: Improving person-environment fit through a consumer-run service. *Community Mental Health Journal, 37,* 215–229.

Collier, P. J., & Fellows, C. (with Holland, B.). (2009). *Students first: Improving first-generation student retention and performance in higher education; Final report of program activities 2005–2009.* http://friends.studentsfirst.pdx.edu/files/SFMP final report 2005–2009 final.doc

Corden, A., & Hirst, M. (2008). Implementing a mixed methods approach to explore the financial implications of death of a life partner. *Journal of Mixed Methods Research, 2,* 208–220.

Creswell, J. W. (2008). *Research design: Qualitative, quantitative, and mixed methods approaches* (3rd ed.). Thousand Oaks, CA: Sage.

Creswell, J. W. (2010). Mapping the developing landscape of mixed methods research. In A. Tashakkori & C. Teddlie (Eds.), *SAGE handbook of mixed methods in social and behavioral research* (2nd ed., pp. 45–68). Thousand Oaks, CA: Sage.

Creswell, J. W., & Plano Clark, V. L. (2011). *Designing and conducting mixed methods research* (2nd ed.). Thousand Oaks, CA: Sage.

Creswell, J. W., Plano-Clark, V. L., Gutmann, M. L., & Hanson, W. E. (2003). Advanced mixed methods research designs. In A. Tashakkori & C. Teddlie (Eds.), *Handbook of mixed methods in social & behavioral research* (pp. 209–240). Thousand Oaks, CA: Sage.

Cunningham, A. J., Edmonds, C. V., Phillips, C., Scoots, K. I., Hedley, D., & Lockwood, G. A. (2000). A prospective, longitudinal study of the relationship of psychosocial work to duration of survival in patients with metastatic cancer. *Psycho-Oncology, 9,* 323–339.

Curry, L. A., O'Cathain, A., Plano Clark, V. L., Aroni, R., Fetters, M., & Berg, D. (2012). The role of group dynamics in mixed methods health sciences research teams. *Journal of Mixed Methods Research, 6,* 5–20.

Davidson, L., Stayner, D. A., Lambert, S., Smith, P., & Sledge, W. H. (1997). Phenomeno-logical and participatory research on schizophrenia: Recovering the person in theory and practice. *Journal of Social Issues, 53,* 767–784.

De Waal, C. (2005). *On pragmatism.* Belmont, CA: Thomson Wadsworth.

DeCoster, V. A., & Cummings, S. (2004). Coping with type-2 diabetes: Do race and gender matter? *Social Work in Health Care, 40,* 37–53.

Denscombe, M. (2008). Communities of practice: A research paradigm for the mixed methods approach. *Journal of Mixed Methods Research, 2,* 270–283.

Denzin, N. K. (1970). *The research act: A theoretical introduction to sociological meth-ods.* Chicago, IL: Aldine.

Denzin, N. K. (1989). *The research act* (3rd ed.). Englewood Cliffs, NJ: Prentice Hall.

Denzin, N. K. (2010). Moments, mixed methods, and paradigm dialogs. *Qualitative Inquiry, 16,* 419–427.

Denzin, N. K. (2012). Triangulation 2.0. *Journal of Mixed Methods Research, 6,* 80–88.

Dewey, J. (1986). *How we think: A restatement of the relation of reflective thinking to the educative process* (Rev. ed.). In *John Dewey: The Later Works, 1925–1953* (Vol. 8). Carbondale: Southern Illinois University Press. (Originally published 1933)

Dobryzkowski, T. M., & Noerager Stern, P. (2003). Out of synch: A generation of first-time mothers over 30. *Health Care for Women International, 24,* 242–253.

Drach-Zahavy, A., & Pud, D. (2010). Learning mechanisms to limit medication admin-istration errors. *Journal of Advanced Nursing, 66,* 794–805.

Farquhar, M. C., Ewing, G., & Booth, S. (2011). Using mixed methods to develop and evaluate complex interventions in palliative care research. *Palliative Care, 25,* 748–757.

Fetterman, D. M. (2009). *Ethnography: Step-by-step* (3rd ed.). Thousand Oaks, CA: Sage.

Fielding, N., & Fielding, J. L. (1986). *Linking data.* Thousand Oaks, CA: Sage.

Fowler, F. J. (2008). *Survey research methods* (4th ed.). Thousand Oaks, CA: Sage.

Gans, K. M., Lovell, J. H., Lasater, T. M., McPhillips, J. B., Raden, M., & Carleton, R. A. (1996). Using quantitative and qualitative data to evaluate and refine a self-help kit for lowering fat intake. *Journal of Nutrition Education, 28,* 157–163.

Glaser, B., & Strauss, A. (1967). *The discovery of grounded theory.* Chicago, IL: Aldine.

Greene, J. C., & Caracelli, V. J. (1997) *Advances in mixed-method evaluation: The chal-lenges and benefits of integrating diverse paradigms.* San Francisco, CA: Jossey-Bass.

Greene, J. C., Caracelli, V. J., & Graham, W. F. (1989). Toward a conceptual framework for mixed-method evaluation designs. *Educational Evaluation and Policy Analysis, 11,* 255–274.

Guba, E. G. (1990). *The paradigm dialog.* Thousand Oaks, CA: Sage.

Guba, E. G., & Lincoln, Y. S. (2005). Paradigmatic controversies, contradictions, and emerging confluences. In N. K. Denzin & Y. S. Lincoln (Eds.), *The SAGE handbook of qualitative research* (3rd ed., pp. 191–215). Thousand Oaks, CA: Sage.

Hacking, I. (1983). *Representing and intervening: Introductory topics in the philosophy of natural science.* New York, NY: Cambridge University Press.

Hammersley, M. (1992). *What's wrong with ethnography? Methodological explorations.* New York, NY: Routledge.

Hammersley, M., & Atkinson, P. (1995). *Ethnography: Principles in practice* (2nd ed.). New York, NY: Routledge.

Houston, H. R., Harada, N., & Makinodan, T. (2002). Development of a culturally sensitive educational intervention program to reduce the high incidence of tuberculosis among foreign-born Vietnamese. *Ethnicity & Health, 7,* 255–265.

Hult, J. R., Wrubel, J., Bränström, R., Acree, M., & Moskowitz, J. T. (2012). Disclosure and nondisclosure among people newly diagnosed with HIV: An analysis from a stress and coping perspective. *AIDS Patient Care and STDs, 26,* 181–190.

James, W. (1995). *Pragmatism.* New York, NY: Dover. (Originally published 1907)

Jick, T. D. (1979). Mixing qualitative and quantitative methods: Triangulation in action. *Administrative Science Quarterly, 24,* 602–611.

Johnson, R. B., & Onwuegbuzie, A. J. (2004). Mixed methods research: A research paradigm whose time has come. *Educational Researcher, 33,* 14–26.

Joseph, J. G., Montgomery, S. B., Emmons, C., Kirscht, J. P., Kessler, R. C., Ostrow, D. G . . . . O'Brien, K. (1987). Perceived risk of AIDS: Assessing the behavioral and psychosocial consequences in a cohort of gay men. *Journal of Applied Social Psychology, 17,* 231–250.

Kenaszchuk, C., Conn, L. J., Dainty, K., McCarthy, C., Reeves, S., & Zwarenstein, M. (2012). Consensus on interprofessional collaboration in hospitals: Statistical agreement of ratings from ethnographic fieldwork and measurement scales. *Journal of Evaluation in Clinical Practice, 18,* 93–99.

Krause, N. (2002). A comprehensive strategy for developing closed-ended survey items for use in studies of older adults. *Journals of Gerontology Series B: Psychological Sciences and Social Sciences, 57B,* S263–S274.

Kuhn, T. S. (1977). The essential tension: Tradition and innovation in scientific research. In *The essential tension: Selected studies in scientific tradition and change* (pp. 225–239). Chicago, IL: University of Chicago Press.

Kuhn, T. S. (1996). *The structure of scientific revolutions* (3rd ed.). Chicago, IL: University of Chicago Press. (Originally published 1962)

Laurie, H. (1992). Multiple methods in the study of household resource allocation. In J. Brannen (Ed.), *Mixing methods: Qualitative and quantitative research* (pp. 145–168). Aldershot, UK: Avebury.

Laurie, H., & Sullivan, O. (1991). Combining qualitative and quantitative data in the longitudinal study of household allocations. *The Sociological Review, 39,* 113–130.

Lawrenz, F., & Huffman, D. (2002). The archipelago approach to mixed method evaluation. *American Journal of Evaluation, 23,* 331–338.

Leech, N. L., & Onwuegbuzie, A. J. (2009). A typology of mixed methods research designs. *Quality & Quantity, 43,* 265–275.

Lewis, S. D., Johnson, V. R., Farris, R. P., & Will, J. C. (2004). Using success stories to share knowledge and lessons learned in health promotion. *Journal of Women's Health, 13,* 616–625.

Lincoln, Y. S., & Guba. E. G. (1985). *Naturalistic inquiry.* Newbury Park, CA: Sage.

Luginaah, I. N., Taylor, S. M., Elliott, S. J., & Eyles, J. D. (2002). Community responses and coping strategies in the vicinity of a petroleum refinery in Oakville, Ontario. *Health and Place, 8,* 177–190.

Luyt, R. (2012). A framework for mixing methods in quantitative measurement development, validation, and revision: A case study. *Journal of Mixed Methods Research, 6,* 294–316.

Maxcy, S. J. (2003). Pragmatic threads in mixed methods research in the social sciences: The search for multiple modes of inquiry and the end of the philosophy of formalism. In A. Tashakkori & C. Teddlie (Eds.), *SAGE handbook of mixed methods in social & behavioral research* (pp. 51–90). Thousand Oaks, CA: Sage.

McIntyre, A. (2008). *Participatory action research.* Thousand Oaks, CA: Sage.

Medlinger, S., & Cwikel, J. (2008). Mosaics, triangles, and DNA: Metaphors for integrated analysis in mixed methods research. *Journal of Mixed Methods Research, 6,* 55–72.

Moran-Ellis, J., Alexander, V., Cronin, A., Dickinson, M., Fielding, J., Sleney, J., & Thomas, H. (2006). Triangulation and integration: Processes, claims, and implications. *Qualitative Research, 6,* 45–59.

Morgan, D. L. (1989). Adjusting to widowhood: Do social networks really make it easier? *The Gerontologist, 29,* 101–107.

Morgan, D. L. (1997). *Focus groups as qualitative research* (2nd ed.). Thousand Oaks, CA: Sage.

Morgan, D. L. (1998). Practical strategies for combining qualitative and quantitative methods: Applications to health research. *Qualitative Health Research, 8,* 362–376.

Morgan, D. L. (2002). Seeking diagnosis for a cognitively impaired family member: Evidence from focus groups. In G. D. Rowles & N. E. Schoenberg (Eds.), *Qualitative Gerontology: A contemporary perspective* (2nd ed., pp. 213–233). New York, NY: Springer.

Morgan, D. L. (2006). "Connected contributions" as a motivation for combining qualitative and quantitative methods. In L. Curry, R. S. Shield, & T. T. Wetle (Eds.), *Improving aging and public health research: Qualitative and mixed methods* (pp. 53–63). Washington, DC: American Public Health Association.

Morgan, D. L. (2007). Paradigms lost and pragmatism regained: Methodological implications of combining qualitative and quantitative methods. *Journal of Mixed Methods Research, 1,* 48–76.

Morgan, D. L. (2008). Purposive sampling. In L. M. Given (Ed.), *The SAGE encyclopedia of qualitative research methods.* Thousand Oaks, CA: Sage.

Morse, J. M. (1991). Approaches to qualitative-quantitative methodological triangulation. *Nursing Research, 40,* 120–123.

Morse, J. M. (2003). Principles of mixed methods and multimethod research design. In A. Tashakkori & C. Teddlie, (Eds.), *Handbook of mixed methods in social and behavioral research* (pp. 189–208). Thousand Oaks, CA: Sage.

Morse, J. M., & Niehaus, L. (2009). *Mixed method design: Principles and procedures.* Walnut Creek, CA: Left Coast Press.

Munro, A., & Bloor, M. (2010). Process evaluation: The new miracle ingredient in public health research? *Qualitative Research, 10,* 699–713.

Murphy, J. P. (1990). *Pragmatism: From Peirce to Davidson.* Boulder, CO: Westview.

Nastasi, B. K., Hitchock, J., Sarkar, S., Burkholder, G., Varjas, K., & Jayasena, A. (2007). Mixed methods in intervention research: Theory to adaptation. *Journal of Mixed Methods Research, 1,* 164–182.

Nastasi, B. K., Jayasena, A., Summerville, M., & Borja, A. P. (2011). Facilitating long-term recovery from natural disasters: Psychosocial programming for tsunami-affected schools of Sri Lanka. *School Psychology International, 32,* 512–532.

Neuendorf, K. A. (2002). *The content analysis guidebook.* Thousand Oaks, CA: Sage.

Nisbett, R. E., & Ross, L. (1980). *Human inference: Strategies and shortcomings of social judgment.* Englewood Cliffs, NJ: Prentice-Hall.

O'Brien, K. (1993). Using focus groups to develop health surveys: An example from research on social relationships and AIDS-preventive behavior. *Health Education Quarterly, 20,* 361–372.

O'Cathain, A., Murphy, E., & Nicholl, J. (2008). Multidisciplinary, interdisciplinary, or dysfunctional: Team working in mixed-methods research. *Qualitative Health Research, 18,* 574–585.

Onwuegbuzie, A. J., Slate, J. R., Leech, N. L., & Collins, K. M. T. (2007). Conducting mixed analyses: A general typology. *International Journal of Multiple Research Approaches, 1,* 4–17

Onwuegbuzie, A. J., Slate, J. R., Leech, N. L., & Collins, K. M. T. (2009). Mixed data analysis: Advanced integration techniques. *International Journal of Multiple Research Approaches, 3,* 13–33.

Organization for Economic and Cooperative Development. (2003). *OECD health data 2003.* Retrieved from http://www.oecd.org/health/healthpoliciesanddata/oecdhealth data2003.htm

Patton, M. Q. (1988). Paradigms and pragmatism. In D. Fetterman (Ed.), *Qualitative approaches to evaluation in education: The silent scientific revolution* (pp. 116–137). Thousand Oaks, CA: Sage.

Patton, M. Q. (2002). *Qualitative research and evaluation methods* (3rd ed.). Thousand Oaks, CA: Sage.

Pavlovskaya, M. E. (2002). Mapping urban change and changing GIS: Other views of economic restructuring. *Gender, Place, and Culture, 9,* 281–289.

Pavlovskaya, M. E. (2004). Other transitions: Multiple economies in Moscow households in the 1990s. *Annals of the American Association of American Geographers, 94,* 329–351.

Plano Clark, V. L., Garrett, A. L., & Leslie-Pelecky, D. L. (2010). Applying three strategies for integrating quantitative and qualitative databases in a mixed methods study of a nontraditional graduate education program. *Field Methods, 22,* 154–174.

Presser, S., Rothgeb, J. M., Couper, M. P., Lessler, J. T., Martin, E., Martin, J., & Singer, E. (Eds.). (2004). *Methods for testing and evaluating survey questionnaires.* New York, NY: Wiley.

Reichardt, C. S., & Cook, T. D. (1979). Beyond qualitative versus quantitative methods. In T. D. Cook & C. S. Reichardt (Eds.), *Qualitative and quantitative methods in evaluation research* (pp. 7–32). Beverly Hills, CA: Sage.

Rescher, N. (2000). *Realistic pragmatism: An introduction to pragmatic philosophy.* Albany: State University of New York Press.

Rossman, G. B., & Wilson, B. L. (1985). Numbers and words: Combing quantitative and qualitative methods in a single large-scale evaluation study. *Evaluation Review, 9,* 627–643.

Rowlingson, K., & McKay, S. (2005). Lone motherhood and socio-economic disadvantage: Insights from quantitative and qualitative evidence. *The Sociological Review, 53,* 30–49.

Rubin, H. J., & Rubin I. S. (2004). *Qualitative interviewing: The art of hearing data* (2nd ed.). Thousand Oaks, CA: Sage.

Sandelowski, M. (2000). Combining qualitative and quantitative sampling, data collection, and analysis techniques in mixed-method studies. *Research in Nursing and Health, 23,* 246–255.

Sandelowski, M., Volis, C. I., & Knafl, G. (2009). On quantizing. *Journal of Mixed Methods Research, 3,* 208–222.

Schensul, J. J., LeCompte, M. D., Trotter, R. T., II, Cromly, E. K., & Singer, M. (1999). *Mapping social networks, spatial data, and hidden populations.* Walnut Creek, CA: AltaMira Press.

Schumacher, K. L., Koresawa, S., West, C., Dodd, M., Paul, S. M., Tripathy, D. . . . Miaskowski, C. (2005). Qualitative research contribution to a randomized clinical trial. *Research in Nursing and Health, 28,* 268–280.

Seal, D. W., Eldrige, G. D., Kacanek, D., Binson, D., & MacGowan, R. J. (2007). A longitudinal, qualitative analysis of the context of substance use and sexual behavior among 18- to 29-year-old men after their release from prison. *Social Science and Medicine, 65,* 2394–2406.

Seccombe, K., & Hoffman K. A. (2007). *Just don't get sick: Access to health care in the aftermath of welfare reform.* New Brunswick, NJ: Rutgers University Press.

Shadish, W, R., Cook, T. D., & Campbell, D. T. (2002). *Experimental and quasi-experimental designs for generalized causal inference.* Boston, MA: Houghton Mifflin.

Shulha, L. M., & Wilson, R. J. (2003). Collaborative mixed methods research. In A. Tashakkori & C. Teddlie (Eds.), *Handbook of mixed methods in social & behavioral research* (pp. 639–670). Thousand Oaks, CA: Sage.

Sieber, S. D. (1973). The integration of fieldwork and survey methods. *American Journal of Sociology, 78,* 1335–1359.

Simmel, G. (1950). *The Sociology of Georg Simmel* (K. H. Wolff, Ed. & Trans.). New York, NY: Free Press.

Slonim-Nevo, V., & Nevo, I. (2009). Conflicting findings in mixed methods research: An illustration from an Israeli study on immigration. *Journal of Mixed Methods Research, 3,* 109–128.

Smith, J. K., & Heshusius, L. (1986). Closing down the conversation: The end of the quantitative-qualitative debate among educational inquirers. *Educational Leadership, 15,* 4–12.

Strauss, A. L., & Corbin, J. M. (1998). *Basics of qualitative research: Grounded theory procedures and techniques* (2nd ed). Thousand Oaks, CA: Sage.

Tashakkori, A., & Teddlie, C. (2010). *SAGE handbook of mixed methods in social & behavioral research* (2nd ed.). Thousand Oaks, CA: Sage.

Teddlie, C., & Tashakkori, A. (2009). *Foundations of mixed methods research.* Thousand Oaks, CA: Sage.

Teddlie, C., & Tashakkori, A. (2010). Overview of contemporary issues in mixed methods research. In A. Tashakkori & C. Teddlie (Eds.), *SAGE handbook of mixed methods in social & behavioral research* (2nd ed., pp. 1–44). Thousand Oaks, CA: Sage.

Thoits, P. A. (1995). Identity relevant events and psychological symptoms: A cautionary tale. *Journal of Health and Social Behavior, 36,* 72–82.

Toch, T. (1999). Outstanding high schools. *U.S. News & World Report.* Retrieved from http://www.usnews.com/usnews/culture/articles/990118/archive_002605.htm

van Staa, A. (2011). Unraveling triadic communication in hospital consultations with adolescents with chronic conditions: The added value of mixed methods research. *Patient Education and Counseling, 82,* 455–464.

Webb, E. J., Campbell, D. T., Schwartz, R. D., & Sechrest, L. (2000). Unobtrusive measures (Rev ed.). Thousand Oaks, CA: Sage.

Weber, R. P. (1990). *Basic content analysis.* Newbury Park, CA: Sage.

Willis, G. B. (2004). *Cognitive interviewing: A tool for improving questionnaire design.* Thousand Oaks, CA: Sage.

Winston, P., Angel, R. J., Burton, L. M., Chase-Lansdale, P. L. Cherlin, A. J., Moffitt, R. A., & Wilson, W. J. (1999). *Welfare, children, and families: A three-city study.* Baltimore, MD: Johns Hopkins University. Project website retrieved from http://web.jhu.edu/threecitystudy

Wuest, J., & Hodgins, M. J. (2011). Reflections on methodological approaches and conceptual contributions in a program of research on caregiving: Development and testing of Wuest's theory of family caregiving. *Qualitative Health Research, 21,* 151–161.

Yin, R. K. (2006). Mixed methods research: Are the methods genuinely integrated or merely parallel? *Research in the Schools, 13,* 41–47.

Youngs, H., & Piggot-Irvine, E. (2012). The application of a multiphase triangulation approach to mixed methods: The research of an aspiring school principal development program. *Journal of Mixed Methods Research, 6,* 184–198.

Yow, V. R. (1994). *Recording oral history: A practical guide for social scientists.* Thousand Oaks, CA: Sage.

Yun, S., Faraj, S., & Sims, H. (2005). Contingent leadership and effectiveness of trauma resuscitation teams. *Journal of Applied Psychology, 90,* 1288–1296.

Author Index

Subject Index

Abduction, in pragmatism, 29
Academic research and applied research
  compared, 230
Action, as a central concept in pragmatism,
  26–32, 34–36, 39–42
Action research, 114
Actions:
  beliefs and experiences linked to,
    26, 28, 31, 60
  changeability of, 26, 27 (figure)
  in Dewey's model, 8, 30 (figure), 31
Actors and behaviors, linked by themes, 182
Added value:
  from follow-up qualitative designs,
    154, 160, 166, 177
  from follow-up quantitative designs,
    180, 193
  from preliminary input designs, 150–151
Addition technique for linking
  of methods, 65 (figure), 66
Additional coverage, 73–77, 80 (table)
  basic designs for, 67, 67 (figure)
  compared to other motivations, 74, 80–81
  division of labor for, 11, 67, 73,
    74–75, 76, 80
  examples of, 73–75
  future directions of, 77
  introduction to, 10, 10 (figure), 11
  for multifaceted projects, 74–75
  parallel studies for, 76–77, 77 (figure), 80
  plus sign notation in, 65 (figure), 66

point of integration for, 77, 81
problematic integration for, 76, 81
uses of, 73–75, 76
Adolescent self-efficacy, example
  of research on, 185
AIDS at-risk groups, example of research on,
  119 (box)
Alternating designs:
  in longer sequential designs,
    205, 206–209, 210
  with a qualitative core, 203–204, 208–209
  with a quantitative core, 201–203, 205–207
  in three-part designs, 198–205
Alternative explanations, illustrating
  the failure of, 176
Alzheimer's caregivers, example of research on,
  6, 31–32, 33–34, 136–137
Anything goes approach, 4, 63–64
Applied research and academic research
  compared, 230
Appropriate responses to research questions,
  20, 41, 59, 81, 99
  and context of research decisions,
    231 (figure), 231–232
  and innovation, 232
  and tacit meaning of
    "appropriate," 230–231
  See also Research methods; Research
    questions
Arrow symbol (→), meaning of,
  65 (figure), 66, 88

Team building, 222
Teamwork:
 challenges involved in, 96, 217–218
 characteristics of, 219–221, 220 (table)
 in the design cycle, 90
 division of labor in, 214, 217, 218,
  220 (table), 221
 multiple-person teams, 219–222
 overview of, 214 (table), 214–215
 questions to ask about, 219
 tension in, with equal priority design, 96
 two-person teams, 218, 219
Technology used in teaching, example of
  research on, 134–135
Testing of hypotheses and theories. See
  Hypothesis testing; Theory testing and
  assessment
Themes, stating results as, 182–188
Theoretical sampling, 144, 208–209
Theory and applications development
  strategy, 129 (table)
 as an emergent approach, 130, 144–145
 grounded theory and, 144–145
 iterative process in, 130, 144, 146–147
Theory and methods, classic advice on linking,
  227 (figure), 227–228
Theory building and creation, 47–48, 49,
  186–187. See also Hypothesis
  generation
Theory testing and assessment, 48, 49,
  186–188. See also Hypothesis testing
Thick versus thin data and narrow versus
  broad coverage, 126
Three principles that summarize the basic
  argument of this book, 20–22, 41–43,
  59–61, 81–83, 99–101, 226
Three-part designs, 198–205
 with a qualitative core, 203–204
 with a quantitative core, 201–203
Top-down approach to linking theory and
  methods, 225, 227 (figure), 229
Training:
 example of research on, 206–207
 for expertise in combining methods,
  214, 216, 217
Transdisciplinarity, 220, 220 (table), 221
Transferability, as a form of generality, 192

Transforming themes, in follow-up
  quantitative designs, 185–186
Treatment interventions, 56. See also
  Experimental interventions; Program
  interventions
Triangulation:
 confusion over the meaning of, 69–70
 in convergent findings, 68–69
Truth, concept of:
 in pragmatism, 26, 27, 39, 40
 in realism and constructivism, 38–39
 universal truths, 26, 39
Tuberculosis, example of research
  on, 190–191
Two-part designs. See Equal priority designs;
  Follow-up qualitative extension designs;
  Follow-up quantitative extension designs;
  Preliminary qualitative input designs;
  Preliminary quantitative input designs

Uncertainty, inquiry for the resolution of, 28
Uncovering of domains, 15, 109, 111, 115
Underserved populations, example of research
  on, 175–176
Understanding, in teamwork, 219, 220 (table)
Universal truths, 26, 39

Validity, 74, 112, 113
Value added. See Added value
Variables:
 categorical, 182
 correlation between, 171–173, 172 (figure)
 dependent, sampling on, 164 (box)
 independent, cases at ends of, 173
 independent and dependent, in hypothesis
  testing, 182–186
 interval, 184
 moderator, 186
 new, and hypothesis generation, 119 (box),
  120
 omitted, in specification error, 111
 operationalization of, 181, 182–188, 189,
  190, 192
 ordinal, 184
 three, in assessing complex theories, 186
Vocabulary, shared, 219, 220 (table). See also
  Language

About the Author

David L. Morgan is a professor in the Department of Sociology at Portland State University. He received his PhD in sociology from the University of Michigan and postdoctoral training at Indiana University. In addition to his widely recognized expertise in focus groups, he also has extensive experience with collection and analysis of survey data. His research interests center on pragmatic approaches to mixed methods research, with an emphasis on practical applications of research design.

⨂SAGE researchmethods

The essential online tool for researchers from the world's leading methods publisher

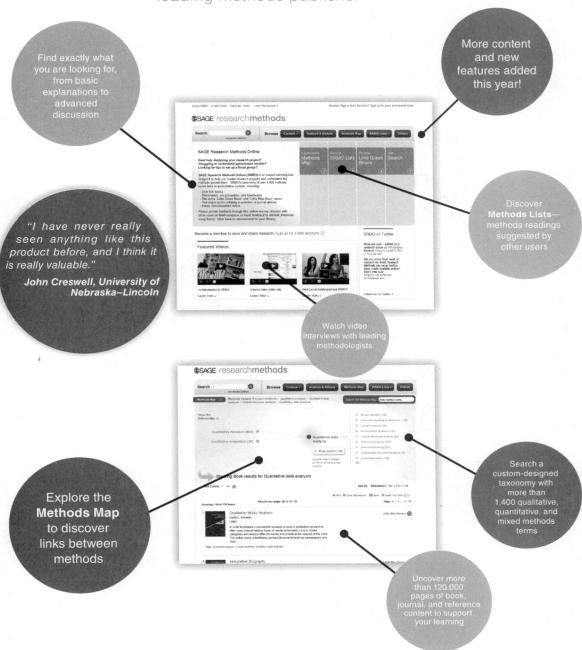

Find exactly what you are looking for, from basic explanations to advanced discussion

More content and new features added this year!

"I have never really seen anything like this product before, and I think it is really valuable."

John Creswell, University of Nebraska–Lincoln

Discover **Methods Lists**— methods readings suggested by other users

Watch video interviews with leading methodologists

Explore the **Methods Map** to discover links between methods

Search a custom-designed taxonomy with more than 1,400 qualitative, quantitative, and mixed methods terms

Uncover more than 120,000 pages of book, journal, and reference content to support your learning

Find out more at
www.sageresearchmethods.com